THREE SPEECHES THAT SAVED THE UNION

Three Speeches that Saved the Union

Clay, Calhoun, Webster, and the Crisis of 1850

Peter Charles Hoffer

NEW YORK UNIVERSITY PRESS

New York

NEW YORK UNIVERSITY PRESS
New York
nyupress.org
© 2025 by New York University

Library of Congress Cataloging-in-Publication Data
Names: Hoffer, Peter Charles, 1944–   compiler.
Title: The Supreme Court footnote : a surprising history / Peter Charles Hoffer.
Description: New York : New York University Press, 2024. |
Includes bibliographical references and index. | Summary: "A history of the most famous,
and infamous, footnotes in leading US Supreme Court cases"— Provided by publisher.
Identifiers: LCCN 2023038945 (print) | LCCN 2023038946 (ebook) |
ISBN 9781479830220 (hardback) |
ISBN 9781479830237 (ebook) | ISBN 9781479830244 (ebook other)
Subjects: LCSH: United States. Supreme Court—Cases—History. |
Constitutional courts—United States. | Judgments—United States.
Classification: LCC KF8741.A53 H64 2024 (print) | LCC KF8741.A53 (ebook) |
DDC 347.73/26—dc23/eng/20231003
LC record available at https://lccn.loc.gov/2023038945
LC ebook record available at https://lccn.loc.gov/2023038946

This book is printed on acid-free paper, and its binding materials are chosen for strength
and durability. We strive to use environmentally responsible suppliers and materials
to the greatest extent possible in publishing our books.

The manufacturer's authorized representative in the EU for product safety is Mare Nostrum
Group B.V., Mauritskade 21D, 1091 GC Amsterdam, The Netherlands.
Email: gpsr@mare-nostrum.co.uk.

Manufactured in the United States of America

10 9 8 7 6 5 4 3 2 1

Also available as an ebook

CONTENTS

Introduction

IN 1849, when he wrote his masterwork, "The Building of the Ship," New England poet Henry Wadsworth Longfellow knew that the Union was in peril. His final passage made clear that the ship in the poem was more than a seagoing vessel. "Thou, too, sail on, O Ship of State! Sail on, O Union, strong and great! Humanity with all its fears, With all the hopes of future years, Is hanging breathless on thy fate!" He believed a critical moment had come in the public life of the still new nation. The debate over slavery divided the sections and the political parties. (Longfellow himself supported abolitionism.) Would that debate sever the ties that bound the states into a Union? Had the slave states chosen to secede at that moment, nothing could have stopped them. Or might words save the Union—if not the poet's, then the nation's leaders'? He pleaded, "In spite of rock and tempest's roar, In spite of false lights on the shore, Sail on, nor fear to breast the sea! Our hearts, our hopes, are all with thee." But was compromise possible?[1]

Surely it was a time when politicians' words counted for something, and nowhere more so than in the great deliberative body, the US Senate. In the years of the "middle period" before the Civil War, a few men's words were so valued that, when they were scheduled to speak, the galleries of the Senate filled and the audience piled out of the chamber into the anteroom. The space itself was one of the architectural gems of the new nation.

> Located in the eastern half of the old north wing in the U.S. Capitol, the "Old Senate Chamber" was a semicircular room 75 feet in diameter covered by a half dome. It was designed by Benjamin Henry Latrobe and constructed by him and his successor, Charles Bulfinch, in 1815–1819.

---

1 Henry Wadsworth Longfellow, "The Building of the Ship" (1849), in *The Building of the Ship, with Illustrations* (Boston: Fields, Osgood, 1870), 76; Nicholas A. Basbanes, *Cross of Snow: A Life of Henry Wadsworth Longfellow* (New York: Knopf, 2020), 251, 252.

Latrobe modeled the chamber after similar rooms he had seen in Paris, which he considered ideally suited for hearing, speaking and seeing. He employed marble columns based on Grecian examples to support the visitor's gallery along the eastern wall. In 1828 Charles Bulfinch added a second gallery supported by slender cast-iron columns along the curving western wall.

The auditory of the chamber was near perfect for this "golden age of debate," although when crowded with visitors the space rapidly heated. Reporters for the *New York Herald* and other newspapers reproduced the speeches, and the speeches appeared, edited by their authors, in the appendix to the *Congressional Globe*, and then reappeared, once again edited by the authors, in pamphlet form. Revisions might be made prior to publication, to sway a larger audience or to avoid giving offense, though these did not materially lengthen or shorten the speeches or alter their purpose.[2]

* * *

For the generation of politicians that inherited the Republic and the Union, the opening months of 1850 seemed a critical moment. The nation had expanded its borders from Canada to Mexico and from the Atlantic Ocean to the Pacific. The war with Mexico had been won, a triumph that added more territory to the country than any event since the Louisiana Purchase of 1803. Vast lands from the mountains of Colorado to the Pacific shores of California offered rich mineral resources, grazing lands, and farmsteads. But the inheritance of this "manifest destiny" was not entirely a blessing. How was this territory to be governed, and most important, was it to be opened to human bondage? Mexican law banned slavery, but was that law binding on the new occupants from the United States? In the acrid debate over the expansion of slavery in the winter of 1850, the national government teetered on the brink of disaster. The story of the Compromise of 1850, as historians have called it, "and of the great debate which ran through it . . . one of the classic and inevitable set pieces in American historical writing . . . the brilliant effect of oratory in

---

2 Donald A. Ritchie, *The U.S. Congress: A Very Short Introduction*, 2nd ed. (New York: Oxford University Press, 2016), 116; Architect of the Capitol, "Old Senate Chamber" (n.d.), www.aoc.gov; *New York Herald*, March 5, 1850, p. 1 (Calhoun), March 9, pp. 1–2 (Webster).

the grand manner . . . combined to create scenes of stunning dramatic effect."[3]

Three men, arguably "the most eloquent men to appear on the American political stage," Henry Clay of Kentucky, John C. Calhoun of South Carolina, and Daniel Webster of Massachusetts, gave speeches occasioned by the application of California for admission to the Union. California had been a part of Mexico, then had briefly declared itself an independent nation (with more than a little help from US instigators), and was finally officially ceded to the United States in the peace negotiations that ended the Mexican-American War, in 1848. Although it had never been a territory of the United States, its leaders wished it to be a free state (no slavery, no slaves), which would have upset the hitherto carefully maintained balance of free and slave states in the upper house of the US Congress. There, faced with the application of California for statehood, senators engaged in a debate whose significance matched the constitutional convention debates of 1787. The difference was that the senators' words, unlike the framers', were public. Could their words save the Union? If so, could a deliberative democracy itself survive such a crisis?[4]

The three senators are familiar to students of the middle period or antebellum era (1815–1860) of our history. Called by one historian "the great triumvirate," Clay, Calhoun, and Webster had all, at some point in their careers, been members of the Senate, secretaries of state, and leaders of their political parties. At various times they had yearned for the presidency, though all had fallen short of success. They rarely made a move without calculating how the others would respond. All had expressed opinions on slavery, opinions that differed substantially.[5]

3 David Potter, *The Impending Crisis: America Before the Civil War, 1848–1861* (New York: Harper & Row, 1976), 97.

4 H. W. Brands, *The Age of Gold: The California Gold Rush and the New American Dream* (New York: Random House, 2002), 246–247. The debates in the constitutional convention of 1787 were closed. Later accounts, principally James Madison's, would become authority, but modern scholarship has questioned Madison's purposes and accuracy.

5 Fergus Bordewich, *America's Great Debate: Henry Clay, Stephen A. Douglas, and the Compromise that Preserved the Union* (New York: Simon & Schuster, 2012), 14; Holman Hamilton, *Prologue to Conflict: The Crisis and Compromise of 1850* (New York: Norton, 1964), 43–62; Merrill D. Peterson, *The Great Triumvirate: Webster, Clay, and Calhoun* (New York: Oxford University Press, 1987), vii, 5, 449–475; H. W. Brands, *Heirs of the Founders: The Epic Rivalry of Henry Clay, John C. Calhoun, and Daniel Webster, the Second Generation of American Giants* (New York: Doubleday, 2018), 1–8, 303–372.

As it happened, and not by chance, all were lawyers. Webster and Clay had large practices, which they maintained while they served in public office. Calhoun, who married into wealth, halted his practice. For all of them, however, practicing law meant knowing and using "terms of art" correctly, but even more important in those days, knowing which words would sway a jury. For lawyers especially, words mattered. Many of the lawyer-politicians gained from their legal practice a surer sense of themselves as advocates of political causes, for legal practice in the antebellum era was as much about verbal agility as about "black letter" (formal lawbook) learning. The leaders of the profession, like Roger B. Taney of Maryland, were distinguished for their skill at untangling issues, not particularly for their mastery of arcane knowledge. Such men were lucid and even passionate in oral argument. Future leaders of the bar like North Carolina's Thomas Ruffin developed a kind of courtroom combat. Ruffin was "hardly ever courteous and not always respectful and frequently abusive." Not everyone fit this model, of course. Young Abraham Lincoln won in court by speaking the language of the jury, and Georgia lawyer Alexander Stephens relied on eloquence. To these lawyer-politicians, by training, experience, and professional ideology, words mattered a great deal.[6]

In this essay, I return to three speeches, presented on the Senate floor between February 5 and March 7, 1850, on the understanding that each was prepared with care and sincerity. Indeed, the speakers' efforts on this occasion were Herculean. Each captured essential elements of American thinking and each revealed the state of American politics. By grouping them together, in their entirety, and commenting on each part, one can see how intractable the slavery issue had become, how near a civil war was, and how it was prevented—at least for a time.[7]

---

6 Peter Charles Hoffer, *Daniel Webster and the Unfinished Constitution* (Lawrence: University Press of Kansas, 2018), 19–20, 23–24; John Niven, *John C. Calhoun and the Price of Union* (Baton Rouge: Louisiana State University Press, 1988), 32, 34; Maurice G. Baxter, *Henry Clay the Lawyer* (Lexington: University Press of Kentucky, 2000); other material quoted from Hoffer, *Uncivil Warriors: The Lawyers' Civil War* (New York: Oxford University Press, 2016), 9.

7 Most biographies and political histories briefly summarize these speeches, even the "classic" ones. The Senate.gov site on classic speeches gives short excerpts. Bordewich, *Great Debate*, 141–181, offers a colorful and dramatic account but reduces the content of the speeches to a page or two; John C. Waugh, *On the Brink of Civil War: The Compromise of 1850 and How It Changed the Course of American History* (Wilmington, DE: Scholarly Resources, 2003), afforded the three speeches ten

To repeat: each of the three speeches is an excellent example of mid-nineteenth-century political oratory, perhaps exceeded only by Lincoln's two inaugurals and his Gettysburg Address. But the three speeches belong together, although separated by days and other Senate speeches, as each in turn added vital elements to the same, ongoing conversation. Gathered here, analyzed piece by piece, and then reassembled, they reveal something that contemporaries understood and Americans today have missed about politics in the age of slavery: like a dark hole, it drew into itself all other issues. One can see how the speakers, reunited in these pages, thought they could save a nation, prevent disunion, and avoid internecine war over slavery.[8]

While nothing today matches the divisive impact on domestic politics that slavery imposed then, emanations of the great 1850 debates still cast shadows over our politics. As in 1850, "the hour seems very dark indeed" as topics of a sectional character dominate the public conversation. Our national legislature is once again marked by political party animosity, so fierce that Congress periodically teeters on unworkability, the nation's bills may go unpaid, and members of Congress routinely behave in uncivil conduct. All had precedents in the 1850s. A riot that shut down the Capitol at the end of a presidential election in 2020 echoed the electoral incivility of the middle period. History, it would seem, does repeat itself, unless we are wise enough to learn its lessons.[9]

* * *

---

pages. Hamilton, *Prologue to Conflict*, gave a summary of the speeches in twenty pages. Other historians' works presented the speeches in similarly truncated fashion.

8 What makes a great speech? Or better put, what makes a speech great? The three speeches herein are great, but why? The most beautiful array of words uttered in an empty theater or on a busy street corner would never be classed as great. Were I to utter Hamlet's famous lines, "except my life, except my life, except my life," from act 2, scene 2, that fragment would never be great, but when Richard Burton spoke these words on the Broadway stage on April 9, 1964, they electrified the audience. (I was there.) Surely, then, the speaker's tone, gesture, and phrasing help make the speech great. Burton found a way to give each of the lines different meanings, so the audience had to listen carefully. Audience attention is thus another element in the great speech. Critics hailed Burton's performance, rightfully, and his appearance for the April through August run of the play was not to be missed. Thus the ripeness of the occasion is another key element of greatness. And of course the speech must be written, for posterity to remember the words. The opening months of 1850 in the Senate Chamber fit this description.

9 Compare Allan Nevins, *Ordeal of the Union*, vol. 1: *Fruits of Manifest Destiny, 1847–1852* (New York: Scribner's, 1947), 257, 260, with Joanne B. Freeman, *The Field of Blood: Violence in Congress and the Road to Civil War* (New York: Farrar, Straus and Giroux, 2018), xxi–xxv.

Although party leaders had repeatedly and energetically attempted to bury the slavery question after the bitterly disputed Missouri Compromise of 1819–1821, in 1846 Pennsylvania Democratic congressman David Wilmot's Proviso in Congress, calling for a ban on slavery in any territory won from Mexico, threw the slavery question back onto the front pages—and enflamed senatorial debate. A majority in the House voted for it, but the Senate blocked it. The war with Mexico concluded two years later; large portions of the Southwest, including the future states of Colorado, New Mexico, and Arizona, were obtained in the Treaty of Guadalupe Hidalgo (1848). California had formed a republic of its own, under the prompting of provocateurs sent by the Polk administration. The fate of slavery in these lands remained uncertain.[10]

After the election of 1848, party leaders on both sides of the aisle once again tried to bridge the widening breach over the expansion of slavery. But beneath the calm of business as usual, ferment was building over the admission of California. The territory's population had zoomed after the discovery of gold at Sutter's Mill in 1848, and the territorial government was preparing a constitution to accompany its application for admission to the Union. On November 11, 1849, the draft California state constitution was ratified by its voters and sent to Washington, DC. The document was long and detailed—its official transcription took hours—but it was clearly a free state constitution.[11]

It began with a statement of rights, the first of which read, "All men are by nature free and independent, and have certain inalienable rights, among which are those of enjoying and defending life and liberty, acquiring, possessing, and protecting property: and pursuing and obtaining safety and happiness." It incorporated an expanded version of the federal Bill of Rights and spoke of persons or inhabitants of the state. Although the sections on political rights limited them to "white male" citizens, the law provided for joint property for wives, a reform based in part on Spanish/Roman law, dueling was deemed illegal, and public education was encouraged. Section 18 of article I, however, was the most important to southern members of the Senate and the Democratic leadership—"Neither slavery, nor involuntary servitude, unless for the

---

10 Joel H. Silbey, *Storm over Texas: The Annexation Controversy and the Road to the Civil War* (New York: Oxford University Press, 2005), 123–149.
11 Brands, *Age of Gold*, 276–287.

punishment of crimes, shall ever be tolerated in this State." Section 3 of the same article seemed directed to the fugitive slave question: "The right of trial by jury shall be secured to all, and remain inviolate forever."[12]

In the House of Representatives, passions over the Wilmot Proviso had not yet subsided when the California question arose. A contest for the Speakership was so tumultuous that for a time no one could gain a majority. (Eventually, Howell Cobb of Georgia was elected.) Members carried weapons into the chamber, and threats of disunion filled the air. When southern members turned to the newly elected president, Louisiana's Zachary Taylor, to resolve the disputes by stalling the admission of California, he threw them out of his office and blustered that he would see California admitted to the Union or else. His special message to the Senate on January 23, 1850, was hardly elegant but made his position clear:

> Under these circumstances I thought, and still think, that it was my duty to endeavor to put it in the power of Congress, by the admission of California and New Mexico as States, to remove all occasion for the unnecessary agitation of the public mind. It is understood that the people of the western part of California have formed a plan of a State constitution and will soon submit the same to the judgment of Congress and apply for admission as a State. This course on their part, though in accordance with, was not adopted exclusively in consequence of, any expression of my wishes, inasmuch as measures tending to this end had been promoted by the officers sent there by my predecessor, and were already in active progress of execution before any communication from me reached California. If the proposed constitution shall, when submitted to Congress, be found to be in compliance with the requisitions of the Constitution of the United States, I earnestly recommend that it may receive the sanction of Congress.

To make the matter even clearer, for Taylor was hardly a master of the English language, he added, "Any attempt to deny to the people of the State the right of self-government in a matter which peculiarly affects

---

12 Herman Belz, "Popular Sovereignty, the Right of Revolution, and California Statehood," in *The California Republic*, ed. Brian P. Janiskee and Ken Masugi (Lanham, MD: Rowman & Littlefield, 2004), 12–26; California Secretary of State, "California State Constitution of 1849," www.sos.ca.gov.

themselves will infallibly be regarded by them as an invasion of their rights, and, upon the principles laid down in our own Declaration of Independence, they will certainly be sustained by the great mass of the American people."[13]

With the petition for admission and the free constitution presented for approval in the Senate, southern voices on the admission question there grew sour and resentful. Leading southern Democrats condemned the admission as a violation of the US Constitution and a danger to the balance of power in the Senate. The Republic seemed in greater peril than at any time since its founding. The Senate itself, the great deliberative body, also faced a great challenge to its rules, its customs, and its importance.[14]

On January 29, as passions in the first session of the thirty-first Congress grew overheated over the admission of California, Clay offered a series of eight resolutions, which he explained and defended in a two-day, five-hour speech over the course of February 5 and 6. He argued for each of them independently. He also, and this is important, argued for moderation in the ensuing debate. He wanted the Senate to be a deliberative body, with members respecting one another. Henry Foote of Mississippi, a proslavery unionist, would try to get the eight resolutions passed together in an "omnibus." Clay did not want an omnibus bill (although he later changed his mind), but both he and Foote hoped that they had given the free states and the slave states' senators enough that they would set aside their differences. No principle would be compromised, he insisted. Calhoun responded on March 4, with a speech that argued slavery was a positive good and conceded nothing in his love for the Union. Clay had visited with Webster a week before Clay presented his resolutions, and Webster promised his support. On the floor of the Senate, Webster tried to bridge the chasm between the two members of the great Senate triumvirate, putting the Union ahead of sectional interests.[15]

---

13 Zachary Taylor, "Regarding Newly Acquired Territories," January 23, 1850, 31st Cong., 1st sess., *Congressional Globe*, appendix, 7; Potter, *Impending Crisis*, 94–95; Waugh, *Brink of Civil War*, 59.
14 Nevins, *Ordeal of the Union*, 275.
15 Potter, *Impending Crisis*, 97; Bordewich, *Great Debate*, 150–151; Nevins, *Ordeal of the Union*, 280–283. The debate continued in the 31st Cong., 1st sess. until September 9–20, 1850, with the admission of California, the Fugitive Slave Act of 1850, and the ban on slave auctions in DC. See the appendix to this volume. Foote was a unique character, a Confederate lawmaker and later convert

Note on Method

There are many fine books on the "crisis" of the 1850s, almost all of them regarding it as the prelude to secession and Civil War. Most, though not all, appear in the footnotes to this book, but they do not obviate the contribution of this book because they do not take the three speeches as seriously as they should. By this I mean they devote relatively few pages to the speeches, summarizing their arguments and politics but not reproducing and analyzing the language and presentation in depth. As David Potter wrote in his Pulitzer Prize–winning account of the 1850s, "Clay, Webster, Calhoun and the others held to a superb standard of debate, and if they did not say very much that had not been said before, they expressed it somewhat better than it had ever been expressed before." The three speeches deserve fuller attention.[16]

It may seem that these three speeches speak for themselves. Not so. The auditory culture of the antebellum years requires an introduction to the modern ear. People really listened back then, not just to the words, but to the speaker's inflection, the verbal gestures. All three of the speakers in this book had characteristic ways of addressing their audiences, aimed to persuade, entertain, and perform. Clay's voice was musical, varying in tone, and captivating. Calhoun's tone was "energetic, rapid, and earnest," often philosophical, lecturing his listeners. Webster was the master orator, never rambling or uttering an undisciplined word; each phrase was indelible, cut from New Hampshire stone, booming, galvanizing—in short, theatrical. But we have no recordings of those speeches.[17]

What is more, one finds that the exact wording in the documentary record may not be entirely accurate. It may not precisely match the freestanding version that the speakers commissioned after the fact. The *Congressional Globe* (1831–1873), in which the proceedings of Congress were

---

to civil rights advocacy who held office under Republican president Rutherford B. Hayes. Foote died in 1880. John E. Gonzales, "Henry Stuart Foote: Confederate Congressman and Exile," *Civil War History* 11 (1965): 384–395.

16 Potter, *Impending Crisis*, 98. The notable exception to this theme of an inescapable crisis is Nevins, *Ordeal of the Union*, 195 (politics as usual), 364 (remove the posturing of the politicians and crises would not have occurred), 398 (defeat of the secessionist movement).

17 Clay: "Henry Cay as an Orator," *New York Times*, January 3, 1888, p. 2; Calhoun, *Life of John C. Calhoun* (New York: Harper, 1848), 73; Webster: Albert E. Pillsbury, *Webster the Orator* (n.p., 1903), 3–7.

recorded, was not an official source, though it was a record taken at the time and, as the Library of Congress reported, after the thirty-second Congress in 1852, "approached verbatim." The first editors of the *Globe*, Francis Preston Blair and John Cook Rives, were Democratic (pro–Andrew Jackson) journalists who hired stenographers to take down the debates as they occurred, but they were not neutral in the politics of the times. By 1849, Blair had left control of the *Globe* to Rives, who proposed to run it impartially. Still, until an official congressional version of the debates appeared (the *Congressional Record* began publication in 1873), the *Globe* was the best source of the debates.[18]

But I have not used the *Globe* as my only source. Members could not only submit a copy of the full text of their speeches to be included in an appendix published at the end of a congressional session but also publish a redacted version (almost always shorter) as a free-standing pamphlet. Webster arranged for the publication of a corrected version of his speech. This version was edited by him, not by the *Globe*, and was closer to his thinking—at least what he wanted readers to know—than the copies in the appendix to the *Globe*. If one lays the two versions alongside one another, in what is called parallel text analysis, common in literary editing, however, one finds that Webster made few substantive changes. I have noted the important omissions and additions in notes.[19]

What is more, all historical documents must be contextualized, that is, set in a time and place. Meanings of terms that seem modern might earlier have contested or variant meanings. Historians are aware of this. Two familiar forms and one less familiar of contextualization that historians produce are the primary source reader and the annotated edition. In the first, the historian presents a series of documents with a general introduction and headnotes for each of the documents. These may be scholarly masterworks, like Harvard University Press's John Harvard Library of American Classics. According to Bernard Bailyn, the

---

18 Williamjames Hull Hoffer, *To Enlarge the Machinery of Government; Congressional Debates and the Growth of the American State, 1855–1889* (Baltimore: Johns Hopkins University Press, 2007), 3–4.
19 Richard J. McKinney, "An Overview of the Congressional Record and Its Predecessor Publications," *Law Library Lights* 45 (2002): 1–8. An example of the historians' preference for the speakers' own published version over the *Globe* appendix version is David Donald, *Charles Sumner and the Coming of the Civil War* (New York: Knopf, 1960), 276n2. "All subsequent refences to *The Crime Against Kansas* are to this contemporary pamphlet edition" regarding Charles Sumner's controversial address on May 19–20, 1856.

first editor-in-chief of the series, the intention was "to make available to the general reader in definitive, reasonably priced editions, major, book-length documents of American cultural history." While that goal was a little ambitious (few of the Belknap volumes made it into classrooms), series like Major Problems from D. C. Heath did and in the hands of students were "designed to encourage critical thinking about history." The Macmillan / Bedford Books topical series in history and culture followed a somewhat different format—short paperback works offering an introduction to the topic, followed by a selection of abbreviated documents, each with its own brief introduction.

In the second format, scholarly editions of letters and speeches of leading Americans, the historical documents are heavily footnoted, each note adding information about the parts of the document. The model was the Julian P. Boyd edition of the *Papers of Thomas Jefferson*, a project that has continued across many years. As historian David Chesnutt has written of the Boyd method, "Modern historical editing dates from the publication of Julian Boyd's first volume of *The Papers of Thomas Jefferson* in 1950. Although there had been earlier compilations of the papers of famous Americans, his carefully prepared texts of Jefferson's letters and other writings, 'warts and all,' set a new standard for accuracy and reliability. His equally careful selection of what to include and what not to include reflected the historian's thoughtful appraisal of what needed to be set before readers so they could begin to understand the essential Jefferson. And Boyd's incisive commentary provided the context needed to place Jefferson in the wider world of the American Revolution and the early national period of American history." The letters' volumes, as I write numbering forty-seven and still unfinished, have spawned ancillary editions of Jefferson's parliamentary writings, literary writings, writings on the Gospels, memorandum books, and legal commonplace book. This and other series, in part supported by grants from the National Historical Publications and Records Commission, are superb examples of the second format, to "promote the preservation and use of America's documentary heritage essential to understanding our democracy, history, and culture."[20]

---

20 David Chesnutt, "The Model Editions Partnership: Historical Editions in the Digital Age," *D-Lib Magazine*, www.dlib.org; National Historical Publications and Records Commission, www.archives.gov/nhprc.

The third format is innovative. In literary biography, a relative hand-ful of documents from a much larger collection are selected, and each, reproduced in full, introduces a chapter. The three works that reflect the very best of this kind of contextualization are Ronald C. White's *The Eloquent President: A Portrait of Lincoln through His Words* (2005), Laurel Thatcher Ulrich's *A Midwife's Tale: The Life of Martha Ballard, Based on Her Diary, 1785–1812*, and Andrew Stauffer's, *Byron: A Life in Ten Letters*. The authors' mastery of the rest of the documentary evidence draws from the selected documents their fullest significance, but what makes this genre of historical editing work is the way that the authors privilege the words of their subjects.[21]

Here I simplify and combine the three methods. After the general introduction above, I introduce each document and then provide a run-ning commentary after each part. The commentary is interwoven with each passage. Notes to the commentary entries appear at the bottom of the page. I take readers back in time and make them part of the audi-ence, listening and responding (as I am certain members of the Senate did to one another) to the speech as it was delivered.

---

21 Ronald C. White, *The Eloquent President: A Portrait of Lincoln through His Words* (New York: Random House, 2005); Laurel Thatcher Ulrich, *A Midwife's Tale: The Life of Martha Ballard, Based on Her Diary, 1785–1812* (New York: Knopf, 1990); Andrew Stauffer, *Byron: A Life in Ten Letters* (Cambridge: Cambridge University Press, 2024).

1

Henry Clay, Speech in the Senate, on Proposed Compromise Resolutions, February 5, 1850

Figure 1.1. Henry Clay. Credit: Library of Congress, Prints & Photographs Division.

ON January 26, 1850, Kentucky's senator Henry Clay, the elder statesman of the Whig Party, wrote to Boyd McNairy about the new Senate session.[1] The foremost issue before Congress was the admission of California to the Union. The proposed state constitution would have made California a "free state," upsetting the balance between free and slave states in the Senate. He admitted that "we are here in the midst of great excitement on the slavery question. I do not yet see land, but hope for the best, whilst fearing the worst." To Thomas Stevenson, another friend, he revealed his plan to offer a series of compromise resolutions. Three days later, an ailing Clay (aged seventy-two and suffering from tuberculosis) offered the Senate "some adjustment" of the dispute. He introduced eight resolutions, which he defended in a five-hour, two-day speech on February 5–6, 1850, here reappearing as chapters 1 and 2.[2]

The eight resolutions included that California would be admitted as a free state; other lands acquired from Mexico as a result of the Mexican-American War would be organized as territories without any provision on slavery; Texas would surrender any claims to that territory; the federal government would assume Texas's debts prior to its admission to the Union in 1845 (for which an allotment of three million dollars would be made); slavery would not be abolished in the District of Columbia; the slave trade (and auctions) would be banned in the District; Congress would not regulate the domestic slave trade elsewhere; and the Fugitive Slave Law would be revised to ease recapture and return of runaways. It was an ambitious and comprehensive program of "compromise and harmony."[3]

Celebrated as the Great Compromiser, Clay boasted a storied career in the service of the Republic. A Virginia-born lawyer with a practice

---

1 Clay, Speech in Senate, February 5, 1850, 31st Cong., 1st sess., *Congressional Globe*, appendix, 115–120. Text here from Henry Clay, *Speech . . . on Taking Up His Compromise Resolutions on the Subject of Slavery* (New York: Stringer and Townsend, 1850). There was very little difference between this version and the version in the appendix.

2 Henry Clay to Boyd McNairy, January 26, 1850, in *Papers of Henry Clay*, ed. Melba Porter Hay and Carol Reardon (Lexington: University Press of Kentucky, 1991), 10:654; Clay to Thomas B. Stevenson, January 26, 1850, in *Papers of Henry Clay*, 10:655.

3 John C. Waugh, *On the Brink of Civil War: The Compromise of 1850 and How It Changed the Course of American History* (Wilmington, DE: Scholarly Resources, 2003), 75.

in Lexington, Kentucky, he had first entered Congress as a senator for a brief time and then the lower house on March 4, 1811, when he was immediately elected Speaker. There he served until 1825. From the House, he went on to negotiate the end of the War of 1812, which he had favored. After a stint as secretary of state under President John Quincy Adams, Clay was elected to represent Kentucky in the Senate in 1831. Although originally a Jeffersonian Republican, he found that his program of internal improvement (called the American System) and his ambitions for the presidency did not lie with the Democratic Party, and he helped found the Whig Party in 1834. His role in the settlement of the Missouri statehood controversy and subsequent disputes over the future of slavery won him the title of Great Compromiser. But his ambition to sit in the White House was continually frustrated.[4]

He was never an abolitionist, and he owned slaves, but he privately viewed and publicly condemned slavery as immoral. He campaigned against the Mexican-American War in part because he saw it as an invitation to expand the empire of slavery. As he told an audience in Lexington in 1847, "My opinions on the subject of slavery are well known. They have the merit, if it be one, of consistency, uniformity, and long duration. I have ever regarded slavery as a great evil, a wrong, for the present, I fear, an irremediable wrong to its unfortunate victims. I should rejoice if not a single slave breathed the air or was within the limits of our country. But here they are, to be dealt with as well as we can, with a due consideration of all circumstances affecting the security, safety and happiness of both races."[5]

Clay's seat was at the back of the chamber (he had just returned to the Senate from retirement, and so was seated in the rear), but as was his wont, he moved about the chamber as he spoke, ending up near the front. Although he had a cold and a cough that day, his voice retained its lovely, bass tone, its almost "hypnotic quality," and its clarity and made him one of the most admired public speakers of the day. "Rather than speaking from finished manuscripts, he tended to rely upon others to report his speeches, and the transcripts were less than perfect. Some

---

4 Robert V. Remini, *Henry Clay, Statesman for the Union* (New York: Norton, 1991), 72–93, 169–192; Michael F. Holt, *The Rise and Fall of the American Whig Party: Jacksonian Politics and the Onset of the Civil War* (New York: Oxford University Press, 1999), 1–2, 137, 160–167.
5 Henry Clay, Speech on the Mexican-American War, November 13, 1847, https://henryclay.org.

of his major speeches were not recorded in any form. It was said that his extemporaneous, emotionally expansive oratorical performances, heightened by his highly effective and fluid facial expressions and theatrical gestures, needed to be witnessed for their full effect."[6]

When reading the speech, note its conversational tone. Clay is sharing his thoughts with his colleagues, like a superb storyteller. The moderation he asks from them matches the modesty of his plea. Only in the last hour of the second day, presented here in chapter 2, does his tone become more urgent, as he warns of the dangers of disunion.

> Mr. President, never on any former occasion have I risen under feelings of such painful solicitude. I have seen many periods of great anxiety, of peril, and of danger in this country, and I have never before risen to address any assemblage so oppressed, so appalled, and so anxious; and sir, I hope it will not be out of place to do here, what again and again I have done in my private chamber, to implore of Him who holds the destinies of nations and individuals in His hands, to bestow upon our country His blessing, to calm the violence and rage of party, to still passion, to allow reason once more to resume its empire. And may I not ask of Him too, sir, to bestow on his humble servant now before him the blessing of his smiles, and of strength and ability to perform the work which now lies before him?

The speaker always addressed the presiding officer, the vice president. He sat at the front of the room, on a raised dais. In this case it was New York's Millard Fillmore, with whom Clay was friendly. Speakers were not supposed to look elsewhere but did when another member interrupted, asking the speaker to "yield the floor" for a motion or to reply to a remark that reflected on them. Courtesy required that the speaker yield, but they did not always extend this courtesy.[7]

---

6 John C. Briggs, "Antebellum Oratory," in *A Companion to American Literature*, ed. Susan Belasco (Hoboken, NJ: Wiley-Blackwell, 2020), 2:258; Fergus Bordewich, *America's Great Debate: Henry Clay, Stephen A. Douglas, and the Compromise that Preserved the Union* (New York: Simon & Schuster, 2012), 134–145; Waugh, *Brink of Civil War*, 71, 72.

7 "No Senator shall interrupt another Senator in debate without his consent, and to obtain such consent he shall first address the Presiding Officer, and no Senator shall speak more than twice upon any one question in debate on the same legislative day without leave of the Senate, which shall be determined without debate." "A Manual for Practice for the Use of the Senate of the United

Clay asking the deity to give him the strength for the task of saving the nation may have seemed a little immodest, but the language of religious piety was a commonplace of senatorial rhetoric. After all, the nation had only just passed through a second "great awakening" of religious effusion. Huge church gatherings and country "camp" meetings brought preachers of all denominations together with crowds seeking salvation. Clay was not notably religious, not belonging to any church until 1847. Other senators were, however, and so was the nation.[8]

> Sir, I have said that I have seen other anxious periods in the history of our country, and if I were to venture, Mr. President, to trace, to their original source the cause of all our present dangers, difficulties, and distraction, I should ascribe it to the violence and intemperance of party spirit. To party spirit! Sir, in the progress of this session we have had the testimony of two Senators here, who, however they may differ on other matters, concur in the existence of that cause in originating the unhappy differences which prevail throughout the country, on the subject of the institution of slavery. Parties, in their endeavors to obtain the one ascendancy over the other, catch at every passing or floating plank in order to add strength and power to each.

Here Clay reminded the senators that he had been there in the waning years of the "first party system" and seen the rise of the "second party system." He had entered politics in the midst of the waning years of the Federalist versus Jeffersonian Republican Party contests, at the end of the first party era, on the eve of the War of 1812. He had helped start that war as one of the "Hawks" in Congress and then helped end the war by negotiating the Treaty of Ghent in 1814. He had run for the presidency

---

States" was written by Thomas Jefferson when he was the vice president and was published in 1801, as he was leaving that office. The content appears in "Jefferson's Manual of Parliamentary Practice," www.govinfo.gov. On Fillmore and Clay, see Paul Finkelman, *Millard Fillmore* (New York: Holt, 2011), 64.

8 On the Second Great Awakening, see Whitney R. Cross, *The Burned-Over District: The Social and Intellectual History of Enthusiastic Religion in Western New York, 1800–1850* (Ithaca, NY: Cornell University Press, 1982), and in politics, Richard J. Carwardine, *Evangelicals and Politics in Antebellum America* (New Haven, CT: Yale University Press, 1993). Clay was not a member of any religious sect until his later years, and even then he was a believer in religious pluralism. Remini, *Clay*, 397, 650. On American religious beliefs in the 1850s, see Jon Butler, *Awash in a Sea of Faith: Christianizing the American People* (Cambridge, MA: Harvard University Press, 1990), 225–256.

in 1824, had served as secretary of state under President John Quincy Adams, and then had been one of the founders of the Whig Party (indeed had given that party its name) in opposition to President Andrew Jackson and the Democratic Party of 1828. Clay officially ran for the highest office as a Whig presidential candidate in 1844, but hankered for it throughout his public career. It was thus more than ironic that he subscribed the present crisis to party spirit, when no one had done more to elevate himself through party spirit than he. He failed to recognize this, instead seeing his party as the nation itself. Many of the senators no doubt saw things differently.[9]

> We have been told by the two Senators to whom I have referred, that each of the parties at the North, in its turn, has moved and endeavored to obtain the assistance of a small party called abolitionists, in order that the scale in its favor might preponderate against that of its adversary. And all around us, every where, we see too many evidences of the existence of the spirit and intemperance of party. I might go to other legislative bodies than that which is assembled in Congress, and I might draw from them illustrations of the melancholy truth upon which I am dwelling, but I need not pass out of this capitol itself.

Although I cannot with certainty determine the two senators, they were likely John Berrien of Georgia and Lewis Cass of Michigan, who had given major speeches earlier in the session, before Clay, on January 29 and anticipated Clay's resolutions. Their comments reminded the upper house that slavery was the central issue. Berrien was a Whig, slaveholder, lawyer, and former US attorney general. Cass was born in New Hampshire, moved with his family to Ohio, and ended up as the territorial governor of Michigan. A Jacksonian Democrat and slave owner, Cass served as Jackson's secretary of war and ran unsuccessfully for the presidency in 1848 against Taylor. Blaming national divisions on the abolitionists was common practice among everyone except the abolitionists. The Liberty Party of 1840 and the Free Soil Party of 1848 represented antislavery efforts to win the presidency but had failed to win

---

9 James C. Klotter, *Henry Clay: The Man Who Would Be President* (New York: Oxford University Press, 2018), 99, 307, 353; Holt, *Rise and Fall of the American Whig Party*, 146.

more than a small fraction of the votes, and they had not threatened the electoral dominance of the Democratic and Whig Parties, although in some northern states they had played a spoiler role.[10]

> I say it, sir, with all deference and respect to that other portion of Congress assembled in the other wing of this capitol; but what have we seen there? During this very session one whole week has been exhausted—I think about a week—in the vain endeavor to elect a doorkeeper of the House. And, Mr. President, what was the question in this struggle to elect a doorkeeper? It was not as to the man or the qualities of the man, or who is best adapted to the situation. It was whether the doorkeeper entertained opinions upon certain national measures coincident with this or that side of the House. That was the sole question which prevented the election of a doorkeeper for about the period of a week.
>
> Sir, I make no reproaches—none, to either portion of that House; I state the fact; and I state the fact to draw from it the conclusion and to express the hope that there will be an endeavor to check this violence of party. Sir, what vicissitudes do we not pass through in this short mortal career of ours? Eight years, or nearly eight years ago, I took my leave finally, and, as I supposed, forever, from this body. At that time I did not conceive of the possibility of ever again returning to it. And if my private wishes and particular inclinations, and the desire during the short remnant of my days to remain in repose and quiet, could have prevailed, you would never have seen me occupying the seat which I now occupy upon this floor. The Legislature of the State to which I belong, unsolicited by me, chose to designate me for this station, and I have come here, sir, in obedience to a sense of stern duty, with no personal objects, no private views, now or hereafter, to gratify.

No reproaches to anyone? Here and in all three speeches, the three men made every effort to avoid ad hominem (personal) attacks on past and present members of either house. Later congressional debates featured furious personal attacks, some of which became physical as well as verbal.

---

10 Daniel Walker Howe, *What Hath God Wrought: The Transformation of America, 1815–1848* (New York: Oxford University Press, 2007), 653, 832–833.

The real battle in the lower house was not over the doorkeeper but over the Speaker of the House. Clay had been in the lower house himself, serving three terms as its Speaker. The House of Representatives was a directly elected body, and over the course of the previous forty years, the number of free white males eligible to vote had grown greatly. The senators were chosen by their state legislatures. Scholars have argued that this part of the "great compromise," including two senators from every state, was a concession to states' rights by the nationalists at the 1787 constitutional convention. Whether that made the upper house a more or less deliberative body, as defenders of that compromise insisted, remains a subject of controversy. Clay retired from the Senate in 1842, returning to his law practice, but his thoughts were never far from his ambition for the White House, and he ran as a Whig for the presidency in 1844. He lost to the "dark horse" Democratic candidate, James K. Polk, a protégé of Andrew Jackson in Tennessee, and himself a Speaker of the lower house and a governor of Tennessee. Polk engineered the annexation of Texas by a joint resolution, after Whigs in the Senate had prevented it.[11]

> I know, sir, the jealousies, the fears, the apprehensions which are engendered by the existence of that party spirit to which I have referred; but if there be in my hearing now, in or out of this Capitol, any one who hopes, in his race for honors and elevation, for higher honors and higher elevation than that which he may occupy, I beg him to believe that I, at least, will never jostle him in the pursuit of those honors or that elevation. I beg him to be perfectly persuaded that, if my wishes prevail, my name shall never be used in competition with his. I beg to assure him that when my service is terminated in this body, my mission, so far as respects the public affairs of this world and upon this earth, is closed, and closed, if my wishes prevail, forever.

In other words, Clay had set aside his ambitions for higher office ("higher elevation").

---

11 Wendy J. Schiller and Charles Stewart III, *Electing the Senate* (Princeton, NJ: Princeton University Press, 2015), 1; Robert W. Merry, *A Country of Vast Designs: James K. Polk, the Mexican War, and the Conquest of the Continent* (New York: Simon & Schuster, 2009), 131–160.

But, sir, it is impossible for us to be blind to the facts which are daily transpiring before us. It is impossible for us not to perceive that party spirit and future elevation mix more or less in all our affairs, in all our deliberations. At a moment when the White House itself is in danger of conflagration, instead of all hands uniting to extinguish the flames, we are contending about who shall be its next occupant. When a dreadful crevasse has occurred, which threatens inundation and destruction to all around it, we are contesting and disputing about the profits of an estate which is threatened with total submersion.

The "conflagration" was a reference to the burning of the White House by British troops in the War of 1812. But the reference also suggested that Clay was prepared to offer himself to save the nation if called upon. The incumbent president, Zachary Taylor, was also a Whig, but no friend of Clay. Although a Louisiana slave owner himself, Taylor did not favor the expansion of slavery and was elevated to the highest office because of his conduct of the Mexican-American War rather than through political favors. He was a strong nationalist. When the motion was made in the House to admit Texas, southern leaders used procedural methods to delay the vote. Two of these, Speaker Howell Cobb and Representative Alexander Stephens, both from Georgia, went to the White House to convince Taylor to deny California admission. He threw them out. Taylor died in July 1850.[12]

Mr. President, it is passion, passion—party, party, and intemperance—that is all I dread in the adjustment of the great questions which unhappily at this time divide our distracted country. Sir, at this moment we have in the legislative bodies of this Capitol and in the States twenty odd furnaces in full blast, emitting heat, and passion, and intemperance, and diffusing them throughout the whole extent of this broad land.

The states to which he referred were those whose representatives had already spoken or presented resolutions from the state governments. The heat was theirs. Some were already calling for secession, led by William

---

12 John S. D. Eisenhower, *Zachary Taylor* (New York: Henry Holt, 2008), 110; Bordewich, *Great Debate*, 164; Holman Hamilton, *Zachary Taylor, Soldier in the White House* (Indianapolis: Bobbs-Merrill, 1951), 2:333.

Yancey, an Alabama newspaperman and briefly a US congressman, and South Carolina's Robert Barnwell Rhett, another journalist turned politician, becoming a senator from South Carolina in December 1850.[13]

> Two months ago all was calm in comparison to the present moment. All now is uproar, confusion and menace to the existence of the Union, and to the happiness and safety of this people. Sir, I implore Senators, I entreat them, by all that they expect hereafter, and by all that is dear to them here below, to repress the ardor of these passions, to look to their country, to its interests, to listen to the voice of reason—not as it shall be attempted to be uttered by me, for I am not so presumptuous as to indulge the hope that anything I may say will avert the effects which I have described, but to listen to their own reason, their own judgment, their own good sense, in determining upon what is best to be done for our country in the actual posture in which we find her.

In public discourse, all was not calm before the Texas application for statehood. It had roiled Congress for almost a decade before outgoing president John Tyler arranged for a treaty with the Republic of Texas, but the treaty failed to garner the necessary two-thirds vote in the Senate. In December 1844, with the cooperation of incoming president James K. Polk, Tyler sought a joint resolution of both houses of Congress that Texas was a US territory, and passage of the resolution (by simple majority votes in both houses) brought it into the Union. Although Mexico did not declare war on the United States for this pragmatic violation of US and Mexican law, a war over the disputed boundary between Texas and Mexico followed nonetheless. That war spawned the Wilmot Proviso, and the huge uproar over the Proviso had not quieted. Clay opposed the annexation and the war but sincerely believed that political compromise was possible and that his moderate language, if not the last words in the debate, could contribute to that compromise by creating an atmosphere of moderation. Words could then become laws, as they had in the Missouri Compromise debates between 1819 and 1821.[14]

---

13 Eric H. Walther, *The Fire-Eaters* (Baton Rouge: Louisiana State University Press, 1992), 60–64, 137–139.
14 Amy S. Greenberg, *A Wicked War: Polk, Clay, Lincoln, and the 1846 US Invasion of Mexico* (New York: Vintage, 2013), 7–8, 61–63.

Like the appeal to religion, the appeal to reason was a staple of antebellum oratory. In romantic culture, passion was the enemy of reason. In
politics, patriotism roused passions. Finding a path between these two
would take Clay the rest of his address. He believed that he had achieved
that feat earlier in his career, however, in the Missouri affair. The point is
that he thought his efforts would bear fruit.[15]

> Sir, to this great object have my efforts been directed during the whole
> session. I have cut myself off from all the usual enjoyments of social life,
> I have confined myself almost entirely, with very few exceptions, to my
> own chamber, and from the beginning of the session to the present time
> my thoughts have been anxiously directed to the object of finding some
> plan, of proposing some mode of accommodation, which would once
> more restore the blessings of concord, harmony and peace to this great
> country.

Why the self-flagellation—confining himself to his home, dedicat-
ing himself to the project of compromise? He knew that everyone else
knew that he was a compulsive gambler and something of a womanizer.
Socializing among the members of Congress with homes, owned and
rented, in the District was a very popular and very expensive social custom. For him to cut himself off from the usual enjoyments of social life
was a sacrifice.[16]

> I am not vain enough to suppose that I have been successful in the ac-
> complishment of this object, but I have presented a scheme, and allow me
> to say to honorable Senators that, if they find in that plan any thing that
> is defective, if they find in it any thing that is worthy of acceptance, but is
> susceptible of improvement by amendment, it seems to me that the true
> and patriotic course is not to denounce it, but to improve it—not to reject
> without examination any project of accommodation having for its object
> the restoration of harmony in this country, but to look at it to see if it be
> susceptible of elaboration or improvement, so as to accomplish the object

---

15 David S. Heidler and Jeanne T. Heidler, *Henry Clay: The Essential American* (New York:
Random House, 2010), 465.
16 See, e.g., Remini, *Clay*, 331, 651. From his early years to the end of his life Clay gambled, which
hurt his public reputation. Drinking and "sociability" were not censured, however.

which I indulge the hope is common to all and every one of us, to restore peace and quiet, and harmony and happiness to this country.

Another plea to be taken seriously. Clay had been stung by his treatment at the presidential polls, and the pain was obvious. Clay's speech was as much about himself as about his proposed omnibus. Another possible reading, suggested by Mark Summers, is that Clay was being modest (more likely Summer's modesty than Clay's, however).

> Sir, when I came to consider this subject, there were two or three general purposes which it seemed to me to be most desirable, if possible, to accomplish. The one was, to settle all the controverted questions arising out of the subject of slavery. It seemed to me to be doing very little if we settled one question and left other distracting questions unadjusted, it seemed to me to be doing but little if we stopped one leak only in the ship of State, and left other leaks capable of producing danger, if not destruction, to the vessel. I therefore, turned my attention to every subject connected with the institution of slavery, and out of which controverted questions had sprung, to see if it were possible or practicable to accommodate and adjust the whole of them.

The project of "settling all controverted questions around the subject of slavery" was the red thread that ran all through antebellum politics—not that all proposals settled all questions but that every controversy arising out of territorial settlement ran into slavery. Attempts to settle the issue led to a series of compromises but not a settlement. Indeed, like a festering infection, slavery spread through the body of national politics, its stench and putrefaction growing worse each year.

> Another principal object which attracted my attention was, to endeavor to form such a scheme of accommodation that neither of the two classes of States into which our country is so unhappily divided should make any sacrifice of any great principle. I believe, sir, the series of resolutions which I have had the honor to present to the Senate accomplishes that object.
>
> Sir, another purpose which I had in view was this: I was aware of the difference of opinion prevailing between these two classes of States. I was

aware that, while one portion of the Union was pushing matters, as it seemed to me, to the greatest extremity, another portion of the Union was pushing them to an opposite, perhaps not less dangerous extremity. It appeared to me, then, that if any arrangement, any satisfactory adjustment could be made of the controverted questions between the two classes of States, that adjustment, that arrangement, could only be successful and effectual by extracting from both parties some concessions—not of principle, not of principle at all, but of feeling, of opinion, in relation to matters in controversy between them.

Clay recognized that the two-party system had held together in the sense that there were northern Democrats and southern Democrats, northern Whigs and southern Whigs. But that fragile unity was breaking along sectional lines, so that northern versus southern interests was becoming a more potent division than Democrat versus Whig. As a westerner (although Kentucky was no longer a frontier state in 1850), Clay had seen an earlier contest between East and West, for example over the cost of western land sales (eastern interests wanted higher prices), transform into the question of the expansion of slavery to the West. The Missouri Compromise line of 36° 30' latitude seemed to quiet that dispute, but only for the Louisiana Purchase lands. But Clay recalled that during the Missouri crisis he had heard "the words civil war and dissolution . . . uttered almost without emotion."[17]

The expansion of slavery into the territory acquired from Mexico reopened the issue. Slavery was common in the New Mexican area when it was part of the Comanche Empire from the 1790s through 1860. Indeed, the capture and resale of Mexican women and men, along with other Native peoples, was a bulwark of the Comanche economy. Mexico had outlawed slavery in 1821, and the Mexican government was continually buying back captives from the Comanche in exchange for guns and ammunition, which they used to capture more slaves. Ironically, when the New Mexico territory became part of the United States following the war with Mexico, had slavery again become legal? Congress barred slavery in all US territories in 1862, and the arrival of American army units

---

17 Henry Clay to Adam Beatty, January 22, 1820, in Calvin Colton, ed., *The Life, Correspondence, and Speeches of Henry Clay* (New York: A. S. Barnes, 1857), 1:61.

after the Civil War ended the Comanche Empire and the Comanche slave trade.[18]

> Sir, I believe the resolutions which I have prepared fulfill that object. I believe, sir, that you will find, upon that careful, rational, and attentive examination of them which I think they deserve, that neither party in some of them make any concession at all; in others the concessions of forbearance are mutual; and in the third place, in reference to the slaveholding States, there are resolutions making concessions to them by the opposite class of States, without any compensation whatever being rendered by them to the non-slaveholding States. I think every one of these characteristics which I have assigned, and the measures which I proposed, is susceptible of clear and satisfactory demonstration by an attentive perusal and critical examination of the resolutions themselves.

The compensation (government payments to private individuals to free their slaves) question was an intractable one, but the idea was still attractive to many politicians. Clay, in his youth, had flirted with it for Kentucky, but to rid the state of slaves not as a general plan of emancipation. It would ensnare Abraham Lincoln in the first years of his presidential term as he contemplated paying to free slaves in the border states. On this and the rest of his resolutions, Clay was not a skilled forecaster of the future of his proposals—the debate would rage on for months, a committee of thirteen that he led in May 1850 would have little success in quieting that furor.[19]

> Let us take up the first resolution. The first resolution, Mr. President, as you are aware, relates to California, and it declares that California, with suitable limits, ought to be admitted as a member of this Union, without the imposition of any restriction either to interdict or to introduce slavery within her limits. Well now, is there any concession in this resolution by either party to the other? I know that gentlemen who come from slave-

---

18 Pekka Hämäläinen, *The Comanche Empire* (New Haven, CT: Yale University Press, 2008), 250–253, 333.
19 On Lincoln: Eric Foner, *The Fiery Trial: Abraham Lincoln and American Slavery* (New York: Norton, 2010), 4, 200; on the committee of thirteen, Colton, ed., *Life, Correspondence, and Speeches of Clay*, 2:426.

holding States say the North gets all that it desires; but by whom does it get it? Does it get it by any action of Congress? If slavery be interdicted within the limits of California, has it been done by Congress—by this Government? No, sir. That interdiction is imposed by California herself. And has it not been the doctrine of all parties that when a State is about to be admitted into the Union, the State has a right to decide for itself whether it will or will not have slavery within its limits?

The process for territories to become states equal in rights and privileges to existing states was laid out in the Northwest Ordinance of 1787 and incorporated in the federal Constitution. (Article IV, section 3, clause 1 declares, "New States may be admitted by the Congress into this Union; but no new State shall be formed or erected within the Jurisdiction of any other State; nor any State be formed by the Junction of two or more States, or Parts of States, without the Consent of the Legislatures of the States concerned as well as of the Congress.") Later convention provided that a territory had to have a population of sixty thousand or so (the population of an average congressional district) and its territorial government, created by Congress, had to draft a constitution and ask to become a state. In 1836 Arkansas sent a constitution and was admitted. Texas had entered the Union as an independent nation and became a state through a treaty with the United States to which the Senate acceded. In 1848 California, also as an independent republic, bypassed the territorial stage by writing a constitution and asking to be admitted. The one uniformity was that the voting population of the state had to vote to seek admission.

> The great principle, sir, which was in contest upon the memorable occasion of the introduction of Missouri into the Union, was, whether it was competent or not competent for Congress to impose any restriction which should exist after she became a member of the Union. We who were in favor of the admission of Missouri contended that no such restriction should be imposed. We contended that, whenever she was once admitted into the Union, she had all the rights and privileges of any preexisting State in the Union, and that among these rights and privileges one was to decide for herself whether slavery should or should not exist within her limits; that she had as much a right to decide upon the intro-

duction of slavery or its abolition as New York had a right to decide upon the introduction or abolition of slavery; and that, although subsequently admitted, she stood among her peers, equally invested with all the privileges that any one of the original thirteen States had a right to enjoy.

Congress could place restrictions on the territories. They were part of the national domain. Once Missouri was a state, however, it existed on an equal footing with the other states, hence was free to make slavery legal. In effect, Clay was engaging in logic chopping in saying that Missouri was a state before it was a state and that it could determine whether it would be slave or free before it had actually achieved statehood. In fact, in 1819 the Tallmadge Amendment to the proposed Missouri Constitution would have barred the importation of slaves into the state and freed every slave born in the state after the age of twenty-five, in effect gradually ending slavery. James Tallmadge was a Jeffersonian Republican New York representative, a leader in the fight for emancipation there (it came in 1827), and his proposal unleashed the fury of southern proslavery members of Congress. Clay opposed it, as he reminded his audience in 1850:[20]

> And so, sir, I think that those who have been contending with so much earnestness and perseverance for the Wilmot proviso ought to reflect that, even if they could carry their object and adopt the proviso, it ceases the moment any State or territory to which it was applicable came to be admitted as a member of the Union. Why, sir, no one contends now, no one believes, that with regard to those Northwestern States to which the ordinance of 1787 applied—Ohio, Indiana, Illinois and Michigan—no one can now believe but that any-one of those States, if they thought proper to do it, have just as much right to introduce slavery within their borders, as Virginia has to maintain the existence of slavery within hers.

Actually, states could change their constitutions to make slavery legal, or at least to aid slaveholders who brought their slaves into the state.[21]

---

20 John R. Van Atta, *Wolf by the Ears: The Missouri Crisis, 1819–1821* (Baltimore: Johns Hopkins University Press, 2015), 16–24, 75–78.
21 After their states achieved statehood, local leaders in Ohio, Indiana, and Illinois sought to suppress the in-migration of free Blacks and the testimony of free Blacks in court cases and torched

Then, sir, if in the struggle for power and empire between the two classes of States a decision in California has taken place adverse to the wishes of the Southern States, it is a decision not made by the General Government. It is a decision respecting which they can utter no complaint toward the General Government. It is a decision made by California herself; which California had unquestionably the right to make under the Constitution of the United States.

Here Clay was throwing the doctrine of states' rights in the face of those who had most often defended it—southern legislators. Irony was a feature of his rhetoric, indeed of all classical rhetoric.

There is, then, in the first resolution, according to the observation which I made some time ago, a case where neither party concedes; where the question of slavery, neither its introduction nor interdiction, is decided in reference to the action of this Government; and if it has been decided, it has been by a different body—by a different power—by California itself, who had a right to make the decision.

Pressing hard on states' rights was the kind of polite aggression that made Clay widely recognized as a great debater. Some historians believe that the southern position was not states' rights per se but southern rights, and in that the federal government's duty to protect southern property rights throughout the nation. This idea, later called "slavery national," was certainly part of the Recaption Clause of the federal Constitution, the Fugitive Slave Act of 1793, and Clay's final proposal, about which we will see more below. Clay knew that this portion of his resolution would be (and indeed had already been) savaged by southern congressmen. There was no reason to hold his scorn in check. But he must now offer something to the South.

Mr. President, the next resolution in the series which I have offered I beg gentlemen candidly now to look at. I was aware, perfectly aware, of the perseverance with which the Wilmot Proviso was insisted upon. I knew

---

Black schools and businesses. Leon F. Litwack, *North of Slavery: The Negro in the Free States, 1790–1860* (Chicago: University of Chicago Press, 1961), 93, 122, 263.

that every one of the free States in this Union, without exception, had by
its legislative body passed resolutions instructing their Senators and re-
questing their Representatives to get that restriction incorporated in any
territorial government which might be established under the auspices of
Congress. I knew how much, and I regretted how much, the free States
had put their hearts upon the adoption of this measure. In the second
resolution I call upon them to waive persisting in it. I ask them, for the
sake of peace and in the spirit of mutual forbearance to other members of
the Union, to give it up—to no longer insist upon it—to see, as they must
see, if their eyes are open, the dangers which lie ahead, if they persevere
in insisting upon it.

Clay preferred the term "free states" to "the North." Why the term
"free states"? Free from what? The answer was free from slavery. By not
talking about North and South, Clay was defusing the sectional character of the debate. What was more, by talking about states rather than
individuals, he deflected blame from individual slaveholders. (Not inci-
dentally, he owned slaves.) This was a vital linguistic tactic if he wanted
to draw support from southern Whigs, many of whom also owned
slaves. The Wilmot Proviso similarly refused to point fingers at individuals, instead focusing on land acquired from Mexico in the war. After
all, Congress could hardly function if accusations were made against
individual members instead of legal entities like states. But with passions
of individual members running high, decorum did not always hold.[22]

When I called upon them in this resolution to do this, was I not bound
to offer, for a surrender of that favorite principle or measure of theirs,
some compensation, not as an equivalent by any means, but some compensation in the spirit of mutual forbearance, which, animating one side,
ought at the same time to actuate the other side? Well, sir, what is it that
is offered them? It is a declaration of what I characterized, and must still
characterize, with great deference to all those who entertain opposite
opinions, as two truths, I will not say incontestable, but to me clear, and I
think they ought to be regarded as indisputable truths.

22 Joanne B. Freeman, *The Field of Blood: Violence in Congress and the Road to Civil War* (New York: Farrar, Straus and Giroux, 2018), 142–144.

True hairsplitting. How was an indisputable fact open to contest? As a matter of style, Clay was accustomed to qualify his remarks, sometimes recasting them in different forms, always careful not to offend. That is why reading his speeches does not give full effect to their impact. One had to see him and hear him to be captivated by his oratory.

> What are they? The first is, that by law slavery no longer exists in any part of the acquisitions made by us from the Republic of Mexico; and the other is, that in our opinion, according to the probabilities of the case, slavery never will be introduced into any portion of the territories so acquired from Mexico. Now, I have heard it said that this declaration of what I call these two truths is equivalent to the enactment of the Wilmot proviso. I have heard this asserted, but is that the case?

The Wilmot Proviso was still looming over the debates in Congress, but the international law question—whether the law of Mexico would follow its cession of territory to another sovereign power—was a complicated one. Clay had diplomatic experience and had served as US secretary of state, and here he treated the Senate to a discourse, complete with a hypothetical or two, on the subject.

> If the Wilmot proviso be adopted in territorial Governments established over these countries acquired from Mexico, it would be a positive enactment, a prohibition, an interdiction as to the introduction of slavery within them; but with regard to these opinions I had hoped, and I shall still indulge the hope, that those who represent the free States will be inclined not to insist—indeed it would be extremely difficult to give to these declarations the form of positive enactment.

Was Clay saying that the ban on slavery could not be enforced on settlers who brought their slaves to the newly acquired territories—not until those territories sought to enter the Union, like California, as free states? Or did Clay imply that a congressional ordinance could not bar slavery in the southwestern territories? But that is exactly what the Missouri Compromise had done—bar slavery in territory acquired in the Louisiana Purchase north of 36° 30'. And Clay had proposed that very ordinance. The question of congressional power over territories was supposedly settled by article IV, section 3, clause 2 of the federal Constitution: "The Congress shall have Power to dispose of and make all needful Rules and Regulations respecting the Territory or other Property belonging to the United States; and nothing in this Constitution shall be so construed as to Prejudice any Claims of the United States, or of any particular State." But other parts of the Constitution, such as the Takings Clause of the Fifth Amendment, "nor shall private property be taken for public use, without just compensation," might be read to prevent Congress from enacting restrictions like that on slavery in the Missouri Compromise or to render the Missouri Compromise null and void. After all, the Fifth Amendment was added to the Constitution after it was ratified, and the ordinary rule of interpretation was that later enactments controlled earlier enactments. That is exactly what Chief Justice Roger Taney's opinion in *Dred Scott v. Sandford* (1857) implied.[23]

> I had hoped that they [the free states] would be satisfied with the simple expression of the opinion of Congress, leaving it upon the basis of that opinion, without asking for what seems to me almost impracticable, if not impossible—for any subsequent enactment to be introduced into the bill by which territorial Governments should be established. And I can only say that the second resolution, even without the declaration of these two truths expressed, would be much more acceptable to me than with them—but I could not forget that I was proposing a scheme of arrangement and compromise, and I could not, therefore, depart from the duty which the preparation of such a scheme seems to me to impose, of offering, while we ask the surrender on one side, of a favorite measure, of offering to the other side some compensation for that surrender or sacrifice.

Tortuous reasoning and tangled prose made Clay's point almost impenetrable. In the end, it amounted to this: please vote for the second proposal. But Clay had another string to his bow: Mexican law.

---

23 *Dred Scott v. Sandford*, 60 U.S. 393, 450 (1857) (Taney, C.J.), but by then the Kansas-Nebraska Act of 1854, replacing the Missouri Compromise, allowed the inhabitants of a territory seeking statehood to decide whether that state should be free or slave—assuming that the Congress allowed the territory to enter the Union as a slave state. So the application of the 36° 30' rule to Kansas Territory was a moot (no longer relevant) question. Kansas's initial application as a slave state (in a disputed draft constitution) led to a miniature civil war in Kansas (so-called Bleeding Kansas) and open violence in Congress. Kansas entered the Union as a free state in 1861.

What are the truths, Mr. President? The first is, that by law slavery does not exist within the territories ceded to us by the republic of Mexico. It is a misfortune, sir, in the various weighty and important topics which are connected with the subject that I am now addressing you upon, that any one of the five or six furnishes a theme for a lengthened speech; and I am therefore reduced to the necessity, I think—at least in this stage of the discussion—of limiting myself rather to the expression of opinions, than going at any great length into the discussion of all these various topics.

Mexico had outlawed slavery in 1829, ending the Spanish colony's long history as a major slaver. In fact, the number of slaves and the value of slaves had been declining long before Mexico won its independence from Spain. The Republic of Mexico had allowed Texas immigrants to own slaves (that is, the slaves they had brought with them from the United States), an exception to Mexican law that ended in 1837, when slavery was abolished there—except by that time the American colonists in Texas had rebelled and created an independent republic in which slavery was legal. Thus the Wilmot Proviso did not apply to Texas—it never did, of course, as its text was related to territory acquired from Mexico. Then again, what were the western and northern borders of Texas? If they extended well into New Mexico, then all bets were off. In effect, the Proviso would have continued the Mexican prohibition on slavery and the slave trade in the rest of the Mexican Southwest.[24]

Now, with respect to the opinion here expressed, that slavery does not exist in the territories ceded to the United States by Mexico, I can only refer to the fact of the passage of the law by the Supreme Government of Mexico abolishing it, I think in 1824, and to the subsequent passage of a law by the legislative body of Mexico, I forget in what year, by which they proposed—although they have never yet carried into full effect—compensation to the owners of slaves for the property of which they were stripped by the act of abolition. I can only refer to the acquiescence of Mexico in the abolition of slavery, from the time of its extinction down to the time of the treaty by which we acquired these countries. But all Mexico, so far as I know, acquiesced in the non-existence of slavery.

---

24 Dennis N. Valdés, "The Decline of Slavery in Mexico," *The Americas* 44 (1987): 167–194.

Unlike Calhoun and Webster, who would do research for their
speeches, Clay relied on his memory, hence the uncertainty about the
dates of Mexican emancipation law.

> Gentlemen, I know, talk about the irregularity of the law by which that
> act was accomplished; but does it become us, a foreign power, to look into
> the mode by which an object has been accomplished by another foreign
> power, when she herself is satisfied with what she has done, and when,
> too, she is the exclusive judge whether an object which is local and mu-
> nicipal to herself has been or has not been accomplished in conformity
> with her fundamental laws?

The doctrine of choice of law, sometimes called conflict of laws, was
an old one. It dated to Roman law and applied in the new nation. Was
a sovereign state required to follow the laws of another member of the
Union? The Comity Clause, aka the Full Faith and Credit Clause, of the
Constitution (article IV, sec. 1: "Full Faith and Credit shall be given in
each State to the Public Acts, Records, and judicial Proceedings of every
other State") bound states to give effect to the judicial decisions of other
states, but not to their statutes. Supreme Court justice and Harvard law
professor Joseph Story had written *Commentaries on the Conflict of
Laws* (1834), in which he declared that a state in which the parties to a
case resided could choose to follow the laws and precedents (older case
law) of the state in which a dispute had arisen or apply its own laws. In
the 1841 edition, he introduced the notion that the law of place where
the transaction occurred should govern. But the book was simply commentary, and both Mexico and Texas were independent republics when
Texas severed itself from Mexico. The issue remains controversial today,
and Clay's disquisition was not going to resolve it.[25]

> Why, Mexico upon this subject showed to the last moment, her anxiety in
> the documents which were laid before the country upon the subject of the
> negotiation of this treatments which were laid before the country upon
> the subject of the negotiation of this treaty, by Mr. Trist. In the very act,

---

25 Joseph Story, *Commentaries on the Conflict of Laws*, 2nd ed. (Boston: Little, Brown, 1841), sec.
280; Kurt H. Nadelman, "Joseph Story's Contributions to American Conflicts Law," *American
Journal of Legal History* 5 (1961): 233.

in the very negotiation by which the treaty was concluded, ceding to us the countries in question, the diplomatic representatives of the Mexican republic urged the abhorrence with which Mexico would view the introduction of slavery into any portion of the territory which she was about to cede to the United States.

The war ended in 1848 with a treaty signed by the Mexican government and by Nicholas P. Trist on behalf of the United States. The negotiations were controversial. Some among the Democrats in Congress along with President Polk wanted a larger cession of Mexican territory. Trist was a veteran negotiator and diplomat who was serving in the State Department when President Polk asked him to negotiate the treaty in 1847. Recalled to the United States before he had finished negotiating with Mexican president Santa Anna, Trist ignored his instructions (to obtain Baja California) and continued to work out the details of what became the Treaty of Guadalupe Hidalgo (1848). Polk fired Trist on his return and refused to pay his expenses, but supported ratification.

> The clause of prohibition was not inserted in consequence of the firm ground taken by Mr. Trist, and his declaration that it was an utter impossibility to mention the subject. I take it then, sir—and availing myself of the benefit of the discussions which took place on a former occasion on this question, and which I think have left the whole country under the impression of the non-existence of slavery within the whole of the territory in the ceded territories—I take it for granted that what I have said, aided by the reflection of gentlemen, will satisfy them of that first truth, that slavery does not exist there by law, unless slavery was carried there the moment the treaty was ratified by the two parties, and under the operation of the Constitution of the United States.

In short, slavery existed only by virtue of positive law. That is, without explicit legal sanction, no one could legally enslave another. Natural law, as understood by most jurists, forbade slavery. The US Supreme Court had said this in the *Amistad* case.[26]

---

26 *United States v. Amistad*, 40 U.S. 518 (1841) (Africans kidnaped from Africa and carried into slavery in Cuba were entitled to their freedom).

Now, really, I must say that upon the idea that *eo instanti* [at that moment] upon the consummation of the treaty, the Constitution of the United States spread itself over the acquired territory, and carried along with it the institution of slavery, the proposition is so irreconcilable with any comprehension or reason that I possess, that I hardly know how to meet it. Why these United States consist of thirty States. In fifteen of them there was slavery; in fifteen of them slavery did not exist. Well, how can it be argued that the fifteen slave States, by the operation of the Constitution of the United States, earned into the ceded territory their institution of slavery, any more than it can be argued on the other side that, by the operation of the same Constitution, the fifteen free States carried into the ceded territory the principle of freedom which they from policy have chosen to adopt within their limits?

Again, slavery exists only by virtue of positive law, and nothing in the treaty or the law of the existing states provided for slavery in the newly acquired territory. This was not quite the same as arguing that slavery could never be extended into the new lands when they became states. Clay was trying to balance the question on the tip of a pin.

Why, sir, let me suppose a case. Let me imagine that Mexico had never abolished slavery there at all—let me suppose that it was existing in point of fact and in virtue of law, from the shores of the Pacific to those of the Gulf of Mexico, at the moment of the cession of these countries to us by the treaty in question. With what patience would gentlemen coming from slaveholding States listen to any argument which should be urged by the free States, that notwithstanding the existence of slavery within those territories, the constitution of the United States abolished it the moment it operated upon and took effect in the ceded territory? Well is there not just as much ground to contend that, where a moiety [half] of the States is free, and the other moiety is slaveholding, the principle of freedom which prevails in the one class shall operate as much as the principle of slavery which prevails in the other?

Clay turned to a hypothetical. Hypothetical reasoning is a staple in legal pleading. One sometimes forgets that Clay the political operator

is also, and here most certainly, Clay the great lawyer. But, a superb im-
provisor, he kept on looking for a formula that would square the circle.

> Can you come, amidst this conflict of interests, principles and legislation
> which prevails in the two parts of the Union, to any other conclusion
> than that which I understand to be the conclusion of the public law of
> the world, of reason, and justice—that the status of law, as it existed at the
> moment of the conquest or the acquisition, remains until it is altered by
> the sovereign authority of the conquering or acquiring power? That is the
> great principle which you can scarcely turn over a page would be justified
> by all considerations which pertain to the happiness and security of man,
> to employ every instrument which God or nature had placed in their
> hands to resist such an attempt on the part of the free States.
>
> And then, if unfortunately civil war should break out, and we should
> present to the nations of the earth the spectacle of one portion of this
> Union endeavoring to subvert an institution in violation of the
> Constitution and the most sacred obligations which can bind men; who
> should present the spectacle in which we should have the sympathies, the
> good wishes, and the desire for our success of all men who love justice
> and truth. Far different, I fear, would be our case—if unhappily we should
> be plunged into civil war—if the two parts of this country should be
> placed in a position hostile toward each other, in order to carry slavery
> into the new territories acquired from Mexico.

So this was his pitch—if you do not buy what Clay was selling, then
the house would come down on all your heads and civil war would
erupt. "Mr. President, we have heard, all of us have read of the efforts of
France to propagate—what, on the continent of Europe? Not slavery, sir;
not slavery, but the rights of man; and we know the fate of her efforts in
a work of that kind." A reference to the French Revolution, which, everyone knew, ended not with a universal expansion of the rights of man
but with a Napoleonic dictatorship and a generation of ruinous wars. It
was also a reference to the Haitian Revolution, in which enslaved people
threw off their bondage but left a bitter taste in the mouths of the former
master class. This was a warning to the abolitionists, though he did not
mention them, that radicalism produces bloodshed and disorder.

But if the two portions of this Confederacy should unhappily be involved in civil war, in which the effort on the one side would be to restrain the introduction of slavery into new territories, and on the other side to force its introduction there, what a spectacle should we present to the contemplation of astonished mankind! An effort not to propagate light, but I must say—though I trust it will be understood to be said with no desire to excite feeling—an effort to propagate wrong in the territories thus acquired from Mexico. It would be a war in which we should have no sympathy, no good wishes, and in which all mankind would be against us, and in which our own history itself would be against us; for, from the commencement of the revolution down to the present time, we have constantly reproached our British ancestors for the introduction of slavery into this country; and allow me to say that, in my opinion, it is one of the best defences which can be made to preserve the institution in this country, that it was forced upon us against the wishes of our ancestors, our own colonial ancestors, and by the cupidity of our British commercial ancestors.

Here Clay anticipated civil war between the two sections, North and South, "two portions of this confederacy" arising from differences over slavery. This prescient remark raises the question of how real the prospect of civil war was to the members of the Senate in 1850. Clay would return to the subject at the end of the second day's speech.

The power then, Mr. President, in my opinion—and I will extend it to the introduction as well as the prohibition of slavery in the new territories—I think the power does exist in Congress, and I think there is that important distinction between slavery outside of the States and slavery inside of the States, that all outside is debatable, all inside of the States is undebatable. The Government has no right to touch the institution within the States; but whether she has, and to what extent she has the right or not to touch it outside of the States, is a question which is debatable, and upon which men may honestly and fairly differ, but which, decided however it may be decided, furnishes, in my judgment, no just occasion for breaking up this happy and glorious Union of ours.

Conclusion: don't destroy the Union over the issue of slavery in the territory taken from Mexico. Clay, plainly afraid of that eventuality, was not given to abstract fears nor easily frightened. He had endured the War of 1812, the Missouri Crisis, and the war with Mexico. When did his concern become fear?

> Now, I am not going to take up that part of the subject which relates to the power of Congress to legislate either within this District—(I shall have occasion to make some observations upon that when I approach the resolution relating to the District)—either within this District or the territories. But I must say, in a few words, that I think there are two sources of power, either of which is, in my judgment, sufficient to warrant the exercise of the power, if it was deemed proper to exercise it, either to introduce or to keep out slavery outside the States, within the territories.

Barring the auction of slaves in the District of Columbia was a time bomb, but one Clay hoped to defuse. The District's government was managed by Congress, so the question was squarely up to the House and the Senate. The American Anti-Slavery Society, led by William Lloyd Garrison, had lit an abolitionist fuse in 1835, flooding Congress with petitions seeking the end of slavery in the District. These were read at the beginning of the new Fall 1835 session in both houses. The right to petition the federal government was guaranteed by the First Amendment, but southern members of Congress, with South Carolina's congressman James Henry Hammond in the lead, asked the lower house to refuse to accept the petitions. The so-called gag rule (the term coined by Massachusetts congressman John Quincy Adams when he protested against Hammond's plan) would roil passions in both houses until 1844, when the petitions were again received and referred to committee without being read.[27]

> Mr. President, I shall not take up time, of which already so much has been consumed, to show that, according to my sense of the Constitution of the United States, or rather according to the sense in which the clause has been interpreted for the last fifty years, the clause which confers on Congress the power to regulate the territories and other property of the United States conveys the authority.

---

27 Peter Charles Hoffer, *John Quincy Adams and the Gag Rule, 1835–1850* (Baltimore: Johns Hopkins University Press, 2018), 61.

Conveying the authority was not the issue; Clay knew that the issue was whether barring slave auctions was the opening wedge of a campaign to end slavery where it already existed, as the reference to "other property" suggested.

> Mr. President, with my worthy friend from Michigan [Lewis Cass]—and I use the term in the best and most emphatic sense, for I believe he and I have known each other longer than he and I have known any other Senator in this hall—I cannot concur, although I entertain the most profound respect for the opinions he has advanced upon the subject, adverse to my own; but I must say, when a point is settled by all the elementary writers of our country, by all the department of our Government, legislative, executive and judicial—when it has been so settled for a period of fifty years, and never was seriously disturbed until recently, that I think, if we are to regard any thing as fixed and settled under the administration of this constitution of ours, it is a question which has thus been invariably and uniformly settled in a particular way. Or are we to come to this conclusion that nothing, nothing on earth is settled under this constitution, but that every thing is unsettled?

In 1848 Michigan Democratic senator Lewis Cass had proposed that instead of extending the Missouri Compromise line to the Pacific, settlers of the territories acquired from Mexico be allowed to determine their slave status. Cass had ambitions for the presidency but had lost to Zachary Taylor. Cass owned one slave, a household maid named Sally. He called her a "servant" but sold her for three hundred dollars. At the same time, he regarded slavery as a moral evil and in 1842 publicly said, "We are no slaveholder, we never have been, we never shall be." Clay continued with a short history lesson.[28]

> Mr. President, we have to recollect it is very possible—sir, it is quite likely—that when that Constitution was framed, the application of it to such territories as Louisiana, Florida, California and New Mexico was

---

28 Cass quoted in William L. G. Smith, *Fifty Years of Public Life: The Life and Times of Lewis Cass* (New York: Derby and Jackson, 1856), 740. Cass had ambitions modeled on William Henry Harrison—go from successful Indian fighting and territorial governorship (of Michigan) to the Senate (when Michigan became a state) to the White House.

CLAY'S SPEECH IN THE SENATE

never within the contemplation of its framers. It will be recollected that when that Constitution was framed the whole country northwest of the river Ohio was unpeopled; and it will be recollected also, that the exercise and the assertion of the power to make governments for territories in their infant state, are, in the nature of the power, temporary, and to terminate whenever they have acquired a population competent for self-government. Sixty thousand is the number fixed by the ordinance of 1787. Now, sir, recollect that when this Constitution was adopted, and that territory was unpeopled, is it possible that Congress, to whom it had been ceded by the states for the common benefit of the ceding State and all other members of the Union—is it possible that Congress had no right whatever to declare what description of settlers should occupy the public lands?

"Unpeopled?" The lands to the west of the Appalachians were certainly peopled by Indigenous communities, and had been for thousands of years before Europeans set foot on North American soil. But Clay knew this, and had spoken out against the Indian Removal Act of 1830.[29]

Clay returned to the future of slavery in the lands acquired from Mexico. Was congressional authority over the territories limited to those (the Northwest and the Southeast) when the Constitution was ratified? Or did Congress have a general power to legislate for all territories? Clay was near the end of the day's session, and the effort was obviously tiring him, perhaps costing him some focus.

Suppose they took up the opinion that the introduction of slavery would enhance the value of the land, and enable them to command for the public treasury a greater amount from that source of revenue than by the exclusion of slaves, would they not have had the right to say, in fixing the rules, regulations, or whatever you choose to call them, for the government of that territory, that any one that chooses to bring slaves may bring them, if it will enhance the value of the property, in the clearing and cultivation of the soil, and add to the importance of the country? Or take the reverse:— Suppose Congress might think that a greater amount of revenue would be

29 Henry Clay, "On Our Relations with the Cherokee Indians," Speech in the Senate, February 4, 1835, in Colton, ed., *Life, Correspondence, and Speeches of Henry Clay*, 6:208–226.

derived from the waste lands beyond the Ohio river by the interdiction of slavery, would they not have a right to interdict it? Why, sir, remember how these settlements were made, and what was their progress. They began with a few. I believe that about Marietta the first settlement was made. It was a settlement of some two or three hundred persons from New England. Cincinnati, I believe, was the next point where a settlement was made. It was settled perhaps by a few persons from New Jersey, or some other State. Did those few settlers, the moment they arrived there, acquire sovereign rights? Had those few persons power to dispose of these territories? Had they even power to govern themselves—the handful of men who established themselves at Marietta or Cincinnati? No, sir, the contemplation of the source of power equally satisfactory, equally conclusive in my mind as that which relates to the territories, and that is the treaty-making power—the acquiring power. Now, I put it to gentlemen, is there not at this moment a power somewhere existing either to admit or exclude slavery from the ceded territory? It is not an annihilated power. This is impossible. It is a subsisting, actual, existing power; and where does it exist? It existed, I presume no one will controvert, in Mexico prior to the cession of these territories. Mexico could have abolished slavery or introduced slavery either in California or New Mexico. That must be conceded. Who will controvert this position?

Again, Clay found that congressional authority over the territories was an "existing" power, that is, it was part of the treaty ratifying power, it was part of the power to acquire new lands, and it thus applied to slavery in those lands.

Well, Mexico has parted from the territory and from the sovereignty over the territory; and to whom did she transfer it? She transferred the territory and the sovereignty of the territory to the Government of the United States. The Government of the United States, then, acquires in sovereignty and in territory over California and New Mexico, all, either in sovereignty or territory, that Mexico held in California or New Mexico, by the cession of those territories. Sir, dispute that who can. The power exists or it does not; no one will contend for its annihilation. It existed in Mexico. No one, I think, can deny that. Mexico alienates the sovereignty over the territory, and her alienee is the Government of the United States.

While it may seem that Clay was belaboring the obvious, repeating himself, he knew where he was going—that the fate of slavery in the newly acquired territories belonged to the federal government. Clay was an accomplished courtroom lawyer, and he was deploying every bit of that experience here.

> The Government of the United States, then, possesses all power which Mexico possessed over the ceded territories, and the Government of the United States can do in reference to them—within, I admit, certain limits of the Constitution—whatever Mexico could have done.

His point was clear: the federal government could bar slavery from the newly acquired territories. The decision was the responsibility not of the present population of those territories nor of future settlers of those territories but of the federal government. Senator Cass, sitting in the chamber, and Stephen Douglas of Illinois, who would soon take up Cass's program of popular sovereignty, must have been squirming. Clay was speaking directly to their proposal, rather than to southern senators.

> There are prohibitions upon the power of congress within the constitution, which prohibitions, I admit, must apply to Congress whenever she legislates, whether for the old States or for new territories; but, within those prohibitions, the powers of the United States over the ceded territories are co-extensive and equal to the power of Mexico in the ceded territories, prior to the cession.

This was not oratory—a speech full of flourishes and allusions and bombast. This was Clay's lawyerly style at its best—calmly explaining to the jury what they must conclude. Lawyers did this routinely in court—make the point so clearly that laymen could not miss it. If it was a little condescending to members of the Senate who were themselves lawyers, Clay was defending his own resolutions, rather than the interests of some client.

> Sir, in regard to this treaty-making power, all who have any occasion to examine into its character and to the possible extent to which it may be carried, know that it is a power unlimited in its nature, except in so far as any limitation may be found in the Constitution of the United States; and upon this

subject there is no limitation which prescribes the extent to which the powers should be exercised. I know, sir, it is argued that there is no grant of power in the constitution, in specific terms, over the subject of slavery any where; and there is no grant in the Constitution to Congress specifically over the subject of a vast variety of matters upon which the powers of Congress may unquestionably operate. The major includes the minor. The general grant of power comprehends all the particulars and elements of which that power consists.

This is the same argument that Alexander Hamilton made in defending his Bank of the United States in 1791. There was no provision in the Constitution for such a bank, but the necessary and proper clause—the "major"—comprehended the bank's establishment by Congress—the "minor." Clay's attachment to Hamiltonian loose construction of the Constitution was natural, for Clay's own program of "internal improvements" of roads, canals, and other federally funded projects (called by Clay the American System) was an extension of Hamilton's program of federal manufacturing and banking activity. As it happened, Clay was a defender of the Second Bank of the United States in the Senate.[30]

> The power of acquisition by treaty draws after it the power of government of the country acquired. If there be a power to acquire, there must be, to use the language of the tribunal that sits below, a power to govern. I think, therefore, sir, without, at least for the present, dwelling farther on this part of the subject, that to the two sources of authority in Congress to which I have referred, and especially to the last, may be traced the power of Congress to act in the territories in question; and, sir, I go to the extent, and I think it is a power in Congress equal to the introduction or exclusion of slavery. I admit the argument in both its forms; I admit if the argument be maintained that the power exists to exclude slavery, it necessarily follows that the power must exist, if Congress choose to exercise it, to tolerate or introduce slavery within the territories.

Clay engaged in almost pure Hamiltonian logic to a purely Hamiltonian end. Hamilton was a founder of the Federalist Party. Clay was

---

30 See, generally, Maurice G. Baxter, *Henry Clay and the American System* (Lexington: University Press of Kentucky, 2021); Michael Trapani, *Panic in the Senate: The Fight over the Second Bank of the United States and the American Presidency* (New York: Algora, 2021), 83–84.

never a Federalist, but there was a lot of similarity between Federalist constitutionalism and Whig political theory. The federal government could introduce slavery or bar it, or ignore it. Existing states could not constrain that power.

> But, sir, I have been drawn off so far from the second resolution—not from the object of it, but from a particular view of it—that it has almost gone out of my recollection. The resolution asserts "That as slavery does not exist by law, and is not likely to be introduced into any of the territory acquired by the United States from the Republic of Mexico, it is inexpedient for Congress to provide by law either for its introduction into or exclusion from any part of the said territory; and that appropriate territorial Governments ought to be established by Congress in all of the said territory, not assigned as the boundaries of the proposed state of California, without the adoption of any restriction or condition on the subject of slavery."

Having established the power of the federal government over slavery in the territories, Clay's resolution declined to use it—to wit, leaving the question of slavery in the newly acquired territory (save for California) unresolved. This was a concession to the South. The hidden issue was the demand of the southern senators to extend the Missouri Compromise line to the New Mexico territory, that is, to prevent the federal government from barring slavery there. New Mexico was not part of the Louisiana Purchase, and thus the Missouri Compromise line did not apply there, but southern senators wanted the line extended to the Pacific. This would have permitted slavery in New Mexico and Arizona (and the southern part of California, not yet admitted as a free state). In fact, because these lands were controlled by the Comanche and their slave trade was well established there, in effect southern senators were adopting Indigenous practices—an irony given how the southern members of Congress had sponsored the dispossession of the Cherokee, Creek, and other Native peoples of the Southeast. Slavery made such ironies commonplace.[31]

---

31 Howe, *What Hath God Wrought*, 352, argues that removal was possible only because some northern Democratic congressmen supported the Indian Removal Act of 1830.

The other truth which I respectfully and with great deference conceive to exist, and which is announced in this resolution, is, that slavery is not likely to be introduced into any of these territories. Well, sir, is not that a fact? Is there a member who hears me that will not confirm the fact?

In a concession to the free states, Clay ignored slavery in the Comanche Empire. Was slavery impossible in arid climates? Slavery certainly existed in Saharan North Africa, but large slave gangs such as those in sugar- and cotton-producing areas of the United States were not economically feasible.

What has occurred within the last three months? In California more than in any other portion of the ceded territory, was it most probable, if slavery was adapted to the interests of the industrial pursuits of the inhabitants, that slavery would have been introduced. Yet, within the space of three or four months, California herself has declared, by a unanimous vote of her convention, against the introduction of slavery within her limits. And, as I remarked on a former occasion, this declaration was not confined to non-slaveholders. There were persons from the slaveholding States who concurred in that declaration. Thus this fact which is asserted in the resolution is responded to by the act of California. Then, sir, if we come down to those mountain regions which are to be found in New Mexico, the nature of its soil and country, its barrenness, its unproductive character, everything which relates to it, and everything which we hear of it and about it, must necessarily lead to the conclusion which I have mentioned, that slavery is not likely to be introduced into them. Well, sir, if it be true that by law slavery does not now exist in the ceded territories, and that it is not likely to be introduced into the ceded territories—if you, Senators, agree to these truths, or a majority of you, as I am persuaded a large majority of you must agree to them—where is the objection or the difficulty to your announcing them to the whole world? Why should you hesitate or falter in the promulgation of incontestable truths?

Clay had intentionally ignored the difference between slavery and the slave trade. The overseas slave trade had been banned by Congress, but the internal slave trade, the carrying of slaves from areas of Virginia and other East Coast slave states to newer slave states like Mississippi and

Texas was big business. The auction houses where slaves were displayed and sold were among the most lucrative commercial establishments in New Orleans, Natchez, and other southwestern cities. If slavery were banned from the Southwest, it would prohibit the transportation and temporary lodging of slaves, a huge business (estimated at 15 percent of the total of slave-produced goods from 1820 to 1860).[32]

> On the other hand, with regard to Senators coming from the free States, allow me here to make, with reference to California, one or two observations. When this feeling within the limits of your States was gotten up; when the Wilmot proviso was disseminated through them, and your people and yourselves attached themselves to that proviso, what was the state of facts? The state of facts at that time was, that you apprehended the introduction of slavery there. You did not know much—very few of us now know much—about these very territories. They were far distant from you. You were apprehensive that slavery might be introduced there. You wanted as a protection to introduce the interdiction called the Wilmot proviso. It was in this state of want of information that the whole North blazed up in behalf of this Wilmot proviso. It was under the apprehension that slavery might be introduced there that you left your constituents. For when you came from home, at the time you left your respective residences, you did not know the fact, which has only reached us since the commencement of the session of Congress, that a constitution had been unanimously adopted by the people of California, excluding slavery from their territory.

Again, Clay was more than a little condescending. Senators from free states were not unaware of the conditions in the southwestern deserts. Addressing them directly, as if their ignorance were the cause of their support for the Proviso, was hardly likely to win their support.

> Well, now, let me suppose that two years ago it had been known in the free States that such a constitution would be adopted; let me suppose that

---

32 Robert H. Gudmestad, *A Troublesome Commerce: The Transformation of the Interstate Slave Trade* (Baton Rouge: Louisiana State University Press, 2002), and Walter Johnson, *Soul by Soul: Life Inside the Antebellum Slave Market* (Cambridge, MA: Harvard University Press, 2000), 6, document the immense commercial success of the internal slave trade.

it had been believed that in no other portion of these ceded territories would slavery be introduced; let me suppose that upon this great subject of solicitude, negro slavery, the people of the North had been perfectly satisfied that there was no danger; let me also suppose that they had foreseen the excitement, the danger, the irritation, the resolutions which have been adopted by Southern Legislatures, and the manifestations of opinion by the people of the slaveholding states—let me suppose that all this had been known at the North at the time when the agitation was first got up upon the subject of this Wilmot proviso—do you believe that it would have ever reached the height to which it has attained? Do any one of you believe it?

The same fever pitch of sectional antagonism arose, almost instantly over the Tallmadge Amendment. Who was Clay fooling, or trying to fool?

And if, prior to your departure from your respective homes, you had had an opportunity of conferring with your constituents upon this most leading and important fact—of the adoption of a constitution excluding slavery in California—do you not believe, Senators and Representatives coming from the free States, that if you had the advantage of that fact told in serious, calm, fire-side conversation with your constituents, they would not have told you to come here and to settle all these agitating questions without danger to this Union?

Not fireside conversations, but agitated public meetings in churches, town halls, and lyceums occurred in the free states during and after the Wilmot Proviso debate and showed that public opinion was moving toward the Free Soil (no expansion of slavery) movement.

What do you want? What do you want who reside in the free States? You want that there shall be no slavery introduced into the territories acquired from Mexico. Well, have not you got it in California already, if admitted as a state? Have not you got it in New Mexico, in all human probability, also? What more do you want? You have got what is worth a thousand Wilmot provisos. You have got nature itself on your side. You have the fact itself on your side. You have the truth staring you in the face that no slavery is existing there.

In other words, Clay was arguing that the extension of slavery to the Southwest was a dead letter. In fact, slavery had already appeared there, and its supporters there and in Congress hoped that conditions were not antipathetic to it. The appeal to nature, however, was more subtle and more imposing. Nature was not just climate but a force that shaped people's lives. For antebellum romantic authors, painters, and poets, nature was a source of virtue. For entrepreneurs, nature was a source of resources to be logged, mined, and planted. Slavery could flourish in market centers in the Southwest. The forests were "a timeless, wild land" to the land speculators, waiting to be exploited. But vegetation of the Southwest was entirely different, with higher elevations offering scattered juniper and pinyon forests, and lower elevations, with little rainfall, featuring deserts.[33]

> Well, if you are men: if you can rise from the mud and slough of party struggles and elevate yourselves to the height of patriots, what will you do? You will look at the fact as it exists. You will say, this fact was unknown to my people. You will say, they acted on one set of facts, we have got another set of facts here influencing us, and we will act as patriots, as responsible men, as lovers of unity, and above all of this Union. We will act on the altered set of facts unknown to our constituents, and we will appeal to their justice, their honor, their magnanimity, to concur with us on this occasion, for establishing concord and harmony, and maintaining the existence of this glorious Union.

Clay here reached into another powerful theme of antebellum culture: manhood. Masculinity was associated with honor—that men would act in a way that gained the approval of other men, that shame was the worst sin, worse than guilt. True men valued harmony, setting aside the petty interests of section. Clay assumed that the model of manhood was self-reliance, and that the self-made man was somehow above political partisanship. Ralph Waldo Emerson's much-read and much-admired "Self-Reliance" (1841) captured this ideal: "There is a time in every man's

---

33 Kevin Waite, *West of Slavery: The Southern Dream of a Transcontinental Empire* (Chapel Hill: University of North Carolina Press, 2021), 48; Alan Taylor, *William Cooper's Town: Power and Persuasion on the Frontier of the Early American Republic* (New York: Knopf, 2007), 32; National Park Service, "Science of the American Southwest" (February 13, 2018), www.nps.gov.

education when he arrives at the conviction that envy is ignorance; that imitation is suicide; that he must take himself for better, for worse, as his portion; that though the wide universe is full of good, no kernel of nourishing corn can come to him but through his toil bestowed on that plot of ground which is given to him to till. The power which resides in him is new in nature, and none but he knows what that is which he can do, nor does he know until he has tried."[34]

> Well, Mr. President, I think, entertaining these views, that there was nothing extravagant in the hope in which I indulged when these resolutions were prepared and offered—nothing extravagant in the hope that the North might content itself even with striking out as unnecessary these two declarations. They are unnecessary for any purpose the free States have in view. At all events, if they should insist upon Congress expressing the opinions which are here asserted, they should limit their wishes to the simple assertion of them, without insisting on their being incorporated in any territorial Government which Congress may establish in the territories.
>
> I pass on from the second resolution to the third and fourth, which relate to Texas and allow me to say, Mr. President, that I approach the subject with a full knowledge of all its difficulties; and of all the questions connected with or growing out of this institution of slavery, which Congress is called upon to pass upon and decide, there are none so difficult and troublesome as those which relate to Texas, because, sir, Texas has a question of boundary to settle, and the question of slavery, or the feelings connected with it, run into the question of boundary.

The eastern and southern boundaries of Texas were established. The northern and western boundaries were not. The eastern section of the state was settled by immigrants from the southern states. The northern and western parts were not so well settled. Federal authority over this question was equally unsettled. Clay was right that the issue was full of difficulties. What exactly were the boundaries of the Republic of Texas?

---

34 Ralph Waldo Emerson, "Self-Reliance," in *Essays, First Series* (1841; new ed., Boston: Phillips, 1857), 40.

The North, perhaps, will be anxious to contract Texas within the narrowest possible limits, in order to exclude all beyond her to make it a free territory; the South, on the contrary, may be anxious to extend those sources of Rio Grande, for the purpose of creating an additional theatre for slavery; and thus, to the question of the limits of Texas, and the settlement of her boundary, the slavery question, with all its troubles and difficulties, is added, meeting us at every step we take.

The question of slavery loomed over everything else.

There is, sir, a third question, also, adding to the difficulty. By the resolution of annexation, slavery was interdicted in all north of 36° 30; but of New Mexico, that portion of it which lies north of 36° 30 embraces I think about one third of the whole of New Mexico east of the Rio Grande; so that you have free and slave territory mixed, boundary and slavery mixed together, and all these difficulties are to be encountered. And allow me to say, sir, that among the considerations which induced me to think it was necessary to settle all these questions, was the state of things that now exists in New Mexico, and the state of things to be apprehended both there and in other portions of the territories. Why, sir, at this moment and I think I shall have the concurrence of the two Senators from that state when I announce the fact—at this moment there is a feeling approximating to abhorrence on the part of the people of New Mexico at the idea of any union with Texas.

The two senators from Texas did not agree with one another. Thomas Jefferson Rusk was a Democrat born in South Carolina, a veteran of the Texas war for independence, a lawyer and for a time chief justice of the Republic, and a strong advocate of Texas extending its boundaries as far west as California. Sam Houston was Rusk's ally in the war for independence and a president of the Republic, then a Democratic senator. Both men owned slaves. But Houston favored the Clay resolutions while Rusk did not.

MR. [THOMAS JEFFERSON] RUSK [DEMOCRATIC SENATOR FROM TEXAS]. Only, sir, on the part of the office-seekers and army followers, who have settled there, and attempted to mislead the people.

Who were "the people"? Rusk meant the landowners in Texas. But the concept of the people was an elusive if potent one in those days. Was it the voters? The citizens? Was it a legal concept? A social concept? Or just a political slogan? Clay's answer was a demographic one—count heads. But first he had to defuse Rusk's snide interruption with humor.

> MR. CLAY. Ah! Sir, that may be, and I am afraid that New Mexico is not the only place where this class composes a majority of the whole population of the country. [Laughter.] Now, sir, if the questions are not settled which relate to Texas, her boundaries, and so forth, and to the territory now claimed by Texas and disputed by New Mexico— the territories beyond New Mexico which are excluded from California—if these questions are not all settled, I think they will give rise to future confusion, disorder and anarchy there, and to agitation here.

The assumption was that Congress had to settle the border lines. It would authorize a survey. In the beginning of the nineteenth century, the Public Land Survey System put in place to survey the national domain was a technological advancement over earlier semiprivate surveying enterprises. The General Land Office carried out the work, hiring surveyors. From 1812 the district land offices mapped out the borders of the national domain. The commissioner of the General Land Office in 1849, appointed by President Taylor, was Justin Butterfield, an Illinois lawyer. It was a patronage appointment. The losing candidate for the job was another Illinois lawyer, Abraham Lincoln. Both men were Whigs.

> There will be, I have no doubt, a party still at the North crying out, if these questions are not settled this session, for the Wilmot proviso, or some other restriction upon them, and we shall absolutely do nothing, in my opinion, if we do not accommodate all these difficulties and provide against the recurrence of all these dangers. Sir, with respect to the state of things in New Mexico, allow me to call the attention of the Senate to what I consider as the highest authority I could offer to them as to the state of things there existing. I mean the acts of their convention, unless that convention happens to have been composed altogether of office-seekers, office-holders, and so forth. Now, sir, I call your attention to what they say in depicting their own situation.

Mr. [Joseph R.] Underwood [Whig senator from Kentucky], at Mr. Clay's request, read the following extract from instructions adopted by the convention, appended to the journal of the convention of the territory of New Mexico, held at the city of Santa Fe, in September, 1849.

"We the people of New Mexico, in convention assembled, having elected a delegate to represent this territory in the Congress of the United States, and to urge upon the Supreme Government a redress of our grievances, and the protection due to us as citizens of our common country, under the constitution, instruct him as follows: That whereas, for the last three years we have suffered under the paralyzing effects of a government undefined and doubtful in its character, inefficient to protect the rights of the people, or to discharge the high and absolute duty of every Government, the enforcement and regular administration of its own laws, in consequence of which, industry and enterprise are paralyzed and discontent and confusion prevail throughout the land. The want of proper protection against the various barbarous tribes of Indians that surround us on every side has prevented the extension of settlements upon our valuable public domain, and rendered utterly futile every attempt to explore or develope the great resources of the territory. Surrounded by the Utahs, Comanches, and Apaches, on the North, East and South, by the Navajos on the West, with Jicarillas within our limits, and without any adequate-protection against their hostile inroads, our flocks and herds are driven off by thousands, our fellow-citizens, men, women and children, are murdered or carried into captivity. Many of our citizens, of all ages and sexes, are at this moment suffering all the horrors of barbarian bondage, and it is utterly out of our power to obtain their release from a condition to which death would be preferable. The wealth of our territory is being diminished. We have neither the means nor any adopted plan by Government for the education of the rising generation. In fine, with a government temporary, doubtful, uncertain, and inefficient in character and in operation, surrounded and despoiled by barbarous foes, ruin appears inevitably before us, unless speedy and effectual protection be extended to us by the Congress of the United States."

There is a series of resolutions, Mr. President, which any gentleman may look at, if he chooses; but I think it is not worth while to take up the time of the Senate in reading them. That is the condition, sir, of New Mexico.

Clay had this missive from New Mexico in his possession when Rusk gibed at the New Mexicans' wish to be independent of Texas. Deploying it when he did was a masterful move, and no more was heard from Rusk.

Well, I suspect that to go beyond it, to go beyond the Rio Grande to the territory which is not claimed by Texas, you will not find a much better state of things. In fact, sir, I cannot for a moment reconcile it to my sense of duty to suffer Congress to adjourn without an effort, at least, being made to extend the benefits, the blessings of government to those people who have recently been acquired by us.

The time had come for adjournment, but no one had moved for it, and Clay was permitted to continue. It was a tribute to him, quietly paid.

Sir, with regard to that portion of New Mexico which lies east of the Rio Grande, undoubtedly if it is conceded to Texas, while she has two parties, disliking each other as much as those office-holders and office-seekers alluded to by the Senator from Texas, if they could possibly be drawn together and governed quietly, peaceably, and comfortably, there might be a remedy, so far as relates to the country east of the Rio Grande; but all beyond it Deseret [the community of the Church of Jesus Christ of Latter-day Saints] and the North of California—would be still open and liable to all the consequences of disunion, confusion and anarchy, without some stable government emanating from the authority of the nation of which they now compose a part, and with which they are but little acquainted. I think, therefore, that all these questions, difficult and troublesome as they may be, ought to be met—met in a spirit of candor and calmness, and decided upon as a matter of duty.

Let Texas have the lands immediately north of the Rio Grande, already won from Mexico, but nothing more. Congress, "the nation," must determine a fair outcome for the rest of the newly acquired lands. After all, the lands were not settled by Texans.

Now, these two resolutions which we have immediately under consideration propose a decision of these questions. I have said, sir, that there is scarcely a resolution in the series which I have offered that does not contain some mutual concession or evidence of mutual forbearance, where the concession was not altogether from the non-slaveholding to the slave-holding states. Now, with respect to this resolution proposing a boundary for Texas, what is it?

Were the question simply one of drawing boundary lines, it would not be so fraught with political consequences. But once again slavery intruded. It was becoming obvious that the slavery question was a brooding omnipotence, not just for California's admission to the Union, but for every other issue that Congress faced this day.

We know the difference of opinion which has existed in this country with respect to that boundary. We know that a very large portion of the people of the United States have supposed that the western limit of Texas was the Nueces [River], and that it did not extend to the Rio Grande. We know, by the resolution of annexation [in 1845, of Texas], that the question of what is the western limit and the northern limit of Texas was an open question—that it has been all along an open question. It was an open question when the boundary was run, in virtue of the act of 1838, marking the boundary between the United States and Texas. Sir, at that time the boundary authorised by the act of 1838 was a boundary commencing at the mouth of the Sabine [River] and running up to its head, thence to Red River, thence westwardly with Red River to, I think, the hundredth degree of west longitude. Well, sir, that did not go so far as Texas now claims, and why—Because it was an open question. War was yet raging between Texas and Mexico; it was not foreseen exactly what might he her ultimate limits.

But sir, we will come to the question of what was done at the time of her annexation. The whole resolution which relates to the question of boundary, from beginning to end, assumes an open boundary, an unascertained, unfixed boundary to Texas on the West. Sir, what is the first part of the resolution? It is that "Congress doth consent that the territory properly included within and rightfully belonging to the Republic of Texas may be erected into a new State." Properly including—rightfully belonging to. The resolution specifies no boundary. It could specify none. It has specified no western or northern boundary for Texas. It has assumed in this state of uncertainty what we know in point of fact existed.

But then the latter part of it: "Said state to be formed subject to the adjustment of all questions of boundary that may arise with other Governments, and the constitution thereof," &c. That is to say, she is annexed with her rightful and proper boundaries, without a specification of them; but inasmuch as it was known that these boundaries at the west and the north were unsettled, the Government of the United States retained to itself the power of settling with any foreign nation what the boundary should be.

Clay now donned the secretary of state mantle he had worn during the John Quincy Adams presidential administration to negotiate (with himself) the boundary of Texas based on an imaginary conversation between Texas and Mexico.

Now, sir, it is impossible for me to go into the whole question and to argue it fully. I mean to express opinions or impressions, rather than to go into the entire argument—The western and northern limit of Texas being unsettled, and the Government of the United States having retained the power of settling it, I ask, suppose the power had been exercised, and that there had been no cession of territory by Mexico to the United States, but that the negotiations between the countries had been limited simply to the fixation of the western and northern limits of Texas, could it not have been done by the United States and Mexico conjointly?

In other words, could Texas and Mexico have agreed on a boundary line? Mexico had agreed, at the end of the war with Texas, to cease hostilities, but there had been no determination of the boundary between Texas and New Mexico, the latter still a part of the Republic of Mexico. The Treaty of Velasco of May 1836 did not specify any western boundary, only that Mexican forces would retreat south of the Rio Grande. The Mexican government did not ratify the treaty, however, and it was not until the end of the Mexican-American War of 1846–1848 that Mexico officially accepted the secession of Texas from Mexico. Clay was thus supplying absent treaty provisions.

Will any one dispute it? I Suppose there had been a treaty of limits of Texas concluded between Mexico and the United States, fixing the Nueces as the western limit of Texas, would not Texas have been bound by it? Why, by the express terms of the resolution she would have been bound by it; or if it had been the Colorado or the Rio Grande, or any other boundary, whatever western limit had been fixed by the joint action of the two powers, would have been binding and obligatory upon Texas by the express terms of the resolution by which she was admitted into the Union.

Next, Clay imagined a negotiated boundary between Mexico and the United States prior to the Mexican-American War. That is, when Texas was annexed, in 1845, the United States might have negotiated a boundary between the state of Texas and the Mexican republic. The United States had done this with Great Britain on several occasions regarding the boundary with Canada. All this was hypothetical, of course, because war soon erupted between the United States and Mexico.

Now, sir, Mexico and the United States conjointly, by treaty, might have fixed upon the western and northern limits of Texas, and if the United States have acquired by treaty all the subjects upon which the limits of Texas might have operated, have not the United States now the power solely and exclusively which Mexico and the United States conjointly possessed prior to the late treaty between the two countries?

It seems to me, sir, that this conclusion and reasoning are perfectly irresistible. If Mexico and the United States could have fixed upon any western limit for Texas, and did not do it, and if the United States have acquired to themselves, or acquired by the treaty in question, all the territory upon which the western limit must have been fixed, when it was fixed, it seems to me that no one can resist the logical conclusion that the United States now have themselves a power to do what the United States and Mexico conjointly could have done. Sir, I admit it is a delicate power—an extremely delicate power. I admit that it ought to be exercised in a spirit of justice, liberality, and generosity toward this the youngest member of the great American family [i.e., California].—But here the power is.

Clay next bowed to the US Supreme Court in what amounted to an extended aside. The Court had heard one such case (article III gave the court original jurisdiction in suits between one state and another state) between Rhode Island and Massachusetts. "The Supreme Court has jurisdiction of a bill filed by the State of Rhode Island against the State of Massachusetts to ascertain and establish the northern boundary between the states, that the rights of sovereignty and jurisdiction be restored and confirmed to the plaintiffs and they be quieted in the enjoyment thereof and their title, and for other and further relief." Webster represented Massachusetts in the case.[35]

> Possibly, sir, upon that question however I offer no positive opinion—possibly, if the United States were to fix it in a way unjust in the opinion of Texas, and contrary to her rights, she might bring the question before the Supreme Court of the United States, and have it there again investigated and decided. I say possibly, sir, because I am not one of that class of politicians who believe that every question is a competent and proper question for the Supreme Court of the United States. There are questions too large for any tribunal of that kind to try; great political questions, national territorial questions, which transcend their limits; for such questions their powers are utterly incompetent. Whether this be one of those questions or not, I shall not decide; but I will maintain that the United States are now invested solely and exclusively with that power which was common to both nations—to fix, ascertain, and settle the western and northern limits of Texas.
>
> Sir, the other day my honorable friend who represents so well the State of Texas [Rusk, again] said, that we had no more right to touch the limits of Texas than we had to touch the limits of Kentucky. I think that was the illustration he gave us—that a state is one and indivisible, and that the General Government has no right to sever it. I agree with him, sir, in that; where the limits are ascertained and certain, where they are undisputed and indisputable. This General Government has no right, nor has any other earthly power the right, to interfere "with the limits of a State whose boundaries are thus fixed, thus ascertained, known, and recognised."—The whole power, at least, to interfere with it is voluntary.

But that was the point—the boundary of Texas was yet undetermined.

> The extreme case may be put—one which I trust in God may never happen in this nation—of a conquered nation, and of a constitution adapting

---

35 *Rhode Island v. Massachusetts*, 37 U.S. 657 (1836).

itself to the state of subjugation or conquest to which it has been reduced; and giving up whole states, as well as parts of states, in order to save from the conquering arms of the invader what remains. I say such a power in case of extremity may exist. But I admit that, short of such extremity, voluntarily, the General Government has no right to separate a state—to take a portion of its territory from it, or to regard it other-wise than as integral, one and indivisible, and not to be affected by any legislation of ours.

Once again, the boundary of Texas was still not determined.

But, then I assume what does not exist in the case of Texas, and these boundaries must beknown, ascertained, and indisputable. With regard to Texas, all was open, all was unfixed; all is unfixed at this moment, with respect to her limits west and north of the Nueces.

What had the Treaty of Guadalupe Hidalgo (and all the money given to Mexico as part of the treaty to settle Mexican boundary claims) achieved?

But, sir, we gave fifteen millions of dollars for this territory that we bought, and God knows what a costly bargain to this now distracted country it has been! We gave fifteen millions of dollars for the territory ceded to us by Mexico. Can Texas justly, fairly, and honorably come into the Union and claim all that she asserted a right to, without paying any portion of the fifteen millions of dollars which constituted the consideration of the grant by the ceding nation to the United States?

Texas benefitted from the payment (ending the hostilities) but was unwilling to concede what the payment implied—that the determination of its western border now belonged to the federal government.

She proposes no such thing. She talks, indeed, about the United States having been her agent, her trustee. Why, sir, the United States was no more her agent or her trustee than she was the agent or trustee of the whole people of the United States. Texas involved herself in war—(I mean to make this no reproach—none, none—upon the past)—Texas brought herself into a state of war, and when she got into that war, it was not the war of Texas and Mexico, but it was the war of the whole thirty United States and Mexico;

it was a war in which the Government of the United States, which created the hostilities, was as much the trustee and agent of the twenty-nine other states composing the Union as she was the trustee and agent of Texas.

And, sir, with respect to all these circumstances—such, for example, as a treaty with a map annexed, as in the case of the recent treaty with Mexico; such as the opinion of individuals highly respected and eminent, like the lamented Mr. Polk, late President of the United States, whose opinion was that he had no right, as President of the United States, or in any character otherwise than as negotiating with Mexico—and in that the Senate would have to act in concurrence with him—that he had no right to fix the boundary; and as to the map attached to the treaty, it is sufficient to say that the treaty itself is silent from beginning to end on the subject of the fixation of the boundary of Texas.

There was no map sent to the Congress, although the commissioner, Colonel John B. Weller, and surveyor, Andrew Grey, were appointed by the US government, and General Pedro Conde and Sr. Jose Illarregui were appointed by the Mexican government, to survey and set the boundary in 1851, but obviously it had no part of the treaty. That is, in ratifying the treaty, Congress did not ratify any boundaries save the Rio Grande. Native lands were often surveyed and described in maps attached to treaties by Indigenous nations with the United States, but the maps had no force in US law, as events (the later relocation of the tribes) invariably proved. The survey was still a matter of contention between the two nations in 1851. It was not settled until the Gadsden Purchase in 1853. A map may be supplied as evidence by one side, but the map itself did not determine the outcome of the litigation—a very controversial subject to this day.[36]

The annexation of the map to the treaty was a matter of no utility, for the treaty is not strengthened by it; it no more affirms the truth of any thing delineated upon that map in relation to Texas than it does any thing in relation to any other geographical subject that composed the map. Mr. President, I have said that I think the power has been concentrated in the Government of the United States to fix upon the limits of the State of

36 Richard Griswold del Castillo, *The Treaty of Guadalupe Hidalgo: A Legacy of Conflict* (Norman: University of Oklahoma Press, 1990), 57–59; Guenter Weissberg, "Maps as Evidence in International Boundary Disputes: A Reappraisal," *American Journal of International Law* 57 (1963): 781–803.

Texas. I have said also that this power ought to be exercised in a spirit of great liberality and justice; and I put it to you, sir, to say, in reference to this second resolution of mine, whether that liberality and justice have not been displayed in the resolution which I have proposed.

In the resolution, what is proposed? To confine her to the Nueces? No, sir. To extend her boundary to the mouth of the Rio Grande, and thence up that river to the southern limit of New Mexico; and thence along that limit to the boundary between the United States and Spain, as marked under the treaty of 1819. Why, sir, here is a vast country. I believe—although I have made no estimate about it that it is not inferior in extent of land, of acres, of square miles, to what—Texas east of the river Nueces, extending to the Sabine, had before. And who is there can say with truth and justice that there is no reciprocity, nor mutuality, no concession in this resolution, made to Texas, even in reference to the question of boundary alone? You give her a vast country, equal, I repeat, in extent nearly to what she indisputably possessed before; a country sufficiently large, with her consent, hereafter to carve out of it some two or three additional states when the condition of the population may render it expedient to make new states. Sir, is there not in this resolution concession, liberality, justice?

Clay had in a single sentence, no more than an aside, allowed Texas to sever, from itself, two or three additional states. He did not mention whether these would be open to slavery.

But this is not all that we propose to do. The second resolution proposed to pay off a certain amount of the debt of Texas. A blank is left in the resolution, because I have not heretofore been able to ascertain the amount.

MR. [HENRY S.] FOOTE [SENATOR FROM MISSISSIPPI]. Will the honorable Senator allow me to suggest that it maybe agreeable to him to finish his remarks to-morrow? If such be the case, I will move that the Senate now go into Executive session.

MR. CLAY. I am obliged to the worthy Senator from Mississippi; I do not think it possible for me to conclude today, and I will yield with great pleasure if. . . .

MR. FOOTE. I now. . . .

MR. CLAY. If the Senator will permit me to conclude what I have to say in relation to Texas, I will then cheerfully yield the floor for his motion.

I was about to remark that, independently of this most liberal and generous boundary which is tendered to Texas, we propose to offer her in this second resolution a sum which the worthy Senator from Texas [Rusk] thinks will not be less than three millions of dollars—the exact amount neither he nor I can furnish, not having the materials at hand upon which to make a statement. Well, sir, you get this large boundary and three millions of your debt paid. I shall not repeat the argument which I urged upon a former occasion, as to the obligation of the United States to pay a portion of this debt, but was struck the other day, upon reading the treaty of limits, first between the United States and Mexico, and next the treaty of limits between the United States and Texas, to find, in the preamble of both those treaties, a direct recognition of the principle from which I think springs our obligation to pay a portion of this debt, for the payment of which the revenue of Texas was pledged before her annexation.

The Treaty of Limits (1828) between the United States and Mexico recognized the border between the two nations as the same as the border between the Spanish colony of Mexico and the United States under the Adams-Onis Treaty of 1819. That border did not include the lands between the Red River and the Rio Grande, claimed by Texas and then won by the United States in the Mexican-American War. Clay was relying on the international law principle that sovereign nations are bound by the treaties they make with one another.

The principle asserted in the treaty of limits with Mexico is, that whereas by the treaty of 1819, between Spain and the United States, a limit was fixed between Mexico and the United States, Mexico comprising then a portion of the possessions of the Spanish Government, although Mexico was at the date of the treaty severed from the crown of Spain, yet she, as having been a part of the possessions of the crown of Spain when the treaty of 1819 was made, was bound by that treaty as much as if it had been made by herself instead of Spain—in other words, that the severance of no part of a common empire can exonerate either portion of that empire from the obligations contracted when the empire was entire and unsevered.

And, Sir, the same principle is asserted in the treaty of 1838, between Texas, and the United States. The principle asserted is, that the treaty of

1828 between Mexico and the United States having been made when Texas was a part of Mexico, and that now Texas being dissevered from Mexico, she nevertheless remains bound by that treaty as much as if no such severance had taken place.

This notion that colonies were bound by treaties made by their imperial powers after they were separated from those imperial powers was, however, far-fetched. It would have bound the United States to agreements made by the British Empire before the Revolution, something that Clay did not consider.

> In other words, the principle is this—that when an independent power creates an obligation or debt, no subsequent political misfortune, no subsequent severance of the territories of that power, can exonerate it from the obligation that was created while an integral and independent power; in other words, to bring it down and apply it to this specific case—that, Texas being an independent power, and having a right to make loans and to make pledges, having raised a loan and pledged specifically the revenues arising from the customs to the public creditor, the public creditor became invested with a right to that fund; and it is a right of which he could not be divested by any other act than one to which his own consent was given—it could be divested by no political change which Texas might think proper to make in consequence of the absorption or merging of Texas into the United States, the creditor, being no party to the treaty which was formed, does not lose his right—he retains his right to demand the fulfilment of the pledge that was made upon this specific fund, just as if there had not been any annexation of Texas to the United States.

The application of this doctrine would have very serious consequences when former Confederate states faced claims for loans they had made during the Civil War.[37]

That was the foundation upon which I arrived at the conclusion expressed in the resolution—that the United States having appropriated

---

37 Harold M. Hyman, *The Reconstruction Justice of Salmon P. Chase*, In Re Turner *and* Texas v. White (Lawrence: University Press of Kansas, 1977), 140–165.

to themselves the revenue arising from the imports, which revenue had
been pledged to the creditor of Texas, the United States as an honorable
and just power ought now to pay the debt for which those duties were solemnly pledged by a power independent in itself, and competent to make
the pledge. Well, sir, I think that when you consider the large boundary
which is assigned to Texas—and when you take into view the abhorrence,
for I think I am warranted in using this expression—with which the people of New Mexico east of the Rio Grande will look upon any political
connexion with Texas—and when, in addition to this, you take into view
the large grant of money that we propose to make, and our liberality in
exonerating her from a portion of her public debt, equal to that grant—
when we take all these circumstances into consideration, I think I have
presented a case in regard to which I confess I shall be greatly surprised
if the people of Texas themselves, whether they come to deliberate upon
these liberal offers, hesitate a moment to accede to them.

Texas cannot complain about the terms of the debt repayment, Clay argued, in what was one of the longest and most convoluted sentences of
the speech. Long sentences were not uncommon in antebellum literature.
Washington Irving, New York journalist and writer, historian, diplomat,
and public intellectual, had sentences that ran on and on, as in his *Sketch
Book* (1820): "There was a delicious sensation of mingled security and awe
with which I looked down, from my giddy height, on the monsters of the
deep at their uncouth gambols: shoals of porpoises tumbling about the bow
of the ship; the grampus, slowly heaving his huge form above the surface;
or the ravenous shark, darting, like a spectre, through the blue waters."[38]

> I have now got through with what I had to say in reference to this resolu-
> tion, and if the Senator from Mississippi wishes it, I will give way for a
> motion for adjournment.
>   (On motion of Mr. Foote the farther consideration of the resolution
> was postponed, and on motion, the Senate adjourned.)

---

38 Self-parody: Of Dutch New Netherland's Wilhelm Kieft, Washington Irving wrote, "In the year
1638, that being the fourth year of his reign, he fulminated against [the English in his province] a
second proclamation, of heavier metal than the former, written in thundering long sentences, not
one word of which was shorter than five syllables." *A History of New York* (1838), in *Works of
Washington Irving* (Ames: University of Iowa, 1897), 159.

2

Henry Clay, Proposed Compromise Resolutions, Cont'd, February 6, 1850

Figure 2.1. Henry Clay addressing the Senate. Credit: Library of Congress, Prints & Photographs Division.

CLAY rested overnight and opened the next day's Senate session with a return to the Texas boundary issue.[1] Obviously, the evening had been spent in consultation with his allies in the Senate, and they brought the issue to his attention.

MR. CLAY. Mr. President, if there be in this vast assembly of beauty, grace, elegance and intelligence any who have come here under an expectation that the humble individual who now addresses you means to attempt any display, any use of ambitious language, any extraordinary ornament or decoration of speech, they will be utterly disappointed. The season of the year, and my own season of life, both admonish me to abstain from the use of any such ornaments; but, above all, Mr. President, the awful subject upon which it is my duty to address the Senate and the country forbids my saying anything but what pertains strictly to that subject, and my sole desire is to make myself, in seriousness, soberness and plainness, understood by you and by those who think proper to listen to me.

When, yesterday, the adjournment of the Senate, took place, at that stage of the discussion of the resolutions which I had submitted which related to Texas and her boundary, I thought I had concluded the whole subject, but I was reminded by a friend that perhaps I was not sufficiently explicit on a single point, and that is, the relation of Texas and the Government of the United States, and that portion of the debt of Texas for which I think a responsibility exists on the part of the Government of the United States. Sir, it was said that perhaps it might be understood, in regard to the proposed grant of three millions, or whatever may be the sum when ascertained, to Texas, in consideration of the surrender of her title to New Mexico this side of the Rio Grande, that we granted nothing—that we merely discharged an obligation which existed upon the Government of the United States, in consequence of the appropriation of the imports receivable in the ports of Texas while she was an independent power.

---

1 Henry Clay, Speech in the US Senate, February 6, 1850, 31st Cong., 1st sess., *Congressional Globe*, appendix, 120–127; text from Henry Clay, *Speech . . . on Taking Up His Compromise Resolutions on the Subject of Slavery* (New York: Stringer and Townsend, 1850).

CLAY'S PROPOSED COMPROMISE RESOLUTIONS, CONT'D · 67

Clay's request looked an awful lot like a bribe. Texas would surrender claims that it could not sustain or effectuate in return for three million dollars from the public treasury. Beneath the surface of this strange proposal was the fact that many men, including politicians, had invested in Texas when it was an independent republic, and Texas could not repay those loans. In effect, the US government would be paying private investors' Texas debt to them. This was the first year of what one historian has called "the plundering generation," a season of unrivalled political corruption. Consider, for example, the grant of federal lands as the right-of-way to railroad companies, which the companies then resold to farmers at a nice profit. But who were the stockholders of the railroads? None other than members of Congress. Such practices, though corrupt, were widely known and almost as widely engaged in.[2]

But that is not my understanding, Mr. President. As between Texas and the United States, the obligation on the part of Texas to pay her portion of the debt referred to, is complete and unqualified, and there is, as between these two parties, no obligation on the part of the United States to pay one dollar of the debt of Texas.

On the contrary, by an express stipulation in the resolutions of admission, it is declared and provided that in no event do the United States become liable or charged with any portion of the debt or liabilities of Texas. It is not, therefore, for any responsibility which exists to the state of Texas, on the part of the Government of the United States, that I think provision ought to be made for that debt. No such thing. As between those two parties, the responsibility on the part of Texas is complete to pay the debt, and there is no responsibility on the part of the United States to pay one cent.

So far, above board. Then comes the revelation that was not news to anyone who had followed Texas's efforts to enter the Union.

But there is a third party, who was no party to the annexation whatever— that is to say, the creditor of Texas, who advanced the money on the faith

---

2 Mark W. Summers, *The Plundering Generation: Corruption and the Crisis of the Union, 1849–1861* (New York: Oxford University Press, 1988), offers abundant evidence of such graft.

of solemn pledges made by Texas to him, to reimburse the loan by the appropriation of the duties received on foreign imports; and he, and he alone, is the party to whom we are bound, according to the view which I have presented of the subject.

Seriously? Creditors of Texas had no part in annexation? They had "advanced money" in the hope of making money, and Texas owed a return to these private citizens that Texas could not pay—until Texas entered the United States. Then the creditors and Texas urged Congress to assume the debt, something like Alexander Hamilton's first message to Congress on the state debts in 1790. Hamilton urged Congress to pass legislation enabling creditors to redeem their loans to the states, as well as the United States, at face value. Clay was again borrowing from Hamilton, although he did not cite the first secretary of the treasury.

> Nor can the other creditors of Texas complain that provision is made only for a particular portion of the debt, leaving the residue of the debt unprovided for, by the Government of the United States, because, in so far as we may extinguish any portion of the debt of Texas under which she is now bound, in so far will it contribute to diminish the residue of the debts of Texas, and leave the funds derived from the public lands held by Texas, and what other resources she may have, applicable to the payment of these debts, with more effect than if the entire debt, including the pledged portion as well as the unpledged portion, was obligatory upon her, and she stood bound by it.

So, Texas should not complain. Part of the debt would be relieved. Why not all of it? Because other states had debts, and Clay was opening a door that would never close.

> Nor can the creditors complain, for another reason. Texas has all the resources which she had when an independent power, with the exception of the duties receivable in her ports upon foreign imports, and she is exempted from certain charges, expenditures and responsibilities which she would have had to encounter if she had remained a separate and independent power: for example, she would have had to provide for a certain amount of naval force and for a certain amount perhaps of military

force, in order to protect herself against Mexico or against any foreign enemy whatever. But by her annexation to the United States she became liberated from all these charges, and, of course, her entire revenues may be applicable to the payment of her debts, those only excepted which are necessary to the support and maintenance of the Government of Texas.

Whether those who had complained to Clay that evening were mollified by his explanation we shall never know. We do know that he listened. That was a part of his political style.

With this explanation upon that part of the subject, I pass to the consideration of the next resolution in the series which I have had the honor to submit, and which relates, if I am not mistaken, to this District. "Resolved, That it is inexpedient to abolish slavery in the District of Columbia, while that institution continues to exist in the State of Maryland, without the consent of that state, without the consent of the people of the District, and without just compensation to the owner of slaves within the District."

This was the object of the antislavery petition campaign of 1835 to 1848, to which Congress responded with the gag rule. Although the gag rule had been lifted, abolitionists still saw the auction and sale of slaves in the District as a blot on the nation's reputation.[3]

Mr. President, an objection at the moment was made to this resolution, by some honorable Senator on the other side of the body, that it did not contain an assertion of the unconstitutionality of the exercise of the power of abolition. I said then, as I have uniformly maintained in this body, as I contended for in 1838, and ever have done, that the power to abolish slavery within the District of Columbia has been vested in Congress by language too clear and explicit to admit, in my judgment, of any rational doubt whatever. What, sir, is the language of the Constitution? "To exercise exclusive legislation, in all case? whatsoever, over such district (not exceeding ten miles square) as may, by cession of particular

3 See Peter Charles Hoffer, *John Quincy Adams and the Gag Rule, 1835–1850* (Baltimore: Johns Hopkins University Press, 2017), 13–27.

States and the acceptance of Congress, become the seat of the Government of the United States." Now, sir, Congress, by this grant of power, is invested with all legislation whatsoever over the District. Not only is it so invested, but it is exclusively invested with all legislation whatsoever over the District. Can we conceive of human language more broad and comprehensive than that which in-vests a legislative body with exclusive power, in all cases whatsoever, of legislation over a given district of territory or country?

The Constitution does not mention slavery. States, like Maryland, were left to determine the status of slavery within their boundaries. But the District was not a state, and Congress was its governing body. Thus, by both the absence of constitutional language guaranteeing the property rights in men to slave owners and the fact that the District was not a state, its slave owners could not claim a constitutional right to their property. But southern legislators feared that ending slavery in the District would be the opening salvo of a federal effort to end the practice everywhere. In fact, slavery did not end in the District until 1862, a year into the Civil War, and then by an act of Congress.

Let me ask, sir, is there any power to abolish slavery in this District? Let me suppose, in addition to what I suggested the other day, that slavery had been abolished in Maryland and Virginia let me add to it the supposition that it was abolished in all the States in the Union; is there any power then to abolish slavery within the District of Columbia, or is slavery planted here to all eternity, without the possibility of the exercise of any legislative power for its abolition? It cannot be invested in Maryland, because the power with which Congress is invested is exclusive. Maryland, therefore, is excluded, and so all the other States of the Union are excluded. It is here, or it is nowhere. This was the view which I took in 1838, and I think there is nothing in the resolution which I offered on that occasion incompatible with the view which I now present, and which the resolution contains.

Clay is reasoning by comparison—Maryland and Virginia could, if they wished, end slavery. It was entirely in their power. So was the fate of slavery where it already existed not in the power of Congress.

While I admitted the power to exist in Congress, and exclusively in Congress, to legislate in all cases whatsoever, and consequently in the case of the abolition of slavery in this District, if it is deemed proper to do so, I admitted on that occasion, as I contend now, that it is a power which Congress cannot, in conscience and good faith, exercise while the institution of slavery continues within the state of Maryland.

Clay alluded to the process of "retrocession." The land in the District was ceded to the federal government from Maryland and Virginia during George Washington's presidency. Periodically thereafter, members of Congress moved to remove portions of that cession from federal control. In 1847 Virginia was successful in 1847 re-accessing the Alexandria portion of the District south of the Potomac River.

The case, sir, is a good deal altered now from what it was twelve years ago, when the resolution to which I allude was adopted by the Senate. Upon that occasion Virginia and Maryland both were concerned in the exercise of the power; but, by the retrocession of that portion of the District which lies south of the Potomac, Virginia became no more interested in the question of the abolition of slavery within the residue of the District than any other slaveholding State in the Union is interested in its abolition. The question now is confined to Maryland. I said on that occasion that, although the grant of power is complete, and comprehends the right to abolish slavery within the District, yet it was a thing which never could have entered into the conception of Maryland or Virginia that slavery would be abolished here while slavery continued to exist in either of those two ceding States.

Why slavery in Virginia or Maryland should influence Congress was obvious—slaveholders in the two states abutting the District regularly brought their slaves (personal servants, coachmen, etc.) with them into the District. Should slavery be outlawed there, the ownership of those men and women would be in doubt. The rule in some slave states was that slaves, once freed in a free state, remained free when they returned to their home state. Clay sought to reassure Maryland and Virginia senators that this would not happen. Nor would runaways find sanctuary in a District that did not allow slavery.

I say, moreover, what the grant of power itself indicates, that, although exclusive, legislation in all cases whatsoever over the District was vested in Congress within the ten miles square, it was to make it the seat of Government of the United States. That was the great, prominent, substantial object of the grant, and that, in exercising all the powers with which we are invested, complete and full as they may be, yet the great purpose—that of the cession having been made in order to create a suitable seat of Government—ought to be the leading and controlling idea with Congress in the exercise of this power. And it is not necessary, in order to render it a proper and suitable seat of Government for the United States, that slavery should be abolished within the limits of the ten miles square.

After all, the government of the United States was not an antislavery body.

And inasmuch as at the time of the cession—when, in a spirit of generosity, immediately after the formation of this constitution—when all was peace, and harmony, and concord—when brotherly affection and fraternal feeling prevailed throughout this whole Union—when Maryland and Virginia, in a moment of generous impulse, and with feelings of high regard toward the members of this Union, chose to make this grant, neither party could have suspected that, at some distant future period, upon the agitation of this unfortunate subject, their generous grant without equivalent was to be turned against them, and that the sword was to be uplifted as it were, in their bosoms, to strike at their own hearts; thus this implied faith, this honorable obligation, this necessity and propriety of keeping in constant view the great object of cession.

Clay captured the great fear of the South that freeing the slaves in nearby territory would incite slaves to rebel or at least to run away. A sword in their bosoms was the kind of language that southern legislatures routinely used to describe this fear.

Those were considerations which in 1838 governed me, as they now influence me, in submitting the reasons which I have submitted to your consideration. Now, as then, I do not think Congress ought ever, as an honorable body, acting bona, fide in good faith, and according to the nature and purposes and objects of the cession at the time it was made—

and, looking at the condition of the ceding States at that time, Congress cannot, without the forfeiture of all those obligations of honor which men of honor and in nations of honor respect as much as if found literally in so many words in the bond itself—Congress cannot interfere with the institution of slavery in this District without the violation of all these obligations, not in my opinion less sacred and less binding than if inserted in the constitutional instrument itself.

But the institution of slavery was not mentioned in the Constitution. There was no right to property in man. Nothing could put that word in the Constitution except an amendment, and that was not going to happen. Invocations of "obligations of honor" would not suffice, as Clay knew.

Well, sir, what does the resolution propose? The resolution neither affirms nor disaffirms the constitutionality of the exercise of the power of abolition in this District. It is silent upon the subject. It says it was inexpedient to do it but upon certain conditions.

The conditions centered on Maryland's consent. Maryland was a slave state and did not end slavery until constitutional revision in 1864, after the Civil War had started. Clay could—perhaps Clay should—have stopped his analysis of the proposal here. But from this distance the reader may have missed where Clay's glance went. It went to the desk where the Maryland senators sat. Unlike Rusk of Texas, their support for his resolutions was vital. At the time, Thomas Pratt and James Pearce were both Whigs. A practicing attorney, Pratt had been governor in the 1840s when his state waged a series of legal battles with Pennsylvania over its refusal to return runaways. This and other issues would induce him to leave the Whig ranks and join the Democrats in 1856. He was stanchly proslavery and pro-South in his politics and was briefly arrested during the Civil War. Pearce, another lawyer and a veteran member of Congress, was a supporter of the compromise plan.

And what are these considerations? Why, first, that the State of Maryland shall give its consent; in other words, that the State of Maryland would release the United States from the obligation of the implied faith which I contend is connected with the act of cession by Maryland to the United States.

What implied faith? Was it implied in the original cession of land for the creation of a federal district? The cession did not mention that it was dependent on the continuation of slavery in the District. That was why Clay said the condition was "implied."

> Well, sir, if Maryland, the only State now that ceded any portion of the territory which remains to us, gives us her full consent; in other words, if she releases Congress from all obligations growing out of the cession, with regard to slavery, I consider it is removing one of the obstacles to the exercise of the power, if it were deemed expedient to exercise the power. But it is removing only one of them.

What had expediency to do with ending slavery in the District? The answer lay in the fact that foreign diplomats and embassies sat in the district, and the British, French, and other foreign powers had ended slavery at home and in their empires. The image of the United States presumably suffered by comparison with these foreign powers when slaves walked the streets of the District.

> There are two other conditions which are inserted in this resolution. The first is the consent of the people of the District.

Free people of color did not have a vote when Virginia retroceded its land from the District. Indeed, when Alexandria returned to Virginia control, free people of color lost whatever minimal rights they had enjoyed in the District. Virginia law was far more stringent. The result was that many free people of color left Alexandria and returned to the District.

> Mr. President, the condition of the people of this District is anomalous. It is a condition in violation of the great principles which lie at the bottom of our own free institutions, and all free institutions, because it is the case of a people who are acted upon by legislative authority, and taxed by legislative authority, without having any voice or representation in the tax-

ing or legislative body. The Government of the United States, in respect to the people of this District, is a tyranny, an absolute Government—not exercised hitherto, I admit, and I hope it never will be exercised, tyrannically or arbitrarily; but it is in the nature of all arbitrary power, because, if I were to give a definition of arbitrary power, I would say that it is that power for property taken by the public, for its use, would not apply to the case of the abolition of slavery in the District, because the property is not taken for the use 'of the public.

Clay here referred to ending slavery through the "takings" doctrine. In one instance of such doctrine, eminent domain, government could take private property from its owners for public use. Eminent domain by the federal government required compensation, under the Fifth Amendment to the Constitution's due process clause. The alternative was to end slavery by confiscation. Governments could take property that had fallen into disuse or was a danger to the public, without compensation. Slaves still had value, however. Note that Clay was applying old English common law property theory to slaves, although slavery was not a subject of England's common law. The next passage revealed Clay's reasons for not "taking" slaves.

Literally, perhaps, it [slavery] would not be taken for the use of the public; but it would be taken in consideration of a policy and purpose adopted by the public, as one which it was deemed expedient to carry into full effect and operation; and, by a liberal interpretation of the clause, it ought to be so far regarded as taken for the use of the public, at the instance of the public, as to demand compensation to the extent of the value of the property. If that is not a restriction as to the power of Congress over the subject of slavery in the District, then the power of Congress stands unrestricted, and that would not be a better condition for the slaveholder in the District than to assume the restriction contained in the [Fifth] amendment. I say it would be unrestricted by constitutional operation or injunction. The great restrictions resulting from the obligations of justice would remain, and they are sufficient to exact from Congress the duty of ascertaining, prior to the abolition of slavery, the value of the property in slaves in the District, and of making full, fair and just compensation for that property.

In 1861, the newly elected president Abraham Lincoln was thinking along these lines—end slavery in the District by compensating
slaveholders.[4]

> Well, Mr. President, I said yesterday there was not a resolution, except the
> first, (which contained no concession by either party), that did not either
> contain some mutual concession by the two parties, or did not contain
> concessions altogether from the North to the South. Now with respect
> to the resolution under consideration. The North has contended that the
> power exists under the constitution to abolish slavery. The South, I am
> aware, has opposed it, and most, at least a great portion of the South,
> have contended for the opposite construction. What does the resolution
> do? It asks of both parties to forbear urging their respective opinions, the
> one to the exclusion of the other, but it concedes to the South all that the
> South, it appears to me, upon this subject, ought in reason to demand, in
> so far as it requires such conditions as amount to an absolute security for
> property in slaves in the District; such conditions as will probably make
> the existence of slavery within the District coeval and coextensive with its
> existence in any of the States out of and beyond the District.

So, the concession to the South was that slavery would remain legal in
the District. But something had to be given in exchange to the free states.

> But, sir, the second clause of this resolution provides "that it is expedi-
> ent to prohibit within the District the trade in slaves bought into it from
> States or places beyond the limits of the District, either to be sold therein
> as merchandise or to be transported to other markets." Well, Mr. Presi-
> dent, if the concession be made that Congress has the power of legis-
> lation, and exclusive legislation, in all cases whatsoever, how can it be
> doubted that Congress has authority to prohibit what is called the slave
> trade in the District of Columbia?

Congress administered the District. Its plenary power was not disputed. But it was constrained by the Fifth Amendment's requirement of

---

4 Eric Foner, *The Fiery Trial: Abraham Lincoln and American Slavery* (New York: Norton, 2010),
182–183 (begin compensation with Delaware).

compensation for property taken. The American Anti-Slavery Society petition campaign of the late 1830s did not mention this requirement, as the AAS did not regard the enslaved as property. Barring the auction of the enslaved in the nation's capital was a lot less than half a loaf to the free states, but it was something.

> Sir, my interpretation of the constitution is this; that, with regard to all parts of it which operate upon the States, Congress can exercise no power which is not granted, or which is not a necessary implication from a granted power.

The first part of Clay's sentence sounded like the strict construction rule that the Jeffersonian Democrats had championed in the 1790s, a bulwark of states' rights thinking in the years after, but the last clause, "which is not a necessary implication," was Hamilton's idea of loose construction, based on the necessary and proper clause of article I. By modifying the former with the latter, Clay was in accord with his own views of internal improvements and other federal projects (like roads) not explicitly mentioned in article I. To repeat: his American System was very Hamiltonian.

> That is the rule for the action of Congress in relation to its legislation upon the States, but in relation to its legislation upon this District, the reverse. I take it to be the true rule that Congress has all power over the District which is not prohibited by some part of the Constitution of the United States; in other words, that Congress has a power within the District equivalent to and co-extensive with, the power which any State itself possesses within its own limits.

A simple but compelling analogy that avoided criticism of Clay's loose construction.

> Well, sir, does any one doubt the power and the right of any slaveholding State in this Union to forbid the introduction, as merchandise, of slaves within their limits? Why, sir, almost every slaveholding State in the Union has exercised its power to prohibit the introduction of slavery as merchandise. It was in the constitution of my own State; and, notwithstand-

ing all the excitement and agitation upon the subject of slavery which occurred during the past year in the State of Kentucky, the same principle is incorporated in the new constitution [of the state]. It is in the constitution, I know, of Mississippi. That State prohibits the introduction of slaves within its limits as merchandise. I believe it to be in the constitution or in the laws of Maryland—in the laws of Virginia—in the laws of most of the slaveholding States.

Here Clay referred to *Groves v. Slaughter* (1841), a US Supreme Court case regarding the importation of the enslaved to Mississippi as merchandise. The state constitution provided that "the introduction of slaves into this state as merchandise or for sale shall be prohibited from and after 1 May, 1833, provided that actual settler or settlers shall not be prohibited from purchasing slaves in any state in this Union and bringing them into this state for their own individual use till the year 1845." The majority opinion on the Court did not reach the constitutional question of whether the Interstate Commerce Clause of the federal Constitution barred Mississippi's law from operating, deciding the case, as it had all of these slave cases, on very narrow technical grounds. The dissenters raised the constitutional issue, but the takeaway was that slave law was entirely controlled by the states. Clay was following the Court in declining to enter the thicket. When the Court, in *Dred Scott v. Sandford* (1857), abandoned its earlier conservatism and hinted that the enslaved, under the Fifth Amendment, could not be barred from the territories without compensation to the owners, the Free Soil states were furious.[5]

It is true that the policy of the different slaveholding States upon this subject has somewhat vacillated—they sometimes adopted it and sometimes excluded it—but there has been no diversity of opinion, no departure from the great principle, that every one of them has the power and authority to prohibit the introduction of the enslaved within their respective limits, if they choose to exercise it.

5 *Groves v. Slaughter*, 40 U.S. 449 (1841); Paul M. Finkelman, *An Imperfect Union: Slavery, Federalism, and Comity* (Chapel Hill: University of North Carolina Press, 1981), 266–268; Don E. Fehrenbacher, *The Dred Scott Case: Its Significance in Law and Politics* (New York: Oxford University Press, 1978), 417–448.

Not entirely true, as border slave states objected to the laws of their free state neighbors regarding the return of alleged runaways. See, for example, *Prigg v. Pennsylvania* (1842) in which Maryland objected to Pennsylvania's 1827 anti-kidnapping law.[6]

> Well, then, sir, I really do not think that this resolution, which proposes to abolish that trade, ought to be considered as a concession by either class of the States to the other class. I think it should be regarded as a common object, acceptable to both, and conformable to the wishes and feelings of both; and yet, sir, in these times of fearful and alarming excitement—in these times when every night that I go to sleep and wake up in the morning, it is with the apprehension of some new and fearful and dreadful tidings upon this agitating subject—I have seen in the act of a neighboring State, among the various contingencies which are enumerated, upon the happening of any one of which delegates are to be sent to the famous convention which is to assemble at Nashville in June next, that among other substantive grounds for the appointment of delegates to that convention—of delegates from the State to which I refer—one is, that if Congress abolish the slave trade in the District of Columbia, that shall be cause for a convention—in other words, it is cause for considering whether this Union ought to be dissolved or not.

In fact, the convention met in Nashville, Tennessee, that June for nine days, with little to show for it, the resolutions for secession tabled and the convention adjourned.[7]

> Is it possible to portray a greater extent of extravagance to which men may be carried by the indulgence of their passions? Sir, the power exists; the duty, in my opinion, exists; and there has been no time—as I may say, in language coincident with that used by the honorable Senator from Alabama there has been no time in my public life when I was not willing to concur in the abolition of the slave trade in this District. I was willing to do it when Virginia's portion of the District was retroceded, that lying South of the Potomac. There is still less ground for objection to doing it

---

6 *Prigg v. Pennsylvania*, 41 U.S. 539 (1842).
7 An older but still useful account is George L. Sioussat, "Tennessee, the Compromise of 1850, and the Nashville Convention," *Mississippi Valley Historical Review* 2, no. 3 (1915): 313–347.

now, when the District is limited to the portion this side of the Potomac, and when the motive or reason for concentrating slaves here in a depot, for the purpose of transportation to distant foreign markets, is lessened with the diminution of the District, by that retrocession of that portion to Virginia. Why should slave-traders who buy their slaves in Maryland or Virginia, come here with their slaves in order to transport them to New Orleans or other Southern markets? Why not transport them from the States in which they are purchased? Why are the feelings of citizens here outraged by the scenes exhibited, and the corteges which pass along our avenues, of manacled human beings, not collected at all in our own neighborhood, but brought from distant parts of neighboring States? Why should they be outraged? And who is there, that has a heart, that does not contemplate a spectacle of that kind with horror and indignation? Why should they be outraged by a scene so inexcusable and detestable as this?

One (ironic) result was that the slave markets of Richmond, Charleston, New Orleans, and Natchez probably gained business that slave sellers in the District lost.[8]

Sir, it is no concession, I repeat, from one class of States or from the other. It is an object in which both of them, it seems to me, should heartily unite, and which the one side as much as the other should rejoice in adopting, inasmuch as it lessens one of the causes of inquietude and dissatisfaction which are connected with this District. Abolish the slave-trade in this district; re-assert the doctrine of the resolution of 1838, that by an implied assent on the part of Congress slavery ought not to be abolished in the District of Columbia, whilst it remains in the State of Maryland; re-assert the principle of that resolution, and adopt the healing measures—or other similar or more healing measures—for I am not attached to any thing that is the production of my own hand, if any thing better should be offered by any body else—adopt the other healing measures which

8 Robert H. Gudmestad, *A Troublesome Commerce: The Transformation of the Interstate Slave Trade* (Baton Rouge: Louisiana State University Press, 2002), 23–26; Walter Johnson, *Soul by Soul: Life Inside the Antebellum Slave Market* (Cambridge, MA: Harvard University Press, 2000), 43–51; Ariela J. Gross, *Double Character: Slavery and Mastery in the Antebellum Southern Courtroom* (Princeton, NJ: Princeton University Press, 2000), 180–181.

are proposed, and which are required by the distracted condition of the country, and I venture to say that, as we have had peace and quiet for the last twenty years, since the termination of the Missouri controversy, we shall have, in all human probability, peace for a longer period to come upon this unhappy subject of slavery.

Finally, Clay came to the most portentous of his resolutions—a strengthening of the existing Fugitive Slave Act of 1793.

The next resolution is: "That more effectual provision ought to be made by law, according to the requirement of the Constitution, for the restitution and delivery of persons bound to service or labor in any State, who may escape into any other State or Territory in the Union." Now, Mr. President, upon that subject I go with him who goes farthest in the interpretation of that clause in the Constitution.

The clause in question was the Rendition Clause, in article IV, clause 3 (not the Extradition Clause for fugitives from justice), but the rendition of those owing labor: "No Person held to Service or Labour in one State, under the Laws thereof, escaping into another, shall, in Consequence of any Law or Regulation therein, be discharged from such Service or Labour, but shall be delivered up on Claim of the Party to whom such Service or Labour may be due." It was not self-executing, so Congress passed the Fugitive Slave Act of 1793, section 3 of which read, "The person to whom such labor or service may be due, his agent or attorney, is hereby empowered to seize or arrest such fugitive from labor, and to take him or her before any Judge of the Circuit or District Courts of the United States, residing or being within the State, or before any magistrate of a county, city, or town corporate, wherein such seizure or arrest shall be made, and upon proof to the satisfaction of such Judge or magistrate, either by oral testimony or affidavit taken before and certified by a magistrate of any such State or Territory, that the person so seized or arrested, doth, under the laws of the State or Territory from which he or she fled, owe service or labor to the person claiming him or her, it shall be the duty of such Judge or magistrate to give a certificate thereof to such claimant, his agent, or attorney, which shall be sufficient warrant for removing the said fugitive from labor to the State or Territory from which he or she fled." Note that state judicial officials were ordered to join in the rendition. No guarantee of due process rights (trial by jury, right to an attorney, presumption of innocence) was included. In *Prigg*, the Court, in a majority decision by Justice Joseph Story, found that the federal government could not compel the state to comply with the act. That was what infuriated the South.

> In my humble opinion, sir, it is a requirement by the Constitution of the United States which is not limited in its operation to the Congress of the United States, but extends to every State in the Union and to the officers of every State in the Union; and I go one step farther; it extends to every man in the Union, and devolves upon them all an obligation to assist in the recovery of a fugitive from labor who takes refuge in or escapes into one of the free States.

This was a view of the nation that was compatible with states' rights. Southern opinion leaders could subscribe to both because they viewed the nation not as primarily a legal entity, but as a cultural entity. The nation, to these white men, was an expression of their values—their whiteness—in what historians have called a *herrenvolk* democracy. Rights and privileges grew out of racial identity. It was thus how these men could extol the "peculiar institution" of slavery as a necessary foundation of the equality of white men.[9]

> And, sir, I think I can maintain all this by a fair interpretation of the Constitution. It will be observed, Mr. President, that this clause in the Constitution is not among the enumerated powers granted to Congress, for, if that had been the case, it might have been urged that Congress alone could legislate to carry it into effect; but it is one of the general powers, or one of the general rights secured by this Constitutional instrument, and it addresses itself to all who are bound by the Constitution of the United States.
>
> Now, sir, the officers of the General Government are bound to take an oath to support the Constitution of the United States. All State officers are

---

9 Paul Quigley, *Shifting Grounds: Nationalism and the American South, 1848–1861* (New York: Oxford University Press, 2011), 16–49; George M. Frederickson, *White Supremacy* (New York: Oxford University Press, 1981), ix.

required by the Constitution to take an oath to support the Constitution of the United States; and all men who love their country and are obedient to its laws, are bound to assist in the execution of those Jaws, whether they are fundamental or derivative. I do not say that a private individual is bound to make the tour of his State in order to assist an owner of a slave to recover his property; but I do say, if he is present when the owner of a slave is about to assert his rights and endeavor to obtain possession of his property, every man present, whether he be an officer of the General Government or the State Government, or a private individual, is bound to assist, if men are bound at all to assist in the execution of the laws of their country.

The polar opposite of the abolitionist argument that every man is bound by conscience to resist the recapture of the enslaved. This was the basis of civil disobedience. According to Henry David Thoreau, who refused to pay taxes to support the Mexican-American War because it aided slavery, "The government itself, which is only the mode which the people have chosen to execute their will, is equally liable to be abused and perverted before the people can act through it. Witness the present Mexican war, the work of comparatively a few individuals using the standing government as their tool; for, in the outset, the people would not have consented to this measure. . . . There are thousands who are in opinion opposed to slavery and to the war, who yet in effect do nothing to put an end to them; who, esteeming themselves children of Washington and Franklin, sit down with their hands in their pockets. . . . Unjust laws exist: shall we be content to obey them, or shall we endeavor to amend them, and obey them until we have succeeded, or shall we transgress them at once?" To Thoreau, the answer had been plain.[10]

Now what is this provision? It is that such fugitives shall be delivered upon claim of the party to whom such service or labor may be due. As has been already remarked in the course of the debate upon the bill upon this subject which is now pending, the language used in regard to fugitives from criminal offences and fugitives from labor is precisely the same. The

---

10 Henry David Thoreau, "Resistance to Civil Government" (1849), in *The Writings of Henry D. Thoreau: Reform Papers*, ed. Wendell Glick (Princeton, NJ: Princeton University Press, 1973), 63–76, 86.

fugitive from justice is to be delivered up, and to be removed to the State having jurisdiction; the fugitive from labor is to be delivered up on claim of the party to whom such service is due.

Well, has it ever been contended on the part of any State that she is not bound to surrender a fugitive from justice, upon demand from the State from which he fled? I believe not. There have been some exceptions to the performance of this duty, but they have not denied the general right; and if they have refused in any instance to give up the person demanded, it has been upon some technical or legal ground, not at all questioning the general right to have the fugitive surrendered, or the obligation to deliver him up as intended by the Constitution.

Plainly wrong, given *Prigg v. Pennsylvania.* Although concurring opinions in *Prigg* agreed with Clay's interpretation, concurring opinions were not the law of the land. The opinion reiterated federal government power to effectuate the Rendition Clause: "If this is so, it would seem upon just principles of construction that the legislation of Congress, if constitutional, must supersede all state legislation upon the same subject, and, by necessary implication, prohibit it. . . . It cannot be that the state legislatures have a right to interfere." At the same time, states could assist: "The Court entertain no doubt whatsoever that the States, in virtue of their general police power, possess full jurisdiction to arrest and restrain runaway slaves, and to remove them from their borders and otherwise to secure themselves against their depredations." But the state was not required to assist: "By the general law of nations, no nation is bound to recognize the state of slavery as to foreign slaves found within its territorial dominions, when it is in opposition to its own policy and institutions, in favor of the subjects of other nations where slavery is recognized. If it does it, it is as a matter of comity, and not as a matter of international right. The state of slavery is deemed to be a mere municipal regulation, founded upon and limited to the range of the territorial laws."[11]

I think, then, Mr. President, that with regard to the true interpretation of this provision of free Constitution there can be no doubt. It imposes an

---

11 *Prigg v. Pennsylvania,* 41 U.S. 539, 540, 541, 542, 611 (1842) (Story, J.).

obligation upon all the States, free or slaveholding; it imposes an obligation upon all officers of the Government, State, or Federal; and, I will add,
upon all the people of the United States, under particular circumstances,
to assist in the surrender and recovery of a fugitive slave from his master.
There has been some confusion, and, I think, some misconception, on
this subject, in consequence of a recent decision of the Supreme Court of
the United States. I think that decision has been entirely misapprehended.
There is a vast difference between imposing impediments and affording
facilities for the recovery of fugitive slaves. The Supreme Court of the
United States has only decided that all laws of impediment are unconstitutional. I know there are some general expressions in the opinion to
which I have referred—the case, of Maryland against Pennsylvania—that
seem to import otherwise.

Conceding that the majority opinion in *Prigg* did not accord with his
view.

But I think, When you come attentively to read the whole opinion, and
the opinion pronounced by all the judges, especially if you take the trouble of doing what I have done, to converse with them as to what their real
meaning was, you will find that the whole extent of the authority which
they intended to establish was that any laws of impediment enacted by
the States were laws that were forbidden by the provision of the Constitution to which I refer; that the General Government had no right, by an
act of the Congress of the United States, to impose obligations upon State
officers not imposed by the authority of their own Constitution and laws.
It is impossible the decision could have been otherwise. It would have
been perfectly extrajudicial.

A fine distinction between the obligation of state officials to assist,
which the opinion did not say, and barring state laws and state officials
from obstructing recapture, which the opinion did say.

The Court had no right to decide the question whether the laws of facility
were or were not unconstitutional. The only question before the Court
was the law of impediment passed by the Legislature of Pennsylvania and
if they had gone beyond the case before them, and undertaken to decide

upon a ease not before them, a principle which was not fairly comprehended within the case before them, it would be what the lawyers term
an obiter dictum, and is not binding; either on that Court itself or any
other tribunal.

Clay is right about the obiter dictum, a part of the opinion not being
necessary to its decision, but if the majority of the justices, as was the
case in *Prigg*, subscribe to the obiter dictum, then it becomes law.

I say it was not possible that, with the case before the Court of a law for
giving facility to the holder of the slave to recover his property again,
it was utterly impossible that any tribunal should pronounce a decision
that such aid and assistance, rendered by the authority of the State, under
this provision of the Constitution of the United States, is unconstitutional
and void. The Court has not said so, or if they have said so, they have
transcended their authority and gone beyond the case which was before
them.

Exactly what leaders of the Republican Party said about the two obiter dicta in Chief Justice Roger Taney's opinion in *Dred Scott*: that persons of African ancestry could never be citizens of the United States and
that the Missouri Compromise barring slavery above a certain latitude
in Louisiana Territory lands was unconstitutional.

Laws passed by States, in order to assist the General Government, so far
from being laws repugnant to the Constitution, would every where be
regarded as laws carrying out, enforcing, and fulfilling the Constitutional
duties which are created by that instrument. Why, sir, as well might it be
contended that if Congress were to declare war—and no one will doubt
that the power to declare war is vested exclusively in Congress; no State
has the right to do it—no one will contend seriously, I apprehend, that
after the declaration of war it would be unconstitutional on the part of
any of the States to assist in the vigorous and effective prosecution of that
war; and yet it would be just as unconstitutional to lend their aid to the
successful and glorious termination of the war in which we might be em-
barked, as it would be to assist in the performance of a high duty which
addresses itself to all the States and all the people of all the States.

Mr. President, I do think that that whole class of Legislation, beginning in the Northern States and extending to some of the Western States, by which obstructions and impedimenta have been thrown in the way of the recovery of fugitive slaves, is unconstitutional, and has originated in a spirit which I trust will correct itself when these States come calmly to consider the nature and extent of their federal obligations.

The latter a reference to the personal liberty laws of many of the northern states.

Of all the States in this Union, unless it be Virginia, the State of which I am a resident [Kentucky] suffers most by the escape of their slaves to adjoining States. I have very little doubt, indeed, that the extent of loss to the State of Kentucky, in consequence of the escape of her slaves is greater, at least, in proportion to the total number of slaves which are held within that commonwealth, even than in Virginia. I know full well, and so does the honorable Senator from Ohio know, that it is at the utmost hazard, and insecurity to life itself, that a Kentuckian can cross the [Ohio] river and go into the interior to take back his fugitive slave to the place from whence he fled.

Recently an example occurred even in the city of Cincinnati, in respect to one of our most respectable citizens. Not having visited Ohio at all, but Covington, on the opposite side of the river, a little slave of his escaped over to Cincinnati. He pursued it; he found it in the house in which it was concealed; he took it out, and it was rescued by the violence and force of a negro mob from his possession—the police of the city standing by, and either unwilling or unable to afford the assistance which was requisite to enable him to recover his property.

The "little slave" was undoubtedly a child. Covington, Kentucky, just outside of Cincinnati on the Ohio River, was a first stop on the Underground Railroad for escaping slaves. It was home to many free Blacks, and they, with white abolitionist aid, provided for the runaways, including breaking runaways out of jail.[12]

---

12 Mary Ellen Snodgrass, *The Underground Railroad: An Encyclopedia of People, Places, and Operations* (London: Rutledge, 2009), 1:13 (list).

Upon this subject I do think that we have just and serious cause of complaint against the free States. I think they fail in fulfilling a great obligation, and the failure is precisely upon one of these subjects which in its nature is the most irritating and inflaming to those who live in the slave States. Now, sir, I think it is a mark of no good neighborhood, of no kindness, of no courtesy, that a man living in a slave State cannot now, with any sort of safety, travel in the free States with his servants, although he has no purpose whatever of stopping there longer than a short time. And on this whole subject, sir, how has the legislation of the free States altered for the worse within the course of the last twenty or thirty years? Why, sir, most of these States, until within a period of the last twenty or thirty years, had laws for the benefit of sojourners, as they were called, passing through or abiding for the moment in the free States, with their servants.

Sir, I recollect a case that occurred during the war. My friend Mr. [Landon] Cheves, of South Carolina, instead of going home in the vacation, went to Philadelphia, taking his family servants with him. Some of the abolitionists of that city took out a habeas corpus, seized the slaves, and the question was brought before the Supreme Court of the State of Pennsylvania, where it was argued for days. It was necessary, during the progress of the arguments, to refer to a great variety of statutes passed from time to time by the Legislature of Pennsylvania, on behalf of the sojourner, guarantying and securing to him the possession of his property during his temporary passage or abode within the limits of that commonwealth. Finally, the court gave their opinion seriatim—each judge his separate opinion, until it came to Judge Breckenridge to deliver his, who was the youngest judge, I think, on the bench. During the progress of the delivery of their opinions they had frequently occasion to refer to the acts passed for the benefit of sojourners; and each of the judges who preceded Mr. Breckenridge always pronounced the word "sudgeners." When it came to Judge Breckenridge to deliver his opinion, he said, "I agree in all that my learned brethren have pronounced upon this occasion, except in their pronunciation of the word 'sojourner.' They pronounced it 'sudgener' but I call it 'sojourner'" [Laughter.] Well, now, sir, all these laws in behalf of these sojourners through the free States are swept away, except I believe in the State of Rhode Island.

But Cheves's slave was returned to him, demonstrating northern compliance. So, not to worry about the personal liberty laws?

MR. [WILLIAM] DAYTON. And New Jersey.

And in other Upper Midwest states as well, extrajudicially.

MR. CLAY. Aye, and in New Jersey. I am happy to hear it; but in most
   of the large States, in most, if not all, of the New England States,
   these laws have been abolished, though the progressive tendency of
   bad neighborhood and unkind action on the part of the free States
   toward the slaveholding States.
      Mr. President, I do not mean to contest the ground—I am not go-
   ing to argue the question, whether, if a man carries his slave voluntarily into the free States and he is not a fugitive, whether that slave,
   by the voluntary action of the master, does or does not become instantly entitled to his freedom. I am not going to argue that question.

If the servant was resident in the free state, free state freedom laws attached. The troublesome cases in law were those in which the master was a sojourner, or passing though, or even just stopping briefly in a harbor or train station. How such northern laws were unneighborly could be understood only if the enslaved were considered not a person but baggage.

   I know what the decision has been at the North, but I mean to say it is unkind, it is unneighborly, it is not in the spirit of fraternal connexion which
   exists between the members of this confederacy, to execute a strict legal
   principle in the way suggested, even supposing it to be right so to do. But
   where there is no purpose of permanent abode, no intention of settling
   finally and conclusively, and placing his slaves within the commonwealth,
   it is but right, and a proof of good neighborhood and kind and friendly
   feeling, to allow the owner of the slave to pass with his property unmo-
   lested through your State.
      Allow me to say upon the subject, though it is perhaps going farther
   into detail than is necessary, that of all the exercise of power of those
   who attempt to seduce from their owners their slaves, there is no

instance in which it is exercised so injuriously to the objects of their charity and benevolence as in the case of the seduction of family slaves from the service of their owner. The slaves in a family are treated with all the kindness that the children of the family receive. Everything which they want for their comfort is given them with the most liberal indulgence; and, sir, I have known more instances than one where, by this practice of the seduction of family servants from their owners, they have been rendered wretched and unhappy in the free States; and in my own family, a slave who had been seduced away, addressed her mistress and begged and implored of her the means of getting back from the state, of freedom to which she had been seduced, to the state of slavery in which she was so much more happy; and in the case to which I have referred the means were afforded her, and she returned to the State of Kentucky to her mistress.

This view of enslavement combined the "positive good" argument with the "moonlight and magnolias" romance novels of the antebellum South. The white people of the South were "the most happiest, most contended, and most prosperous people on earth," according to Virginia lawyer and proslavery essayist George Fitzhugh, and "the institution of slavery gives full development and full play to the affections." Edmund Ruffin, a Virginia planter and agronomist, added that the master class "always speaks to the slave in a kind and subdued tone." Even if a slave-holding society was devastated by want, every domestic slave is as much as before assured of his customary food and other allowances.[13]

Then, Mr. President, I think that the existing laws upon the subject, for the recovery of fugitive slaves, and the restoration and delivering of them up to their owners, being found inadequate and ineffective, it is incumbent on Congress—and I hope hereafter, in a better state of feeling, when more harmony and good -will will prevail among the members of this confederacy, it will be regarded by the free States themselves as a fail of their duty also—to assist in allaying this irritating and disturbing subject to the peace of our Union; but, at all events, whether they do it or not, it is our

---

13 George Fitzhugh, *Sociology for the South* (Fredericksburg, VA: Recording Printing, 1850), 3, 10; Edmund Ruffin, *The Political Economy of Slavery* (Washington, DC: Lemuel Towers, 1853).

duty to do it. It is our duty to make the law more effective, and I shall go with the Senator from the South who goes farthest in making penal laws and imposing the heaviest sanctions for the recovery of fugitive slaves, and the restoration of them to their owners.

Mr. President, upon this part of the subject, however, allow me to make an observation or two. I do not think the States, as States, ought to be responsible for all the misconduct of particular individuals within those States. I think that the States are only to be held responsible when they act in their sovereign capacity. If there are a few persons, indiscreet, mad, if you choose—fanatics, if you choose so to call them—who are for dissolving this Union, as we know there are some at the North, and for dissolving it in consequence of the connexion which exists between the free and slaveholding States, I do not think that any State in which such madmen as they are to be found, ought to be held responsible for the doctrines they propagate, unless the State itself adopts those doctrines.

Back again to Massachusetts's Samuel Hoar's mission of 1844, and to South Carolina's ill reception of Hoar, this time blaming Massachusetts for sending him to free her sailors from Charleston jails.

Sir, there have been, perhaps, mutual causes of complaint; and I know, at least I have heard, that Massachusetts, for some of her unfriendly laws on the subject of the recovery of fugitive slaves, urges as the motive for the passage of those laws the treatment which a certain minister of hers experienced in Charleston, some years ago. Mr. [Samuel] Hoar, I think, is the name of the individual who was sent to South Carolina to take care of the free negroes of Massachusetts that might pass to Charleston in the vessels of Massachusetts. I think it was a mission that it was hardly worthy of Massachusetts to create. I think she might have omitted to send Mr. Hoar upon any such mission; but she thought it right to send him. And he went there for the purpose of asserting, as he said, the rights of those free people of color before the courts of justice, and of testing the validity of certain laws in South Carolina with regard to the prohibition of free negroes from coming into her ports. I believe that was the object, that was the purpose of his mission. He went there to create no disturbance, as I understand, except so far as asserting those rights and privileges, in the sense in which Massachusetts held them, might create disturbance. He was virtually driven out of Charleston, as I believe he or some other emissary of the same kind was driven out of New Orleans. I do not mean to say whether it was right or wrong to expel him. What I mean to say is, that Massachusetts, or some of her citizens, has said, that, after finding this treatment towards those whom she chooses to consider citizens, on the part of South Carolina, she determined on that course of legislation by which she has withdrawn all aid and assistance for the recovery of fugitives, and interposes obstacles; and then she pleads the treatment of Mr. Hoar as an apology. I think that furnished her with no sufficient apology. If South Carolina treated her ill, it is no reason why she should ill treat Kentucky and Virginia, and other slaveholding States that had done her no wrong.

In fact, the Massachusetts freedom cases regarded slaves resident in the state, not sojourners or fugitives. Massachusetts state courts did not aid abolitionists in freeing from arrest runaways after the passage of the 1850 Fugitive Slave Act, and the state Freedom Act came in 1855.[14]

But she thought so. I mention both cases—the case of the expulsion of Mr. Hoar from Charleston, and the passage of the laws of Massachusetts—not by way of approbation of either, but to show that there have been, unhappily, mutual causes of agitation, furnished by one class of States as well as by the other; though, I admit, not in the same degree by the slave States as by the free States. And I admit, also, that the free States have much less cause for anxiety and solicitude on this subject of slavery than the slave states, and that far more extensive excuses, if not justification, ought to be extended to the slave than the free States, on account of the difference of the condition of the respective parties.

Again, the enslaved not being a person, he or she was not considered one of the "respective parties."

Mr. President, passing from that resolution, I will add only a single observation, that when the bill comes up to be finally acted on, I will vote most cordially and heartily for it.

---

14 Earl Maltz, *Fugitive Slave on Trial: The Anthony Burns Case and Abolitionist Outrage* (Lawrence: University Press of Kansas, 2010), 87.

MR. [JOHN] DAVIS, OF MASSACHUSETTS. Will the honorable
Senator permit me to interrupt him for a moment? I want to say one
word in behalf of the state of Massachusetts, with his permission.

Davis was a former governor of Massachusetts, a lawyer, and a Whig;
he passed away in 1854.

MR. CLAY. Certainly, certainly.

MR. DAVIS. I have never, although most likely he may have, heard
the apology stated by the honorable Senator for passing the law to
which he has referred; but on the contrary I have always understood
that the law which Massachusetts had, for restoring fugitive slaves,
was repealed because the courts below, as they understood it, had
pronounced their law unconstitutional. That is the ground which
they took; whether they were wise in the legislation they adopted, I
shall not undertake to say. But I wish to say one word in regard to the
mission, as it is termed by the honorable Senator from Kentucky, to
South Carolina. If I call the facts to my recollection correctly, they
are these. We are the owners of much shipping; we employ many sailors, and among them we employ free colored men, men whom we
in Massachusetts acknowledge to be citizens of the United States and
citizens of the commonwealth, and entitled to the rights of citizens.
These citizens were taken from our vessels when they arrived in
South Carolina, and were held in custody till the vessels sailed again.
This our citizens complained of, whether justly or unjustly, that it was
an encroachment, in the first place, upon the rights of citizens, and,
in the next place, that it was a great inconvenience to men engaged
in commerce. If I remember rightly, and I think I do, the state of
Massachusetts authorized its Governor to propose, at the expense to
the State, to some suitable and proper person, who was a citizen of
South Carolina, to test the right to hold her citizens in custody in this
way, in the courts of the State, or in the courts of the United States.
If I remember rightly, that was declined by one or more citizens of
South Carolina. Then the mission, to which the honorable Senator
refers, was instituted, and the termination of it I believe he has correctly stated. I wish it to appear that Massachusetts had no aggressive
purpose whatever, but simply wished that the judiciary should decide

the question existing between them. She wanted nothing more, asked nothing more.

MR. CLAY. Mr. President, I hear with much pleasure this explanation. I have been informed, however, by an eminent citizen of Massachusetts, whose name it is unnecessary to mention—he is not a member of this body—that the motive for the repeal of these laws, or for the passage of these laws, at least one of the motives, was the treatment of Mr. Hoar in Charleston. However, I am glad to hear that it proceeded from another cause, and that is what I conceive to be a misconception of what the true opinion of the judges of the Supreme Court was. When the true exposition of that opinion comes to be known in Massachusetts, I trust that the Legislature of that State will restore the laws facilitating the recovery of fugitive slaves, which she repealed in consequence of that misconception.

The Negro Seamans Acts of southern states were liberalized in the 1850s.[15]

Mr. President, I have a great deal yet to say, and I shall, therefore, pass from the consideration of this seventh resolution with the observation, which believe I have partly made before, that the most stringent provision upon this subject which can be devised will meet with my hearty concurrence and co-operation, in the passage of the bill which is under the consideration of the Senate.

The last resolution declares "That Congress has no power to prohibit or obstruct the trade in slaves between the slaveholding States; but that the admission or exclusion of slaves brought from one into another of them depends exclusively upon their own particular laws." This is a concession, not, I admit, of any real constitutional provision, but a concession from the North to the South of what is understood, I believe, by a great number at the North, to be a constitutional provision. If the resolution should be adopted, take away the decision of the Supreme Court of the United States on this subject, and there is a great deal, I know, that might be said on both sides, as to the right of Congress to regulate the trade between the States, and, consequently, the trade in slaves between the

---

15 Michel Schoeppner, "Peculiar Quarantines: Negro Seaman Acts and Regulatory Authority in the Antebellum South," *Law and History Review* 31 (2013): 571–572.

States; but I think the decision of the Supreme Court has been founded upon correct principles, and I trust it will forever put an end to the question whether Congress has or has not the power to regulate the intercourse and trade in slaves between the different States.

Another reference to *Groves*. Actually, the Court's majority decision did not go into the interstate commerce question. It was the dissent that did.

Such, Mr. President, is the series of resolutions which in an earnest and anxious desire to present the olive branch to both parts of this distracted, and at the present moment unhappy country, I have thought it my duty to offer. Of all men upon earth I am the least attached to any productions of my own mind. No man upon earth is more ready than I am to surrender any thing which I have proposed, and to accept in lieu of it any thing that is better; but I put it to the candor of honorable Senators on the. other side and upon all sides of the House, whether their duty will be performed by simply limiting themselves to objections to any one or to all of the series of resolutions that I have offered. If my plan of peace, and accommodation, and harmony, is not right, present us your plan. Let us see the counter project. Let us see how all the questions that have arisen out of this unhappy subject of slavery can be better settled, more fairly and justly settled to all quarters of the Union, than on the plan proposed in the resolutions which I have offered. Present me such a scheme, and I will hail it with pleasure, and will accept it without the slightest feeling of regret that my own was abandoned.

He could have stopped here, once again, but earlier speakers had offered an alternative to his plan, and although he said he was perfectly willing for the Senate to adopt such reasonable alternatives, I don't believe he was. But let the listener decide. The most prominent of these, proposed by southern senators, was to extend the Missouri Compromise line of 36° 30′ to the Pacific Ocean. This would have allowed slavery in much of the territory acquired from Mexico, including in Southern California.

Sir, while I was engaged in anxious consideration upon this subject, the idea of the Missouri compromise, as it has been termed, came under my review, was considered by me, and finally rejected as in my judgment less

worthy of the common acceptance of both parts of this Union than the
project which I have offered for your consideration.

It certainly would not have met with approval in the free states. But
Clay had a lot more to say about his own role in the Missouri Compromise. It had nothing to do with his eight resolutions. It was a long digression. Webster would do the same with respect to his voting record on
the admission of Texas. Clay's digression is worth our attention because
it is one of the occasions in which he reveals his innermost thinking.

Before I enter into a particular examination, however, of that Missouri
compromise, I beg to be allowed to correct a great error which is pre-
vailing, not merely in this Senate but throughout the whole country, in
respect to my agency in the Missouri compromise, or rather in respect to
the line of 36 deg. 30 minutes which was established in 1820 by an act of
Congress. I do not know whether any thing has excited more surprise in
my mind, as to the rapidity with which important historical transactions
are obliterated and pass from the mind, than when I understood everywhere that I had been the author of the line of 30 deg. 30 min., which
was established upon the occasion of the admission of Missouri into the
Union. It would take too much time to go over the whole of that important error in the public affairs of the country. I shall not do it, although I
have got ample materials before me, derived from a careful examination
of the journals of both houses.

Like the famous Roman orator and lawyer Cicero, Clay promised not
to spend time on the details, then spent a good deal of time on the details of the Missouri admission question.

I will not occupy your time by going in detail through the whole transaction, but I will content myself with saying that so far from my having
presented as a proposition this line of 36 deg. 30 min., upon the occasion of the consideration whether Missouri should be admitted into the
Union or not, it did not originate in the house of which I was a member.
It originated in this body, as those who will cast their recollection back,
and I am sure the honorable Senator from Missouri, (Mr. [Thomas Hart]
Benton,) more correctly than any body else, must bring to his recollec-

tion the fact that at the Congress when the proposition was first made to admit Missouri—or rather to allow her to hold a convention and frame a constitution and decide whether she should or should not be admitted into the Union—the bill failed by a disagreement between the two houses, the House insisting on and the Senate dissenting from the provisions contained in the ordinance of 1787. The House insisting on the interdiction of slavery, and the Senate rejecting the proposition of the interdiction of slavery, the bill fell through; it did not pass at that session of Congress.

In 1819 the lower house voted in favor of New York's James Tallmadge's amendment to the Missouri territory's proposed constitution. Tallmadge asked that no additional slaves could be brought into the state and all persons born in the state were to be free. The slave state representatives voted as a bloc against the amendment, and one, from Georgia, threatened "blood will flow" if it passed. Clay, then in the House, voted against it.[16]

At the next session it was renewed, and at the time of its renewal Maine was knocking at our door to be admitted into the Union. In the House there was a majority for the restriction as to slavery in Missouri; in the Senate there was a majority opposed to all restriction. In the Senate; therefore, in order to carry through the Missouri bill, or the provision for her admission—or rather authorizing her to determine the question of her admission—that bill was coupled with the bill for the admission of Maine. They were connected together, and the Senate said to the House, "You want a bill for the admission of Maine passed, but you shall not have it, unless you take along with it a bill for the admission of Missouri also." There was a majority, a very large one, in the Senate, for coupling both together.

Well, sir, the bill went through all the usual stages of disagreement of committees of conference, and there were two committees of conference on the occasion before the matter was finally settled. And it was finally settled to disconnect the two bills—to admit Maine separately, without any connection with Missouri, and to insert in the Missouri bill

---

16 John R. Van Atta, *Wolf by the Ears: The Missouri Crisis, 1819–1821* (Baltimore: Johns Hopkins University Press, 2015), 82, 93, 94.

a clause proposed in the Senate of the United States by Mr. [Jesse Burgess] Thomas, Senator from Illinois, restricting slavery north of the line 36 deg. 30 min., and leaving it open south of that line, either to admit it or not to admit it. Well, sir, the bill finally passed. The committees of conference of the two houses recommended the detachment of the two cases, and the passage of the Missouri bill with the clause 36 deg. 30 min. in it; and so it passed, so it went to Missouri, so it for a moment quieted the country, by means of the introduction of the clause 36 deg. 30 min.

You will find, I repeat, sir, if you will take the trouble to look at the journals, that on as many as three or four different occasions Mr. Thomas in every instance presented the proposition of 36 deg. 30 min. It was finally agreed to; and I take occasion to say that among those who voted for the 36 deg. 30 min. were the majority of the Southern members—my friend from Alabama, (Mr. [William R.] King,) in the Senate, Mr. Pinckney, from Maryland, and indeed the majority of the Southern Senators voted in favor of the line 36 deg. 30 min.; and the majority of the Southern members in tie other house, at the head of whom was Mr. [William] Lowndes himself, voted also for that [latitude] line.

William R. King, a lawyer and cotton planter, was the vice president of the United States under Franklin Pierce in 1853, for a brief period, dying a month after the inauguration. He was a supporter of the Compromise of 1850. William Pinkney was a Jeffersonian Republican senator from Maryland, a diplomat, and formerly a member of the House. William Lowndes was a member of the House from South Carolina. These were all leading politicians in their day.

I have no doubt I did also; but, as I was Speaker of the House at the time, and the journal does not show how the Speaker votes except in the case of a tie, I was not able to ascertain, by a resort to the records, how I did vote; but I have very little doubt that I voted, in common with my other Southern friends, for the adoption, in a spirit of compromise, it is true, of the line 36 deg. 30 min. Well, sir, so the matter ended in 1820.

During that year Missouri held her convention, adopted her constitution, sent her delegates to Congress, seeking to be admitted into the Union; but she had inserted a clause in her constitution containing a prohibition of free people of color from that State. She came here with her constitution containing that prohibition, and immediately the Northern members took exception to it. The flame which had been repressed during the previous session now burst forth with double violence throughout the whole Union. Legislative bodies all got in motion to keep out Missouri, in consequence of her interdiction of free people of color from within her limits.

I did not arrive at Congress that session till January, and when I got here I found both bodies completely paralyzed in consequence of the struggle to exclude Missouri from the Union on account of that prohibition. Well, sir, I made the first effort in the House to settle it. I asked for a committee of thirteen, and a committee of thirteen was granted to me, representing all the old States of the Union. The committee met. I presented to them a resolution, which was adopted by the committee and reported to the House—not unlike the one to which I will presently call the attention of the Senate—and we should have carried it in the House but for the votes of Mr. Randolph, of Virginia, Mr. Edwards, of North Carolina, and Mr. Burton, of North Carolina two of the three, I believe, no longer living.

These three Southern votes were all cast against the compromise, which was prepared by the committee, or rather by myself, as chairman of the committee of thirteen, and defeated it. Well, sir, in that condition the thing remained for several days. The greatest anxiety pervaded the country—the public mind was unsettled—men were unhappy—there was a large majority of the House then, as I hope and trust there is now a large majority in Congress, in favor of an equitable accommodation or settlement of the question; and the resolution would have been adopted, I believe, but when it came to the vote of yeas and nays, unfortunately then—mere unfortunately then, I hope, than now, if there should be occasion for it now there were few Leonidases willing to risk themselves for the safety and security of their country.

Leonidas, today made famous by the movie *The 300 Spartans*, was the elected coruler of Sparta during the Persian invasion of Greece in 480 BCE. He and his men, along with their allies, fought the Persians at the Battle of Thermopylae, delaying their advance. While the battle was not a victory (indeed the Spartan contingent was wiped out), Leonidas's efforts became a symbol of military courage in the service of his country.

I endeavored to avail myself of that good feeling, as far as I could; and, after a few days had elapsed, brought forward another proposition; a new one, perfectly unpracticed in this country, either before or since, as far as I know. I proposed a joint committee of the two houses; that of the House to consist of twenty three members, (the number of the Senate committee I do not recollect) and that this committee should be appointed by ballot; for at that time Mr. [John R.] Taylor, of New York, was in the chair, and Mr. Taylor was the very man who had first proposed the restriction upon Missouri.

Memory failed Clay. Taylor was indeed a New Yorker who supported the Tallmadge Amendment, but it was Tallmadge, not Taylor, who proposed it. As the narrative continued, it became obvious that Clay's purpose was to demonstrate how he had saved the nation. And how he was ready to do it again.

He [Taylor] proposed that she should only be admitted on the principle of the ordinance of 1787; I proposed therefore, that the committee be appointed by ballot. Well, sir, my motion was carried by a large majority; and members came to me from all quarters of the House, and said, "Whom, Mr. Clay, do you want to have with you on the committee?" I made out my list of twenty-three members, and I venture to say that that happened on that occasion which will hardly ever happen again, eighteen of the twenty-three were elected on the first ballot, and the remaining five on my list having the largest number of votes, but not the majority, I moved to dispense with any farther balloting, and that these five should be added to the eighteen, thus completing the committee of twenty-three. One or two gentlemen, Mr. Livermore, of New Hampshire, and one or two others, declined to serve on the committee; and, very much to my regret, and somewhat to my annoyance, the lamented Mr. Randolph and another person were placed in their situation—I forgot whether done by ballot or by the Speaker; it is enough to say they were put on the committee. Well, sir, the Senate immediately agreed to the proposition, appointed its committee, and we met in this hall on the Sabbath day, within two or three days of the close of the session, when the whole nation was waiting with breathless anxiety for some final and healing measure upon the distracting subject-which occupied our attention.

Clay's detailed recollection was a digression, an elderly politician re-calling his youthful experience, setting the historical record straight, as he remembered it. The antebellum orator was a storyteller, and his fellow senators appreciated this fact, although they must have been wondering if Clay would rehearse the whole of his congressional experience for them.

We met thereon that day, and, accordingly, the moment we met, Mr. Randolph made a suggestion which I knew would be attended with the greatest embarrassment and difficulty. He contended that over the two committees of the two houses the chairman of the House committee [Clay] had a right to preside, and he was about to insist at some length that the two committees should be blended together, and that I should preside over both. I instantly interposed, and said that I did not think that was the correct mode, but that the chairman of the committee of each house should preside over his own committee, and that when the committee of one house matured and adopted a proposition, it should be submitted to the other committee, and if agreed to by them, it should then be reported to the two houses, and its adoption recommended

That course was agreed upon, and Mr. Holmes, I believe, of Maine, presided over the committee of the Senate, and I presided over the committee of the House. I did then, what I have protested I would not, do at this session, took too much the lead in the discussion. I brought forward the proposition which I will refer to presently; and I did more, I took the trouble to ascertain the views of each member of the committee—I polled the committee, if I may use the expression. I said, now, gentlemen, we do not want a proposition carried thereby a simple majority and reported to the House, there to be rejected. I am for something practical something conclusive, something decisive upon this agitating question, and it should be carried by a good majority.

How will you vote, Mr. A.? how will you vote, Mr. B.? how will you vote, Mr. C.? and I polled them in that way. Well sir, to my very great happiness, a sufficient number responded affirmatively, that they would vote for the proposition, to enable me to know that, if they continued to vote that way in the two houses, of which I had not a particle of doubt in the world, the proposition would be carried in the two houses. Accordingly, it having been agreed upon by both committees, and reported to their respective houses, it was finally adopted. This joint resolution for the admission of Missouri was passed in 1821.

I find I have been furnished with one which was proposed, but not adopted. The right one is contained in those statutes at large; I have seen it there. Well, sir, the resolution was finally adopted. I can state, without reading it, what its provisions are. It declares that, if there be any provision in the Constitution of Missouri, incompatible with the Constitution of the United States, Missouri shall forbear to enforce the repugnant provisions of her constitution, and that she shall by some solemn and authentic act declare that she will not enforce any provisions of her constitution which are incompatible with the constitution of the United States; and upon her passage of such a solemn and authentic act, the President of the United States—who was at that time Mr. Monroe—shall make proclamation of the fact; and thereupon, and without any farther legislation of Congress, Missouri shall be admitted into the Union. Now, sir, I want to call your attention to this period of history, and to the transactions which took place during the progress of the discussion upon the resolution.

During the discussion which took place in the House at that time, from day to day, and from night to night—for the discussions frequently ran into the night—we who were for admitting Missouri into the Union said to our brethren from the North, "Why, gentlemen, if there be any provision in the Constitution of Missouri which is repugnant to the constitution of the United States, it is a nullity. The Constitution of the United States, by virtue of its own operation—its own self-operation—vacates it. Any tribunal on earth, before which the question may be brought, must pronounce the Constitution of the United States paramount, and must pronounce invalid the repugnant provision of the constitution of Missouri." Well, sir, the argument was turned, and twisted, and used in every possible variety of form. All was in vain. An inflexible majority stood out to the last against the admission of Missouri; and yet the resolution.

Mr. [Joseph R.] Underwood. I have it here.

Joseph R. Underwood was a Whig senator from Kentucky, a Unionist, and a supporter of the Compromise. Obviously, he was given a copy of the resolution by Clay and read it on cue.

Mr. Clay. If you will read it, I shall be obliged to you.

Mr. Underwood read the resolution as follows:

> Resolution providing for the admission of the State of Missouri into the Union on a certain condition. Resolved by the Senate and House of Representatives of the United States of America in Congress assembled, That Missouri shall be admitted into this Union on an equal footing With the original States in all respects whatever, upon the fundamental condition that the fourth clause of the 26th section of the third article of the Constitution, submitted on the part of said state to Congress, shall never be construed to authorise the passage of any law, and that no law shall be passed in conformity thereto, by which any citizen of either of the States of this Union shall be excluded from the enjoyment of any of the privileges and immunities to which such citizen is entitled under the Constitution of the United States: Provided, That the Legislature of the said state, by a solemn public act, shall declare the assent of the said State to the said fundamental condition, and shall transmit to the President of the United States, on or before the fourth Monday in November next, an authentic copy of the said act; upon the receipt whereof the President, by proclamation, shall announce the fact; whereupon, and without any farther proceeding on the part of Congress, the admission of the said State into the Union shall be considered as complete. [Approved March 2, 1821]

MR. CLAY. There is the resolution, sir, and you see it is precisely what I have stated. After all this excitement throughout the country, reaching to such an alarming point that the Union itself was supposed to be in the most imminent peril and danger, the parties were satisfied by the declaration of an incontestable principle of Constitutional law, that when the Constitution of a State is violative in its provisions of the Constitution of the United States the constitution of the United States is paramount, and the constitution of the State in that particular is a nullity and void.

That was all. They [the holdouts in the North] wanted something as a justification, and this appeared, at least, a justification of the course they took. There is a great deal of language there of a high-sounding character—that it shall be a fundamental act, a solemn act, an authentic act; but, after all, when you come to strip it of its verbiage, it is nothing but the announcement of the principle that the

Constitution of the United States is paramount over the local Constitution of any one of the States of the Union.

Clay had used the narrative to demonstrate that he was never a pure states' rights advocate. The federal Constitution was supreme in the areas in which it spoke distinctly.

> Mr. President, I may draw from that transaction in our history which we are now examining, this moral; that now, as then, if we will only suffer our reason to have its scope and sway, and to still and hush the passion and excitement that has been created by the occasion, the difficulty will be more than half removed, in the settlement, upon just and amicable principles, of any questions which unhappily divide us at this moment.

Finally, Clay returned to the question on the floor, and applied the lessons of the Missouri Compromise controversy (as he saw them) to the those who advocated the extension of the Missouri Compromise line.

> But, sir, I wish to contrast the plan of accommodation which is proposed by me with that which was offered by the Missouri compromise line being extended to the Pacific ocean, and to ask of gentlemen from the South, and gentlemen from the North, too, which is most proper, which most just, and to which there is the least cause of objection. Now, sir, what was done by the Missouri line? Slavery was positively interdicted North of that line. The question of the admission or exclusion of slavery South of that line was not settled. There was no provision that slavery should be introduced or established South of that line. In point of fact, it existed in all the territory South of the line of 36 deg. 30 min., embracing Arkansas and Louisiana. It was not necessary then, to my mind, to insert a clause admitting slavery at that time. But, sir, if there is a power to interdict, there is a power to admit: and I put it to gentlemen from the South are they prepared to be satisfied with the line of 36 deg.
> MR. FOOTE.—[asking the president of the Senate for recognition]
> MR.: CLAY.—That nothing short of a positive recognition of slavery south of the line of 36° 30' would satisfy him. Well, is there any body who believes that you could get twenty votes in this body, or a proportional number in the other House, to a declaration in favor

of the recognition of slavery south of the line of 36° 30'? It is impossible. All that you can get, all that you can expect to get, all that was proposed at the last session, was action on the north of the line, and non-action as regards slavery south of that line. It is interdicted on one side, without any corresponding provision for its admission on the other side of the line of 36° 30'.

Now, sir, when I came to consider the subject, and to compare the provisions of the line of 36° 30 min.—the Missouri compromise line—with the plan which I propose for the accommodation of this question, what said I to myself? Why, if I offer the line of 36 deg. 30 m., interdicting slavery north of it, and leaving the question open south of that line, I offer that which is illusory to the north; I offer that which will deceive them, if they suppose that slavery will be introduced south of that line. It is better for them, I said to myself—it is better for the whole South, that there should be non-action on both sides, than that there should be action interdicting slavery on one side, without action for the admission of slavery on the other side of the line. Is it not so?

How nonaction north of the 36° 30' latitude would please Free Soilers is unclear to me, as it must have been to free state senators in 1850. Clay was playing a shell game with both sides—find the pea (of slavery) under the shell (of the Missouri Compromise) as Clay moved around the other shells so quickly that no one would notice that the pea has vanished.

What, then, is gained by the South, if the Missouri line is extended to the Pacific, with an interdiction of slavery north of it? Why, sir, one of the very arguments which have been most often and most seriously urged by the South has been this, that we do not want you to legislate upon the subject at all; you ought not to touch it; you have no power over it. I do not concur, as is well known from what I have said upon this occasion, in this view of the subject. But that is the Southern argument. We do not want you to legislate at all on the subject of slavery; but if you adopt the Missouri line and extend it to the Pacific, and interdict slavery north of that line, you do legislate upon the subject of slavery, and you legislate without a corresponding equivalent of legis-

lation on the subject of slavery south of the line. For, if there be legislation interdicting slavery north of the line, the principle of equality
would require that there should be legislation admitting slavery south
of the line.

A nice point, well scored, against those southern senators who objected to federal intrusion in matters of slavery, but would, if the Missouri line were extended, have given to the federal government once
more the power to exclude slavery from territories north of the line.

Sir, I have said that I never could vote for it, and I repeat that I never can,
and never will vote for it; and no earthly power shall ever make me vote
to plant slavery where slavery does not exist. Still, if there be a majority—
and there ought to be such a majority for interdicting slavery north of the
line, there ought to be an equal majority—if equality and justice be done
to the South—to admit slavery south of the line. And if there be a majority ready to accomplish both of these purposes, though I cannot concur
in the action, yet I would be one of the last to create any disturbance,
I would be one of the first to acquiesce in such legislation, though it is
contrary to my own judgment and my own conscience.

Clay, having made the opposite point, now swallowed hard and accepted that his view might not be the majority view. As a dutiful member of the Senate, he would accept its decision.

I think, then, it would be better to keep the whole of these territories
untouched by any legislation by Congress on the subject of slavery, leaving it open, undecided, without any action of Congress in relation to it;
that it would be best for the South, and best for all the views which the
South has, from time to time, disclosed to me as correspondent with her
wishes. I know it may be said with regard to these ceded territories, as it
is said with regard to California, that non-legislation implies the same
thing as the exclusion of slavery. That we cannot help. That Congress is
not reproachable for. If nature has pronounced the doom of slavery upon
those territories—if she has declared, by her immutable laws, that slavery
cannot and shall not be introduced there, whom can you reproach but
nature or nature's God?

Congress you cannot; Congress abstains; Congress is passive; Congress is non-active in regard to the subject of slavery south and north of the line; or rather Congress, according to the plan which proposes to extend no line, leaves the entire theatre of these territories un-touched by legislative enactment, either to exclude or admit slavery.

Well, sir, I ask again—if you will listen to the voice of calm and dispassionate reason—I ask of any man from the South to rise and tell me if it is not better for his section of the Union that Congress should remain passive, on both sides of any ideal line, than that it should interdict slavery on one side of the line and be passive in regard to it on the other side of the line!

Having spoken for hours over the course of two days, Clay was exhausted, but he still wanted to warn against the dissolution of the Union.

Sir, I am taxing both the physical and intellectual powers which a kind Providence has bestowed upon me, too much—too much by far—though I beg to be permitted, if the Senate will have patience with me, to conclude what I have to say, for I do not desire to trespass another day upon your time and patience, as I am approaching, though I have not yet nearly arrived at, the conclusion.

MR. [WILLIE P.] MANGUM. If the Senator will permit me, I will
   move an adjournment.

Mangum was a Whig from North Carolina and recognized that Clay was on his last legs.

MR. CLAY. No, sir, no: I will conclude. I think I can get on better to-day than I shall be able to do if the subject be postponed. Sir, this Union is threatened with subversion. I want, Mr. President, to take a very rapid glance at the course of public measures in this Union presently. I want, however, before I do that, to ask the Senate to look back upon the career which this country has run since the adoption of this constitution down to the present day.

Clay wanted to end on a high note. His celebratory view of history excluded Native peoples, the enslaved, and immigrants, the role of women, and the persecution of religious minorities, including the Mormons, however. It was an example of the *herrenvolk* republic ideal.

> Was there ever a nation upon which the sun of heaven has shone that has exhibited so much of prosperity? At the Commencement of this Government our population amounted to about four millions; it has now reached upward of twenty millions. Our territory was limited chiefly and principally to the border upon the Atlantic ocean, and that which includes the southern shores of the interior lakes of our country. Our country now extends from the Northern provinces of Great Britain to the Rio Grande and the Gulf of Mexico on one side, and from the Atlantic ocean to the Pacific on the other side—the largest extent of territory under any Government that exists on the face of the earth, with only two solitary exceptions. Our tonnage, from being nothing, has risen in magnitude and amount so as to rival that of the nation who has been proudly characterized as "the mistress of the ocean."
>
> We have gone through many wars—wars too with the very nation from whom we broke off in 1776, as weak and feeble colonies, and asserted our independence as a member of the family of nations. And, sir, we came out of that struggle, unequal as it was—armed as she was at all points, in consequence of just having come out of her long struggle with other European nations, and unarmed as we were at all points, in consequence of the habits and nature of our country and its institutions—we came, I say, out of that war without any loss of honor whatever—we emerged from it gloriously. In every Indian war—and we have been engaged in many of them—our armies have triumphed; and without speaking at all as to the causes of the recent war with Mexico, whether it was right or wrong, and abstaining from any expression of opinion as to the justice or propriety of the war, when once commenced all must admit that, with respect to the gallantry of our armies, the glory of our triumphs, there is no page or pages of history which record more brilliant successes.

Clay, recall, had opposed the Mexican-American War. But he had to say something praiseworthy about President Taylor, a Whig, and one of the two generals who had successfully waged that war. (The other was Winfield Scott, also a Whig.)

With respect to one commander of an important portion of our army I need say nothing here; no praise is necessary in behalf of one who has been elevated by the voice of his country to the highest station she could place him in, mainly on account of his glorious military career. And of another, less fortunate in many respects than some other military commanders, I must take the opportunity of saying, that for skill, for science, for strategy, for ability and daring fighting, for chivalry of individuals and of masses, that portion of the American army which was conducted by the gallant Scott, as the chief commander, stands unrivalled either by the deeds of Cortez himself, or by those of any other commander in ancient or modern times.

But there was a dark cloud on the horizon.

Sir, our prosperity is unbounded—nay, Mr. President, I sometimes fear that it is in the wantonness of that prosperity that many of the threatening ills of the moment have arisen. Wild and erratic schemes have sprung up throughout the whole country, some of which have even found their way into legislative halls; and there is a restlessness existing among us which I fear will require the chastisement of Heaven to bring us back to a sense of the immeasurable benefits and blessings which have been bestowed upon us by Providence.

The wild schemes included early versions of annexing additional lands for slavery in the Caribbean and Central America,[17]

At this moment—with the exception of here and there a particular department in the manufacturing business of the country—all is prosperity and peace, and the nation is rich and powerful. Our country has grown to a magnitude, to a power and greatness, such as to command the respect, if it does not awe the apprehensions, of the powers of the earth, with whom we come in contact. Sir, do I depict with colors too lively the prosperity which has resulted to us from the operations of this

---

17 Walter Johnson, *River of Dark Dreams: Slavery and Empire in the Cotton Kingdom* (Cambridge, MA: Harvard University Press, 2013), 303–422 (Cuba); Matthew Karp, *This Vast Southern Empire: Slaveholders at the Helm of American Foreign Policy* (Cambridge, MA: Harvard University Press, 2016), 70–83 (Brazil).

Union? Have I exaggerated in any particular her power, her prosperity, or her greatness?

Clay wanted to defend the Union, but he had to accept a sectional frame of analysis. That is, he had to defend the contributions of the North to the country as a whole. Then he would turn to the contributions of the South. By dividing his account in this way, he conceded that sectionalism had become the dominant form of political discourse. It was a savage irony, and one that he could not escape.

> And now, sir, let me go a little into detail with respect to sway in the councils of the nation, whether from the North or the South, during the sixty years of unparalleled prosperity that we have enjoyed. During the first twelve years of the administration of the Government Northern counsels rather prevailed; and out of them sprang the Bank of the United States, the assumption of the State debts, bounties to the fisheries, protection to our domestic manufactures—I allude to the act of 1789—neutrality in the wars of Europe, Jay's treaty, the alien and sedition laws, and war with France. I do not say, sir, that these, the leading and prominent measures which were adopted during the administrations of Washington and the elder Adams, were carried exclusively by Northern counsels—they could not have been—but mainly by the ascendancy which Northern counsels had obtained in the affairs of the nation.

This was an odd account of a period when Virginians (George Washington, Thomas Jefferson, James Madison, and James Monroe) dominated the executive branch and the emergence of the Jeffersonian Republican Party came to control Congress. Perhaps Clay meant the first decade of the federal government, when the Federalist Party was in the majority.[18]

> So, sir, of the later period—for the last fifty years. I do not mean to say that Southern counsels alone have carried the measures which I am about to enumerate. I know they could not exclusively have carried them, but

---

18 Stanley M. Elkins and Eric McKitrick, *The Age of Federalism: The Early American Republic, 1788–1800* (New York: Oxford University Press, 1995), 691–693.

I say that they have been carried by their preponderating influence, with the co-operation, it is true—the large co-operation in some instances—of the Northern section of the Union. And what are those measures? During that fifty years, or nearly that period, in which Southern counsels have preponderated, the embargo and other commercial restrictions of non-intercourse and non-importation were imposed; war with Great Britain, the Bank of the United States overthrown, protection enlarged and extended to domestic manufactures—I allude to the passage of the act of 1815 or 1816—the Bank of the United States re-established, the same bank put down, re-established by Southern counsels and put down by Southern counsels, Louisiana acquired, Florida bought, Texas annexed, war with Mexico, California and other territories acquired from Mexico by conquest and purchase, protection superseded, and free trade established, Indians removed west of the Mississippi, and fifteen new States admitted into the Union, all very possible, sir, that in this enumeration I may have omitted some of the important measures which have been adopted during this later period of time—the last fifty years—but these I believe to be the most prominent ones.

Now, sir, I do not deduce from the enumeration of the measures adapted by the one side or the other any just cause of reproach either upon one side or the other; though one side or the other has predominated in the two periods to which I have referred. These measures were, to say the least, the joint work of both parties, and neither of them have any just cause to reproach the other.

Clay's point was that both North and South supported the recharter of the bank. I think the hidden agenda was a little different. He was also defending himself for his role in the establishment of the Second Bank of the United States, at the time strongly opposed by states' rights legalists and local bank entrepreneurs, and later by President Andrew Jackson. The so-called bank war of Jackson's second administration was one of the reasons for the emergence of the Whig Party.

But sir, I must say, in all kindness and sincerity, that least of all ought the South to reproach the North, when we look at the long list of measures which, under her sway in the counsels of the nation, have been adopted; when we reflect on even opposite doctrines have been from time to time advanced by her; that the establishment of the Bank of the United States, which was done under the administration of Mr. Madison, met with the co-operation of the South—I do not say the whole South—I do not, when I speak of the South or the North, speak of the entire South or the entire North; I speak of the prominent and larger proportion of Southern and Northern men. It was during Mr. Madison's administration that the Bank of the United States was established.

My friend, whose sickness—which I very much deplore—prevents us from having his attendance upon this occasion (Mr. Calhoun,) was the chairman of the committee, and carried the measure through Congress. I voted for it with all my heart. Although I had been instrumental with other Southern votes in putting down the [first] Bank of the United States, I changed my opinion and co-operated in the establishment of the Bank of 1816.

The same bank was again put down by Southern counsels, with Gen. Jackson at their head, at a later period. Again, with respect to the policy of protection. The South in 1815—I mean the prominent Southern men, the aforementioned Lowndes, Mr. Calhoun, and others—united in extending a certain measure of protection to domestic manufactures as well as the North. We find a few years afterward the South interposing most serious objections to this policy, and one member of the South, threatening on that occasion, a dissolution of the Union or separation.

A not so veiled reference to Calhoun's doctrine of nullification during the Tariff of 1828–1833 wars. Clay was violating more than one convention of senatorial courtesy. He was attacking an absent member, attacking a dying member, and singling out another member. He knew that Calhoun was a leader of the southern Democratic cohort in the Senate.[19]

Now, sir, let us take another view of the question—and I would remark that all these views are brought forward not in a spirit of reproach, but of conciliation—not to provoke, or exasperate, but to quiet, to produce harmony and repose, if possible.

---

19 David Potter, *The Impending Crisis: America Before the Civil War, 1848–1861* (New York: Harper & Row, 1976), 83–85. But not the southern Whigs.

Not an apology, and no one mistook it for one.

> What have been the territorial acquisitions made by this country, and
> to what interests have they conduced? Florida, where slavery exists, has
> been introduced; Louisiana, or all the most valuable part of that State—
> for although there is a large extent of territory north of the line 36 deg.
> 30 min. in point of intrinsic value and importance, I would not give
> the single State of Louisiana—the whole of it—all Louisiana [territory],
> I say, with the exception of that which lies north of 36 deg. 30 min.
> including Oregon, to which we obtained title mainly on the ground
> of its being a part of the acquisition of Louisiana; all Texas; all the ter-
> ritories which have been acquired by the Government of the United
> States during its sixty years operation have been slave territories, the
> theatre of slavery, with the exception that I have mentioned of that ly-
> ing north of the line 36 30. And here, in the case of a war made essen-
> tially by the South—growing out of the annexation of Texas, which was
> a measure proposed by the South in the councils of the country, and
> which led to the war with Mexico—I do not say all of the South, but the
> major portion of the South pressed the annexation of Texas upon the
> country—that measure, as I have said, led to the war with Mexico, and
> the war with Mexico led to the acquisition of those territories which
> now constitute the bone of contention between the different members
> of the Confederacy.

By the "Confederacy" here Clay referred to the Union of the states, but
the use of the term was, to modern ears, more than a little portentous.

> And now, sir, for the first time after the three great acquisitions of Texas,
> Florida, and Louisiana have been made and have redounded to the ben-
> efit of the South now, for the first time, when three territories are at-
> tempted to be introduced without the institution of slavery, I put it to
> the hearts of my countrymen of the South, if it is right to press matters
> to the disastrous consequences which have been indicated no longer ago
> than this very morning, on the occasion of the presentation of certain
> resolutions—even extending to a dissolution of the Union.

Clay had been the first to speak that morning.

Mr. President, I cannot believe it.

MR. UNDERWOOD. Will the Senator give way for an adjournment?

MR. CLAY. Oh, no; if I do not weary the patience of the Senate, I prefer to go on. I think I can begin to see land. I shall soon come to the conclusion of what I have to say. Such is the Union, and such are the glorious fruits which are now threatened with subversion and destruction.

This final portion of Clay's address was directed not to his resolutions but, speaking on the fly (off message as it were), to the threat to the Union.

Well, sir, the first question which naturally arises, is, supposing the Union to be dissolved for any of the causes or grievances which are complained of, how far will dissolution furnish a remedy for those grievances? If the Union is to be dissolved for any existing cause, it will be because slavery is interdicted or not allowed to be introduced into the ceded territories; or because slavery is threatened to be abolished in the District of Columbia; or because fugitive slaves are not restored, as in my opinion they ought to be, to their masters. These, I believe, would be the causes, if there be any causes which can lead to the dreadful event to which I have referred.

Let us suppose the Union dissolved; what remedy does it, in a severed state, furnish for the grievances complained of in its united condition? Will you be able at the South to push slavery into the ceded territory? How are you to do it, supposing the North, or all the States north of the Potomac, in possession of the navy and army of the United States? Can you expect, I say, under these circumstances, that if there is a dissolution of the Union can carry slavery into California and New Mexico? Sir, you cannot dream of such an occurrence. If it were abolished in the District of Columbia and the Union were dissolved, would the dissolution of the Union restore slavery in the District of Columbia? Is your chance for the recovery of your fugitive slaves safer in a state of dissolution or of severance of the Union than when in the Union itself?

Why, sir, what is the state of the fact? In the Union you lose some slaves and recover others; but here let me revert to a fact which I ought to have noticed before, because it is highly creditable to the courts and juries of the free States. In every instance, as far as my information extends, in which an appeal has been made to the courts of justice to recover penalties from those who have assisted in decoying slaves from their masters—in every instance, as far as I have heard, the court has asserted the rights of the owner, and the jury has promptly returned an adequate verdict on his behalf. Well, sir, there is then some remedy while you are a part of the Union for the recovery of your slaves, and some indemnification for their loss.

Now the list of hypothetical consequences followed, all hypothetical of course, but not so far from what would happen in a little over a decade. Lawyers argued in hypotheticals all the time. He spoke as if addressing a jury rather than a bench—speaking to individual senators rather than a gathering of lawmakers. For the next fifteen minutes (the time it takes to read the following passages aloud) Clay appeared to ramble, repeating himself. As his language grew more fraught, one has to conclude that his concern was not contrived. This is as close to real life as one gets in the *Globe*, no buffers no spin, no script, rather Clay wearing his heart on his sleeve. Listening, we are there. I do not interrupt it, as Clay's meaning is clear.

What would you have, if the Union was severed? Why, then the several parts would be independent of each other—foreign countries—and slaves escaping from one to the other would be like slaves escaping from the United States to Canada. There would be no right of extradition, no right to demand your slaves; no right to appeal to the courts of justice to indemnify you for the loss of your slaves. Where one slave escapes now by running away from his master, hundreds and thousands would escape if the Union were dissevered—I care not how or where you run the line, or whether independent sovereignties be established. Well, sir, finally, will you, in case of a dissolution of the Union, be safer with your slaves within the separated portions of the States than you are now? Mr. President, that they will escape much more frequently from the border States no one will deny.

And, sir, I must take occasion here to say that, in my opinion, there is no right on the part of any one or more of the States to secede from the Union. War and dissolution of the Union are identical and inevitable, in my opinion. There can be a dissolution of the Union only by consent or by war. Consent no one can anticipate, from any existing state of things, is likely to be given, and war is the only alternative by which a dissolution could be accomplished.

If consent were given—if it were possible that we were to be separated by one great line—in less than sixty days after such consent was given war would break out between the slaveholding and non-slaveholding portions of this Union—between the two independent parts into which it would be erected in virtue of the act of separation.

In less than sixty days, I believe, our slaves from Kentucky, flocking over in numbers to the other side of the river, would be pursued by their owners. Our hot and ardent spirits would be restrained by no sense of the right which appertains to the independence of the other side of the river, should that be the line of separation. They would pursue their slaves into the adjacent free States; they would be repelled, and the consequence would be that, in lets than sixty days, war would be blazing in every part of this now happy and peaceful land.

And, sir, how are you going to separate the States of this Confederacy? In my humble opinion, Mr. President, we should begin with at least three separate Confederacies. There would be a Confederacy of the North, a Confederacy of the Southern Atlantic slaveholding States, and a Confederacy of the valley of the Mississippi. My life upon it, that the vast population which has already concentrated and will concentrate on the head-waters and the tributaries of the Mississippi will never give their consent that the mouth of that river shall be held subject to the power of any foreign State or community whatever.

There were many in Kentucky who wanted to join the Confederacy, but the Unionists prevailed.

Such, I believe, would be the consequences of a dissolution of the Union, immediately ensuing, but other Confederacies would spring up from time to time, as dissatisfaction and discontent were disseminated throughout the country—the Confederacy of the lakes, perhaps the Confederacy of New England, or of the Middle States. Ah, sir, the veil which covers these sad and disastrous events that lie beyond it, is too thick to be penetrated or lifted by any mortal eye or hand.

Mr. President, I am directly opposed to any purpose of secession or separation. I am for staying within the Union, and defying any portion of this confederacy to expel me or drive me out of the Union. I am for staying within the Union and fighting for my rights, if necessary, with the sword, within the bounds and under the safeguard of the Union. I am for vindicating those rights, not by being driven out of the Union harshly and unceremoniously by any portion of this confederacy. Here I am within it, and here I mean to stand and die, as far as my individual wishes or purposes can go—within it to protect my property and defend myself, defying all the power on earth to expel me or drive me from the situation in which I am placed.

And would there not be more safety in fighting within the Union than out of it? Suppose your rights to be violated, suppose wrong to be done you, aggressions to be perpetrated upon you, can you not better vindicate them—if you have occasion to resort to the last necessity, the sword, for a restoration of those rights—within, and with the sympathies of a large portion of the population of the Union, than by being without the Union, when a large portion of the population have sympathies adverse to your own? You can vindicate your rights within the Union better than if expelled from the Union, and driven from it without ceremony and without authority.

In sum, the Union was indissoluble, a permanent bond, to which states had acceded. Clay anticipated Lincoln's First Inaugural. The entire preceding demonstrated how much Clay genuinely loved the Union, the actual Union, the idea of Union, and the ideal of Union. Even if southern senators did not buy into his resolves, they must have credited his sincerity.

Sir, I have said that I thought there was no right on the part of one or more States to secede from the Union. I think so. The Constitution of the United States was made not merely for the generation that then existed, but for posterity—unlimited, undefined, endless, perpetual posterity. And every State that then came into the Union, and every State that has since come into the Union, came into it binding itself, by indissoluble bands, to remain within the Union itself, and to remain within it by its posterity forever.

Like another of the sacred connexions, in private life, it is a marriage which no human authority can dissolve or divorce the parties from. And if I may be allowed to refer to some examples in private life, let me say to the North and to the South, what husband and wife say to each other We have mutual faults; neither of us is perfect; nothing in the form of humanity is perfect; let us, then, be kind to each other—forbearing, forgiving each other's faults—and above all, let us live in happiness and peace together.

The analogy of marriage was surprising, for marriage was a subject of private domestic law, left to the states, rather than public law. But marriage law was changing, as divorce was becoming legal without legislative consent in many states. In the South, a veritable "family crisis" precipitated divorce law reform. Kentucky changed its law in 1809. Either member of the couple could go to court and seek divorce for a number of reasons.[20]

Mr. President, I have said, what I solemnly believe, that dissolution of the Union and war are identical and inevitable; that they are convertible terms; and such a war as it would be, following a dissolution of the Union! Sir, we may search the pages of history, and none so ferocious, so bloody, so implacable, so exterminating—not even the wars of Greece, including those of the Commoners of England and the revolutions of France—none, none of them all would rage with such violence, or be characterized with such bloodshed and enormities as would the war which must succeed, if that event ever happens, the dissolution of the Union.

And what would be its termination? Standing armies, and navies, to an extent stretching the revenues of each portion of the dissevered members, would take place. An exterminating war would follow—not, sir, a war of two or three years duration, but a war of interminable duration—and exterminating wars would ensue, until, after the struggles and exhaustion of both parties, some Philip or Alexander, some Caesar or Napoleon, would arise and cut the Gordian knot, and solve the problem

---

20 Loren Schweninger, *Families in Crisis in the Old South: Divorce, Slavery, and the Law* (Chapel Hill: University of North Carolina Press, 2012), 6–7.

of the capacity of man for self-government, and crush the liberties of both the severed portions of this common empire.

Again, something like that happened in both the North and the South during the Civil War. It brought a draft to both sides; it enlisted hundreds of thousands of men; it cost over six billion dollars to the respective sides. The war did seem interminable. It did result in catastrophic destruction of property and loss of life. Freedom of the press, the sacredness of private property, and other rights were severely curtailed. Clay's vision may have seemed fantastical, but it was not. His mixture of shrewd concessions and his melodramatic warnings fit the times.[21]

Can you doubt it? Look at all history—consult her pages, ancient or modern—look at human nature; look at the contest in which you would be engaged in the supposition of war following upon the dissolution of the Union, such as I have suggested; and I ask you if it is possible for you to doubt that the final disposition of the whole would be some despot treading down the liberties of the people—the final result would be the extinction of this last and glorious light which is leading all mankind, who are gazing upon it, in the hope and anxious expectation that the liberty which prevails here will sooner or later be diffused throughout the whole of the civilized world. Sir, can you lightly contemplate these consequences? Can you yield yourself to the tyranny of passion, amid dangers which I have depicted in colors far too tame of what the result would be if that direful event to which I have referred should ever occur?

Sir, implore gentlemen, I adjure them, whether from the South or the North, by all that they hold dear in this world—by all their love of liberty—by all their veneration for their ancestors—by all their regard for posterity—by all their gratitude to Him who has bestowed on them such unnumbered and countless blessings—by all the duties which they owe to mankind—and by all the duties which they owe to themselves, to pause, solemnly to pause at the edge of the precipice, before the fearful and dangerous leap is taken into the yawning abyss below, from which none who ever take it shall return in safety. Finally, Mr. President, and in conclusion,

---

21 Charles Royster, *The Destructive War: William Tecumseh Sherman, Stonewall Jackson, and the Americans* (New York: Random House, 1993), 110 (Sherman's view), 242 (Lincoln's view).

I implore, as the best blessing which Heaven can bestow upon me, upon earth, that if the direful event of the dissolution of this Union is to happen, I shall not survive to behold the sad and heart-rending spectacle.

The response to Clay's appeal was not as he had hoped. Although his friends in and out of Congress lauded the effort, his critics were merciless. Immediately after he spoke, a squad of southern senators attacked him along with his proposals. Chief among them was Mississippi's planter soldier Jefferson Davis. Davis was a graduate of the US Military Academy but not a career soldier (unlike Taylor), then a volunteer officer and something of a hero in the Mexican-American War. He had been on Clay's case since January 29, when he accused Clay of undermining

principles . . . deemed sacred and necessary to secure the safety of the Union. Now an honorable and distinguished Senator, to whom the country has been induced to look for something that would heal the existing dissensions, instead of raising new barriers against encroachment, dashes down those heretofore erected and augments the existing danger.

Nothing in Clay's defense of his proposals alleviated Davis's fears. Now he led a legion of proslavery senators to besiege Clay's position. There was no apology for slavery—unlike during the generation of the framers. Slavery was not a necessary evil, as men like Thomas Jefferson, James Madison, and St. George Tucker (all of whom owned the enslaved) thought, but a positive good according to Davis, who owned over a hundred enslaved men and women on his cotton plantation. He compared the life of the enslaved favorably to the life of the northern industrial worker. Slavery was good for the enslaved, good for the master, and good for the country, and the practice should be extended from the Mississippi River to the Pacific Ocean.[22]

---

22 Allan Nevins, *Ordeal of the Union*, vol. 1: *Fruits of Manifest Destiny, 1847–1852* (New York: Scribner's, 1947), 272; William C. Davis, *Jefferson Davis: The Man and His Hour* (New York: HarperCollins, 1991), 194; Fergus Bordewich, *America's Great Debate: Henry Clay, Stephen A. Douglas, and the Compromise that Preserved the Union* (New York: Simon & Schuster, 2012), 148–149; John C. Waugh, *On the Brink of Civil War: The Compromise of 1850 and How It Changed the Course of American History* (Wilmington, DE: Scholarly Resources, 2003), 78–79; Davis, January 29, 1850, in *Papers of Jefferson Davis*, ed. Lydia L. Crist (Houston: Rice University Press, 1983), 4:64.

Senator Henry Foote of Mississippi rushed to Clay's aid by offering to submit the proposals to a committee and bundle them into an omnibus bill. Clay was named to the committee, of course, but was dismayed that he was no longer in command of his plan. In particular, like Fortinbras, the Norwegian king who lurks at the edges of Hamlet's Denmark, John C. Calhoun's presence, or rather his foreboding absence, threw shade over the debate. And then Calhoun himself arrived, speech in hand.

Figure 3.1. John C. Calhoun, in the US Capitol, March 1849. Credit: Library of Congress, Prints & Photographs Division.

3

John C. Calhoun's Speech on the Compromise of 1850, March 4, 1850

O N March 4, 1850, John C. Calhoun was sixty-eight and shriv-eled by tuberculosis.[1] He had spent the majority of his adult life in public service. He was, at various times, a member of the House of Representatives, the secretary of war, the vice president, and a senator. Trained in law in Connecticut, he did not practice law after marrying well and inheriting a plantation and its enslaved popula-tion and enjoying the prestige of the master class of South Carolina. Although he was initially a nationalist, by the middle of the 1820s his attention turned to the interests of South Carolina and slavery. The state legislature asked him to craft, secretly, an exposition and pro-test against the Tariff of 1828 (although at the time he was presiding over the Senate, which had passed the measure). His essay argued for a concurrent majority doctrine, a strong version of states' rights in which any state that objected to an act of Congress could legally defy it. This incorporated the doctrine of nullification, although it was nowhere mentioned in the Constitution. Thus a strict constructionist relied on a loose construction of the Constitution: "If it be conceded, as it must be by every one who is the least conversant with our insti-tutions, that the sovereign powers delegated are divided between the General and State Governments, and that the latter hold their portion by the same tenure as the former, it would seem impossible to deny to the States the right of deciding on the infractions of their powers, and the proper remedy to be applied for their correction." By 1850, he had become the iron fist of the proslavery corps in the Senate, determined not to back down an inch to the hated abolitionists and their allies. It was not party nor personal ambition (any longer) that

---

1 John C. Calhoun, Speech, March 4, 1850, 31st Cong., 1st sess., *Congressional Globe*, 451–456, delivered on the Senate floor by Virginia senator James Mason. Text from LC ms. 166.267, John C. Calhoun Papers.

motived him, but the love of a way of life that depended on a master and a servile class.[2]

During 1849 Calhoun had labored, unsuccessfully, to create a unified southern bloc in the Senate. Signatories to his proposed "address" to the southern people fell far short of a majority, however. He thus knew the stakes and prepared his speech carefully, far more so than had Clay. Unlike his great rival, Calhoun did not read it. Instead, borne into the chamber on a chaise, he listened as James Mason of Virginia read the speech, Calhoun's deep-set eyes traveled about the chamber, almost daring anyone to object or interrupt. For Calhoun's manner had always been professorial, dry, logical, and moralistic.

The ideas in the speech were not new; indeed, he had made many of the same arguments on previous occasions. The tension that had been mounting between the North and the South had now brought the Union close to the breaking point, and Calhoun presented himself before crowded galleries to assert that the equilibrium that had long existed between the two sections had been destroyed. Although the elements of Clay's compromise calling for the abolition of slavery in the District of Columbia and the admission of California as a free state were familiar to Calhoun, he did not take this opportunity to respond to them directly. They were not negotiable to Calhoun and his followers. In his view, the sovereignty of the slave states was at stake, and the slavery question was moved squarely to the forefront of the debate.[3]

According to the Library of Congress accession notes, "Calhoun's speech, covering forty-two pages in manuscript, had been prepared with great care, in spite of his feeble condition. He had, however, been unable to write it out himself and dictated it over the course of two days to his secretary, Joseph Alfred Scoville (1815–1864), who would later be his biographer. Calhoun then revised the text, making corrections and emendations in his own hand that are apparent in the manuscript." It is that manuscript that is reproduced here.[4]

---

2 John Niven, *John C. Calhoun and the Price of Union* (Baton Rouge: Louisiana State University Press, 1988), 154–163; nullification: Avalon Project, Yale Law School, http://avalon.law.yale.edu.

3 David Potter, *The Impending Crisis: America Before the Civil War, 1848–1861* (New York: Harper & Row, 1976), 85–87; Allan Nevins, *Ordeal of the Union*, vol. 1: *Fruits of Manifest Destiny, 1847–1852* (New York: Scribner's, 1947), 279, Library of Congress, from LC ms. 166.267, John C. Calhoun Papers.

4 Robert C. Byrd, *The Senate, 1789–1989* (Washington, DC: Government Publishing Office, 1989), 190, quoting the *New York Herald*.

Calhoun would return to the Senate on March 5, then again on March 7, to listen to the speech given by Daniel Webster in favor of Clay's resolutions, and he appeared there for the final time on March 13. On March 9, he wrote to Edmund Hubbard, "The view [of my speech] I hope will meet with your approval. It has met with the hearty approbation of all the southern representation here, except open traitors to the cause of the South [Clay, of course, as well as Foote, Mangum, and Underwood]. . . . Our true course is to place before the country in their full strength our just complaints, and it leave it to our aggressors to offer terms of settlement." Presumably Clay was one of the traitors. Calhoun died on March 31, 1850.[5]

The speech came as a rebuttal to Clay but did not address his proposals directly. It was instead a summation of Calhoun's own views, and his attempt to save the Union by conceding to one section of it—the slave South—all that it asked.[6]

> I have, senators, believed from the first that the agitation of the subject of slavery would, if not prevented by some timely and effective measure, end in disunion. Entertaining this opinion, I have, on all proper occasions, endeavored to call the attention of both the two great parties which divided the country to adopt some measure to prevent so great a disaster, but without success. The agitation has been permitted to proceed with almost no attempt to resist it, until it has reached a point when it can no longer be disguised or denied that the Union is in danger. You have thus had forced upon you the greatest and gravest question that can ever come under your consideration: How can the Union be preserved?

Calhoun thus began where Clay had ended—with secession. Calhoun averred that he had been consistent in his love for the Union over the course of his career. One might find that hard to believe considering his conversion to states' rights ideology in 1828. In his thinking, however, his view of the Constitution, featuring nullification of federal law as a remedy available to every state, did not conflict with love of the

---

5 See, e.g., John C. Calhoun to J. R. Mathewes, March 6, 1850, in *Papers of John C. Calhoun*, ed. Clyde N. Wilson (Columbia: University of South Carolina Press, 2003), 27:219; Calhoun to Edmund Hubbard, March 9, 1850, *Papers of Calhoun*, 27:226; Robert V. Remini, *Daniel Webster: The Man and His Time* (New York: Norton, 1997), 667.
6 Potter, *Impending Crisis*, 100–101.

Union. Indeed, his purpose in speaking this day was to preserve the Union, as he had on previous occasions. The danger to the Union came from northern extremists. Was this disingenuous? The reverence for the Union in his generation was almost spiritual. Was he blind to the threat that sectionalism posed to the Union? Not really—for him slavery was simply part of the American way of life, and those who opposed slavery must accept this. The rest of the speech was thus an elaboration of this theme. Actually, nullification had a distinguished pedigree in the South, derived from the writings of two Virginia luminaries, Thomas Jefferson and James Madison, in opposition to the Alien and Sedition Acts of 1798. Their so-called Kentucky and Virginia Resolves, respectively, had argued that states could interpose themselves between acts of Congress and citizens of the states, a doctrine very much like nullification.[7]

> To give a satisfactory answer to this mighty question, it is indispensable to have an accurate and thorough knowledge of the nature and the character of the cause by which the Union is endangered. Without such knowledge it is impossible to pronounce with any certainty, by what measure it can be saved; just as it would be impossible for a physician to pronounce in the case of some dangerous disease, with any certainty, by what remedy the patient could be saved, without similar knowledge of the nature and character of the cause which produce it. The first question, then, presented for consideration in the investigation I propose to make in order to obtain such knowledge is: What is it that has endangered the Union?

---

7 Paul C. Nagel, *One Nation Indivisible: The Union in American Thought, 1776–1861* (New York: Oxford University Press, 1964), 101; Terri Diane Halperin, *The Alien and Sedition Acts of 1798* (Baltimore: Johns Hopkins University Press, 2016), 100–106; Peter Charles Hoffer, *The Free Press Crisis of 1800: Thomas Cooper's Trial for Seditious Libel* (Lawrence: University Press of Kansas, 2011), 56, 57–58, 62, 71; Niven, *Calhoun*, 323–325. But Madison did not agree with nullification at all—"The true question therefore is whether there be a Constitutional right in a single state to nullify a law of the U.S. We have seen the absurdity of such a claim in its simple naked and suicidal form. . . . They can not say that the right meant was a Constl. right to resist the Constitutional authority: for that is a contradiction in terms, as much as a legal right to resist a law. . . . The same zealots, must again say, as they do, with a like boldness & incongruity, that the Govt. of the U.S. wch. has been so deemed & so called from its birth to the present time; which is organized in the regular forms of Representative Govts, and like them operates directly on the individuals represented; and whose laws are declared to be the supreme law of the land, with a physical force in the Govt. for executing them, is yet no Govt, but a mere agency, a power of Attorney, revocable at the will of any of the parties granting it." Madison, "On Nullification" (1834), Madison Papers, University of Virginia.

Clay's answer was party spirit, a reckless partisanship. Calhoun knew better. In this sense his address was more honest than Clay's. Or at least Calhoun, on this point, was directly answering Clay. The entire purpose of national parties was to mute sectional discord. But now the parties were divided by section, and the sections divided by free and enslaved. The metaphor of a dangerous disease was a barely veiled reference to his own condition. In a way, he had linked his own bodily infirmity to the sickness afflicting the Union.

> To this question there can be but one answer—that the immediate cause is the almost universal discontent which pervades all the States composing the Southern section of the Union. This widely extended discontent is not of recent origin. It commenced with the agitation of the slavery question and has been increasing ever since. The next question, going one step further back, is: What has caused this widely diffused and almost universal discontent?

Discontent and unease were white discontent and unease, shared by masters and non-slaveholders. The enslaved, being chattel property, were not counted in Calhoun's calculations, here and elsewhere.[8]

> It is a great mistake to suppose, as is by some, that it originated with demagogues who excited the discontent with the intention of aiding their personal advancement, or with the disappointed ambition of certain politicians who resorted to it as the means of retrieving their fortunes. On the contrary, all the great political influences of the section were arrayed against excitement, and exerted to the utmost to keep the people quiet. The great mass of the people of the South were divided, as in the other section, into Whigs and Democrats. The leaders and the presses of both parties in the South were very solicitous to prevent excitement and to preserve quiet; because it was seen that the effects of the former would necessarily tend to weaken, if not destroy, the political ties which united them with their respective parties in the other section.[9]

---

8 Mark V. Tushnet, *Slave Law in the American South* (Lawrence: University Press of Kansas, 2003), 12–13.

9 For that, see James G. Randall, "The Blundering Generation," *Mississippi Valley Historical Review* 27 (1940): 12.

Those who know the strength of party ties will readily appreciate the immense force which this cause exerted against agitation and in favor of preserving quiet. But, great as it was, it was not sufficient to prevent the widespread discontent which now pervades the section.

No; some cause far deeper and more powerful than the one supposed must exist, to account for discontent so wide and deep. The question then recurs: What is the cause of this discontent? It will be found in the belief of the people of the Southern States, as prevalent as the discontent itself, that they can not remain, as things now are, consistently with honor and safety, in the Union. The next question to be considered is: What has caused this belief?

This was a remarkable and dramatic series of admissions—concluding that it was the South's concern that drove the nation toward crisis. The admissions were then the basis for the rest of the argument. Of course, by this time, such a conclusion was hardly news—it was the (almost) uniform South that opposed the admission of California as a free state. (The exceptions included Clay from Kentucky, a slave state, Taylor from Louisiana, Thomas Hart Benton from Missouri, and others.) But notice how Calhoun is using a dramatic device to withhold the answer to his own question. He is "foreshadowing" to create suspense.

One of the causes is, undoubtedly, to be traced to the long-continued agitation of the slave question on the part of the North, and the many aggressions which they have made on the rights of the South during the time. I will not enumerate them at present, as it will be done hereafter in its proper place.

Was Calhoun exaggerating? On the one hand, northern abolitionists were few. Free Soil advocates were far more numerous, although they did not advocate the overthrow of the slave system where it already existed. But fear can be out of proportion to real danger. On the other hand, the key word, often repeated in the southern press, was aggression. Aggression was a response to fears. What were these? One usually associates aggression with violent acts—assault and battery in legal terms. But assault can also be with words. This is what the abolitionists were doing, at least since the 1830s. With pamphlets, petitions to Congress, speeches to open meetings, and conferences, abolitionists were accusing the slave owners of gross immorality. It was a war of words. The more active escalation would ironically come after the passage of the Fugitive Slave Law of 1850, but there had already been cases of forcible assistance rendered to runaway slaves. How words and symbolic deeds, all of which took place elsewhere, should be called aggression against the South requires an understanding of a culture of honor. Honor was a characteristic of gentility, and only gentlemen possessed it. It was a fear of being shamed or committing a shameful act, although accusations of shaming might lead to violence.[10]

> There is another [cause] lying back of it—with which this is intimately connected—that may be regarded as the great and primary cause. This is to be found in the fact that the equilibrium between the two sections in the government as it stood when the Constitution was ratified and the government put in action has been destroyed. At that time there was nearly a perfect equilibrium between the two, which afforded ample means to each to protect itself against the aggression of the other; but, as it now stands, one section has the exclusive power of controlling the government, which leaves the other without any adequate means of protecting itself against its encroachment and oppression.
>
> The result of the whole is to give the Northern section a predominance in every department of the government, and thereby concentrate in it the two elements which constitute the federal government: a majority of States, and a majority of their population, estimated in federal numbers. Whatever section concentrates the two in itself possesses the control of the entire government.

If one sets aside the fact, which Calhoun surely knew, that the southern interest had dominated the federal government for many years, here was the rub: slavery was protected from federal interference not just by the Constitution—for the Constitution did not mention slavery—but by the three branches of the federal government when controlled by southern interests, if not by southerners. But by March 1850, the presidency

---

10 In general, see Bertram Wyatt-Brown, *Southern Honor: Ethics and Behavior in the Old South* (New York: Oxford University Press, 1982), 350. On words in Congress, see Hoffer, *Gag Rule*, 28–44.

was in the hands of a southern Whig who, though a slave owner himself, was a not a fan of expanding the reign of slavery, and the House of Representatives increasingly reflected Free Soil views as the free population of the country was growing more rapidly in the North than in the South. Only the Senate and the federal courts remained relatively safe havens for slave interests. The federal courts had acted repeatedly to enforce the Fugitive Slave Act of 1793, but state courts and state legislatures in the North had not always cooperated. That left the Senate—so long as it was balanced between free and slave states. The admission of California as a free state would upset that balance. This was a nakedly sectional view of national government, that is, that the nation was forever divided into two antagonistic parts, held together by the Senate.[11]

> But we are just at the close of the sixth decade and the commencement of the seventh. The census is to be taken this year, which must add greatly to the decided preponderance of the North in the House of Representatives and in the Electoral College. The prospect is, also, that a great increase will be added to its present preponderance in the Senate, during the period of the decade, by the addition of new States. Two Territories, Oregon and Minnesota, are already in progress, and strenuous efforts are making to bring in three additional States from the Territory recently conquered from Mexico; which, if successful, will add three other States in a short time to the Northern section, making five States, and increasing the present number of its States from fifteen to twenty, and of its senators from thirty to forty.

The assumption that Minnesota, settled by immigrants from Scandinavia and migrants from the Upper Midwest, and Oregon, settled by families traveling the Overland Trail from the Midwest, would become free states was a sound one. The states coming from the Mexican Cession—New Mexico, Colorado, and Arizona—were still up for grabs. (Although New Mexico and Arizona did not become states until 1912,

---

11 The importance of sectionalism, replacing party divisions, was well understood at the time. A brilliant exposition of it is Frederick Jackson Turner, "Geographic Sectionalism in American History," *Annals of the American Association of Geographers* 16 (1926): 85–93. "As soon as we cease to be dominated by the political map, divided into rectangular states, and by the form of the constitution in contrast with actualities, groups of states and geographic provinces, rather than individual states press upon the historian's attention."

Calhoun could not have known this.) Clay offered that the environment of those states was unsuitable for slavery, but that thinking was incorrect. It was unsuitable for extensive cotton cultivation, but slavery had existed in those states from time immemorial, although not African or chattel slavery. If those were to be slave states, the balance in the Senate could be restored.

Note that here and in the other speeches "African slavery" is used as a synonym for "Black slavery," not for slavery in Africa.

> On the contrary, there is not a single Territory in progress in the Southern section, and no certainty that any additional State will be added to it during the decade. The prospect then is, that the two sections in the Senate, should the efforts now made to exclude the South from the newly acquired Territories succeed, will stand, before the end of the decade, twenty Northern States to fourteen Southern (considering Delaware as neutral), and forty Northern senators to twenty-eight Southern. This great increase of senators, added to the great increase of members of the House of Representatives and the Electoral College on the part of the North, which must take place under the next decade, will effectually and irretrievably destroy the equilibrium which existed when the government commenced.

Calhoun's calculus of numbers, of immigrants, of representatives, of states, and of the Electoral College voters who chose the president, often a part of his speeches in the Senate, was almost morbidly fatalistic. Southern eyes were cast on "all Mexico," but that program failed. Southern "filibuster" attempts to overturn Central American nations had not yet begun. But in prospect was the acquisition of Cuba and Brazil and additional land from Mexico, but those futuristic plans would not come to pass. Where was slavery to go? For Calhoun, like his fellow southern senators, believed that slavery must expand or explode in slave rebellions. Even if the enslaved remained quiescent, without new lands to cultivate, the profits of the internal slave trade would whither.

> Had this destruction been the operation of time without the interference of government, the South would have had no reason to complain; but such was not the fact. It was caused by the legislation of this government,

which was appointed as the common agent of all and charged with the protection of the interests and security of all.

This was a return to Calhoun's "concurrent majority" theory of the Constitution, first espoused in his Exposition of 1828. As his posthumously published *Disquisition on Government* explained, "The concurrent majority is an indispensable element in forming constitutional governments; and why the numerical majority, of itself, must, in all cases, make governments absolute. The necessary consequence of taking the sense of the community by the concurrent majority is, as has been explained, to give to each interest or portion of the community a negative on the others."[12]

> The legislation by which it has been effected may be classed under three heads: The first is that series of acts by which the South has been excluded from the common territory belonging to all the States as members of the federal Union—which have had the effect of extending vastly the portion allotted to the Northern section, and restricting within narrow limits the portion left the South.
>
> The next consists in adopting a system of revenue and disbursements by which an undue proportion of the burden of taxation has been imposed upon the South, and an undue proportion of its proceeds appropriated to the North.
>
> And the last is a system of political measures by which the original character of the government has been radically changed. I propose to bestow upon each of these, in the order they stand, a few remarks, with the view of showing that it is owing to the action of this government that the equilibrium between the two sections has been destroyed, and the whole powers of the system centered in a sectional majority.

There were three "counts," or charges, against the federal government—legislative, fiscal, and political. All reflected, in Calhoun's opinion, a shift from the original purpose of government. Like Clay before him and Webster subsequently, Calhoun was an originalist—the source of authority for his arguments lay in the original language of the Constitution.

---

12 John C. Calhoun, *Disquisition on Government* (New York: Appleton, 1853), 35.

I have not included the territory recently acquired by the treaty with Mexico. The North is making the most strenuous efforts to appropriate the whole to herself, by excluding the South from every foot of it. If she should succeed, it will add to that from which the South has already been excluded 526,078 square miles, and would increase the whole which the North has appropriated to herself to 1,764,023, not including the portion that she may succeed in excluding us from in Texas. To sum up the whole, the United States, since they declared their independence, have acquired 2,373,046 square miles of territory, from which the North will have excluded the South, if she should succeed in monopolizing the newly-acquired Territories, about three-fourths of the whole, leaving to the South but about one-fourth. Such is the first and great cause that has destroyed the equilibrium between the two sections in the government.

Calhoun was fond of quantitative evidence. Here he had researched and presented the actual area. Maps available for this calculation included, notably, Samuel Augustus Mitchell's 1846 *New Map of Texas, Oregon, and California*, in part based on William H. Emory's *Map of Texas and the Country Adjacent* (1844). These widely popular commercial maps made travel over the Overland Trail to Oregon and California far easier.

The next is the system of revenue and disbursements which has been adopted by the government. It is well known that the government has derived its revenue mainly from duties on imports. I shall not undertake to show that such duties must necessarily fall mainly on the exporting States, and that the South, as the great exporting portion of the Union, has in reality paid vastly more than her due proportion of the revenue; because I deem it unnecessary, as the subject has on so many occasions been fully discussed. Nor shall I, for the same reason, undertake to show that a far greater portion of the revenue has been disbursed in the North, than its due share; and that the joint effect of these causes has been to transfer a vast amount from South to North, which, under an equal system of revenue and disbursements, would not have been lost to her. If to this be added that many of the duties were imposed, not for revenue but for protection—that is, intended to put money, not in the Treasury, but directly into the pocket of the manufacturers—some conception may be formed of the immense amount which in the long course of sixty years has been transferred from South to North. There are no data by which it can be estimated with any certainty; but it is safe to say that it amounts to hundreds of millions of dollars. Under the most moderate estimate it would be sufficient to add greatly to the wealthy of the North, and thus greatly increase her population by attracting immigration from all quarters to that section.

Calhoun here referred to the contentious debate over the tariff. The 1828 so-called Tariff of Abominations was a protective tariff, an aid to northeastern manufacturing interests over southern importing and exporting interests. It was the cause of *South Carolina Exposition and Protest*, a pamphlet written by vice president Calhoun at the behest of the state legislature. In that document, Calhoun argued that the state could "nullify" a federal law even when the subject of the law was one of the powers explicitly given to Congress (in this case the power to lay and collect tariffs). The controversy escalated when President Andrew Jackson warned the state that he would send gunboats to Charleston to ensure that the tariff was collected. The controversy cooled in 1833 when Congress passed a tariff far less unfavorable to the state.[13]

This, combined with the great primary cause, amply explains why the North has acquired a preponderance in every department of the government by its disproportionate increase of population and States. The former, as has been shown, has increased, in fifty years, 2,400,000 over that of the South. This increase of population during so long a period is satisfactorily accounted for by the number of immigrants, and the increase of their descendants, which have been attracted to the Northern section from Europe and the South, in consequence of the advantages derived from the causes assigned.

Actually, Calhoun was being more than a little disingenuous. The reason why the Irish and the Germans tended to remain in the North's

---

13 Calhoun was a profoundly cynical political economist, believing that self-interest was the most important motivation among men. Alexander Tabberok and Tyler Cowen, "The Public Choice Theory of John C. Calhoun," *Journal of Institutional and Theoretical Economics* 148 (1992): 655–674. On nullification, see William W. Freehling, *Prelude to Civil War: The Nullification Controversy in South Carolina, 1816–1836* (New York: Harper & Row, 1966).

cities and spread over the Midwest and West rather than spread over the South was that they did not want to compete with the enslaved and did not have the necessary capital to acquire land. The few immigrants who did travel south played an important role in the region's economy, however.[14]

> If they had not existed—if the South had retained all the capital which has been extracted from her by the fiscal action of the government; and if it had not been excluded by the Ordinance of 1787 and the Missouri Compromise, from the region lying between the Ohio and the Mississippi Rivers, and between the Mississippi and the Rocky Mountains north of 36° 30'—it scarcely admits of a doubt that it would have divided the immigration with the North, and by retaining her own people would have at least equaled the North in population under the census of 1840, and probably under that about to be taken.

Here Calhoun is massaging the numbers and ignoring the causes of internal migration. Many white southerners were migrating to the cotton lands of Alabama and Mississippi, bringing their slaves with them. They were not excluded from internal migration at all.[15]

> She would also, if she had retained her equal rights in those territories, have maintained an equality in the number of States with the North, and have preserved the equilibrium between the two sections that existed at the commencement of the government. The loss, then, of the equilibrium is to be attributed to the action of this government.

It was true that slavery was excluded from the Northwest Territory, but it was not excluded and in fact flourished in the lands that became Missouri, Alabama, Mississippi, Louisiana, Arkansas, and Florida

---

14 Only 5 percent of the southern white population was foreign-born in 1850, according to the census. By 1860, only one in fifteen was foreign-born. Ira Berlin and Herbert Gutman, "Natives and Immigrants, Free Men and Slaves: Urban Working Men in the Antebellum South," *American Historical Review* 88 (1983): 1175–1200.

15 Adam Rothman, *Slave Country: American Expansion and the Origins of the Deep South* (Cambridge, MA: Harvard University Press, 2005), documents this migration of slaves into the Black Belt.

and in the annexation of Texas. These seven slave states offset Maine, Ohio, Indiana, Illinois, Michigan, Iowa, and Wisconsin, all free states.

> There is a question of vital importance to the Southern section, in refer-
> ence to which the views and feelings of the two sections are as opposite
> and hostile as they can possibly be. I refer to the relation between the
> two races in the Southern section, which constitutes a vital portion of
> her social organization. Every portion of the North entertains views and
> feelings more or less hostile to it. Those most opposed and hostile regard
> it as a sin, and consider themselves under the most sacred obligation to
> use every effort to destroy it.

Not quite true. Northern opinion was hardening around free soil and free labor, but not around belief in the social equality of the races. In general northern whites were as racialist in their opinions as southern whites. The difference lay not in the relation between the two races but in the enslavement of one race by the other.[16]

> Indeed, to the extent that they conceive that they have power, they
> regard themselves as implicated in the sin, and responsible for not sup-
> pressing it by the use of all and every means. Those less opposed and
> hostile regard it as a crime—an offense against humanity, as they call
> it and, altho not so fanatical, feel themselves bound to use all efforts to
> effect the same object; while those who are least opposed and hostile
> regard it as a blot and a stain on the character of what they call the "na-
> tion," and feel themselves accordingly bound to give it no countenance
> or support.

A fair if very simplified description of the two kinds of antislavery opinion—immediate and gradual.

> On the contrary, the Southern section regards the relation as one
> which can not be destroyed without subjecting the two races to the
> greatest calamity, and the section to poverty, desolation, and wretch-

16 Leon Litwack, *North of Slavery: The Negro in the Free States, 1790–1860* (Chicago: University of Chicago Press, 1961), 97–99, documents examples of this racism.

edness; and accordingly they feel bound by every consideration of interest and safety to defend it.

This was the same argument that Thomas Jefferson, St. George Tucker, and other apologists for slavery made in the 1780s—the enslaved, freed, would fall on poverty and crime. Calhoun may or may not have been suggesting that with the end of slavery the South itself would be plunged into poverty.[17]

> Unless something decisive is done, I again ask, What is to stop this agitation before the great and final object at which it aims—the abolition of slavery in the States—is consummated? Is it, then, not certain that if something is not done to arrest it, the South will be forced to choose between abolition and secession? Indeed, as events are now moving, it will not require the South to secede in order to dissolve the Union. Agitation will of itself effect it, of which its past history furnishes abundant proof—as I shall next proceed to show.

"Were these the only choices?"—to die in the coop or to die trying to fly the coop, a question asked by Babs in the animated feature film *Chicken Run* (2000). If the South had done nothing when Abraham Lincoln was elected president, would slavery have been ended? By seceding, the South precipitated the ruin of slavery that it feared. But Calhoun, as intelligent as he was, did not see this third choice.

> It is a great mistake to suppose that disunion can be effected by a single blow. The cords which bind these States together in one common Union are far too numerous and powerful for that. Disunion must be the work of time. It is only through a long process, and successively, that the cords can be snapped until the whole fabric falls asunder. Already the agitation of the slavery question has snapped some of the most important, and has greatly weakened all the others.

---

17 Thomas Jefferson, *Notes on the State of Virginia* (1782/1785; Philadelphia: Pritchard and Hall, 1788), 146; Paul Finkelman, "The Dragon St. George Could Not Slay: Tucker's Plan to End Slavery," *William and Mary Law Review* 47 (2006): 1221–1222.

By contrast, this was Calhoun at his best: realistic, thoughtful, and conservative. The cords that bound the nation were many—financial, cultural, and religious, as well as political and legal. And slavery, always a potential sword, was cutting those ties.

> If the agitation goes on, the same force, acting with increased intensity, as has been shown, will finally snap every cord, when nothing will be left to hold the States together except force. But surely that can with no propriety of language be called a Union when the only means by which the weaker is held connected with the stronger portion is force. It may, indeed, keep them connected; but the connection will partake much more of the character of subjugation on the part of the weaker to the stronger than the union of free, independent, and sovereign States in one confederation, as they stood in the early stages of the government, and which only is worthy of the sacred name of Union.

Here is a reminder that Calhoun was always a believer in the importance of the Union. His states' rights philosophy comported with that loyalty—until it no longer did.

> Having now, senators, explained what it is that endangers the Union, and traced it to its cause, and explained its nature and character, the question again recurs, How can the Union be saved?

But here is where his attachment to southern ways led him astray. "There is but one way" is hardly the moderation and conciliation that Clay begged of the Senate. Instead of consensus, Calhoun urged concession. Or else.

> To this I answer, there is but one way by which it can be, and that is by adopting such measures as will satisfy the States belonging to the Southern section that they can remain in the Union consistently with their honor and their safety. There is, again, only one way by which this can be effected, and that is by removing the causes by which this belief has been produced. Do this, and discontent will cease, harmony and kind feelings between the sections be restored, and every apprehension of danger to the Union removed.

The question, then, is, How can this be done? There is but one way by which it can with any certainty; and that is by a full and final settlement, on the principle of justice, of all the questions at issue between the two sections. The South asks for justice, simple justice, and less she ought not to take. She has no compromise to offer but the Constitution, and no concession or surrender to make. She has already surrendered so much that she has little left to surrender.

Again, no room for compromise, making Calhoun's speech a direct answer to Clay's. But Calhoun, recalling his lawyerly background, asks for justice. The free states have been unjust to the South. The abolitionists have been unjust. A "full and final settlement" made no sense in political terms, where time and circumstance change. Only the decision that a high court can render would finally settle a dispute. In short, unlike Clay, who saw the Senate as a supremely political body, Calhoun recasts the Senate as the high court of the nation and sees the resolution of the sectional quarrel as a legal one.

Such a settlement would go to the root of the evil, and remove all cause of discontent, by satisfying the South that she could remain honorably and safely in the Union, and thereby restore the harmony and fraternal feelings between the sections which existed anterior to the Missouri agitation. Nothing else can, with any certainty, finally and for ever settle the question at issue, terminate agitation, and save the Union.

But can this be done? Yes, easily; not by the weaker party, for it can of itself do nothing—not even protect itself—but by the stronger. The North has only to will it to accomplish it—to do justice by conceding to the South an equal right in the acquired territory, and to do her duty by causing the stipulations relative to fugitive slaves to be faithfully fulfilled—to cease the agitation of the slave question, and to provide for the insertion of a provision in the Constitution, by an amendment, which will restore to the South, in substance, the power she possessed of protecting herself before the equilibrium between the sections was destroyed by the action of this government. There will be no difficulty in devising such a provision—one that will protect the South, and which at the same time will improve and strengthen the government instead of impairing and weakening it.

The solution was an amendment to the Constitution guaranteeing the right to property in men and women and the right of those who held the enslaved in bondage to take the enslaved with them, in safety, wherever they went in the United States. It would make slavery national rather than sectional. It would become a centerpiece of compromise negotiations in the Senate in 1860–1861, after secession had begun.

> But will the North agree to this? It is for her to answer the question. But, I will say, she can not refuse if she has half the love of the Union which she professes to have, or without justly exposing herself to the charge that her love of power and aggrandizement is far greater than her love of the Union. At all events, the responsibility of saving the Union rests on the North, and not on the South. The South can not save it by any act of hers, and the North may save it without any sacrifice whatever, unless to do justice and to perform her duties under the Constitution should be regarded by her as a sacrifice.

The absent voice in Calhoun's address was that of the Black people themselves. The "North" was white. The "South" was white. The profound silence of these millions, free and enslaved, is deafening to modern ears.

> It is time, senators, that there should be an open and manly avowal on all sides as to what is intended to be done. If the question is not now settled, it is uncertain whether it ever can hereafter be; and we, as the representatives of the States of this Union regarded as governments, should come to a distinct understanding as to our respective views, in order to ascertain whether the great questions at issue can be settled or not. If you who represent the stronger portion, cannot agree to settle them on the broad principle of justice and duty, say so; and let the States we both represent agree to separate and part in peace.

Whether Calhoun, as he spoke, had moved from a defense of the Union to a plea to let the slave South go in peace, he did not nod in its direction.

If you are unwilling we should part in peace, tell us so; and we shall know what to do when you reduce the question to submission or resistance. If you remain silent, you will compel us to infer by your acts what you intend. In that case California will become the test question. If you admit her under all the difficulties that oppose her admission, you compel us to infer that you intend to exclude us from the whole of the acquired Territories, with the intention of destroying irretrievably the equilibrium between the two sections. We should be blind not to perceive in that case that your real objects are power and aggrandizement, and infatuated, not to act accordingly.

The threat was in the open. The South, if not appeased, would secede, and if necessary would defend itself with force. After all, the North was the guilty party, infatuated with power and driven to aggrandizement. One with foresight of the future could almost hear the South Carolina Declaration of the Cause of Secession: "An increasing hostility on the part of the non-slaveholding States to the institution of slavery, has led to a disregard of their obligations, and the laws of the General Government have ceased to effect the objects of the Constitution. . . . For twenty-five years this agitation has been steadily increasing, until it has now secured to its aid the power of the common Government. . . . It has announced that the South shall be excluded from the common territory, that the judicial tribunals shall be made sectional, and that a war must be waged against slavery until it shall cease throughout the United States."[18]

I have now, senators, done my duty in expressing my opinions fully, freely, and candidly on this solemn occasion. In doing so I have been governed by the motives which have governed me in all the stages of the agitation of the slavery question since its commencement. I have exerted myself during the whole period to arrest it, with the intention of saving the Union if it could be done; and if it could not, to save the section where it has pleased providence to cast my lot, and which I sincerely believe has justice and the Constitution on its side. Having faithfully done my duty to the best of my ability, both to the Union and my section, throughout

18 Declaration of the Immediate Causes Which Induce and Justify the Secession of South Carolina from the Federal Union, December 24, 1860, South Carolina Secession Convention, Charleston, SC.

this agitation, I shall have the consolation, let what will come, that I am free from all responsibility.

The Republican statesman, like the Roman senator Cato, had a duty to express opinions freely and without bias. In his own mind, Calhoun had done no less. Let the outcome be what it would be. In a sense, the speech did not advance his cause, however, for everything in it he had said already. But his attachment to the Union was still strong, and surely that meant something. The immediate reaction in the chamber was solemn silence. Henry Foote worried that Calhoun's insistence on a constitutional amendment would be another obstacle to compromise. When Foote told Calhoun this, Calhoun replied, "I make my speeches for myself." Historians disagree about the impact of the speech. For one leading historian, Calhoun had "contributed powerfully to the achievement of compromise" by warning that secession must be taken seriously, but another historian found the proposal for a constitutional amendment as "far-fetched as the speech was devious." In the end, Calhoun's dire prophecy was the most accurate, of the three speeches, but the rest of the Senate waited for Daniel Webster's contribution.[19]

---

19 Foote and Calhoun quoted in John C. Waugh, *On the Brink of Civil War: The Compromise of 1850 and How It Changed the Course of American History* (Wilmington, DE: Scholarly Resources, 2003), 93, 94; Potter, *Impending Crisis*, 101, dismissed Foote's concern; Sean Wilentz, *The Rise of American Democracy: Jefferson to Lincoln* (New York: Norton, 2005), 639, agreed with Foote.

4

Daniel Webster, Speech on the Union, March 7, 1850

Figure 4.1. Daniel Webster, daguerreotype by Matthew Brady, ca. 1847. Credit: Library of Congress, Prints & Photographs Division.

WEARY, ill, saddened by the recent deaths of his only son and all but one of his daughters, his once prosperous law practice winding down, in debt, sixty-nine-year-old Daniel Webster approached his last term in the Senate with less than enthusiasm.[1] Despite his genuine diplomatic achievements as secretary of state under President John Tyler (the Webster-Ashburton Treaty line marking part of the border between Canada and the United States still stands), his departure was hastened by accusations of partisanship and peculation.[2]

In the public eye, Webster had appeared to be very much a Massachusetts man and a northern man. Born and educated in New Hampshire, he had practiced law and defended the economic interests of the Boston merchants, and then the Massachusetts textile factory owners, for thirty-five years. "To his political opponents, there seemed something shifty about Webster's career in politics. He went from populist defender of the yeoman farmer to free trade advocate of the overseas merchants to spokesman for tariff protection for New England manufacturing. Was it political ambition that drove him; Webster looking for a popular stance to propel him from Congress to the presidency? If so, with all due respect to his actual achievements, he had no clue. He took unpopular positions, New England positions, when the region was increasingly atypical of the rest of the country. Admired as a political advocate and for a time certain of reelection to Congress, he never quite got the hang of what the mass of voters wanted. In the end, he seemed out of place—a crotchety defender of older values when successful presidential candidates spoke for more popular positions in a democratic vernacular."[3]

Early in February 1850, Henry Clay visited Webster, and the Massachusetts man assured Clay that he would be supportive when Clay's resolutions were debated. After Calhoun had finished his speech, Web-

---

1 Webster, Speech in US Senate, March 7, 1850, 31st Cong., 1st sess., *Congressional Globe*, appendix, 269–276; Text, revised, March 18, 1850 (Washington, DC: Gideon, 1850). Comparing the two versions shows minor alterations—changes in a few words and the addition of a few clarifying phrases. I have reproduced the text Webster edited with annotations drawn from the appendix entry in the *Globe*.
2 Peter Charles Hoffer, *Daniel Webster and the Unfinished Constitution* (Lawrence: University Press of Kansas, 2021), 127–138.
3 Hoffer, *Webster and the Unfinished Constitution*, 12.

ster consulted with close friends and decided on a course of action. Like Calhoun, Webster would not respond directly to Clay, but Webster would stand with the Union. On March 7, 1850, he rose from his desk in the middle of the room and walked to the front of the chamber. His hand resting on the Speaker's desk, supporting his broad shoulders and leonine head, his booming voice still commanding the chamber, "God-like Daniel" began his "Seventh of March" speech. His tone was not con-versational, like Clay's, or pedantic, like Calhoun's, but hortatory, calling on members of the Senate to heed and obey. Crowds, hearing of his forthcoming performance, filled the visitors' gallery and spilled onto the floor of the chamber. He had been an opponent of slave power through-out his career. Slavery was a curse; freedom was its cure. But now he put the safety of the Union ahead of all other concerns.[4]

But, a very large but, Webster did not exactly endorse Clay's propos-als. Although, like Clay, a Whig, and surely privy to Clay's plan before Clay spoke, Webster hedged, dodged, called for compromise, praised the Union, and supported the fugitive slave provisions, as they were already enforced in Massachusetts. If Clay was the politician, and Calhoun the ideologue, Webster was the peacemaker. Whether his efforts were su-perb or merely self-congratulatory remains an open question.[5]

> Mr. President: I wish to speak to-day, not as a Massachusetts man, nor as a Northern man, but as an American, and a member of the Senate of the United States. It is fortunate that there is a Senate of the United States; a body not yet moved from its propriety, not lost to a just sense of its own dignity and its own high responsibilities, and a body to which the country looks, with confidence, for wise, moderate, patriotic, and healing counsels.

The original text of the speech, reported in the *Globe*, said "doctrine" rather than "counsels." What this meant in the original was not clear.

---

4 David Potter, *The Impending Crisis: America Before the Civil War, 1848–1861* (New York: Harper & Row, 1976), 97; Robert V. Remini, *Daniel Webster: The Man and His Time* (New York: Norton, 1997), 666–667; Fergus Bordewich, *America's Great Debate: Henry Clay, Stephen A. Douglas, and the Compromise that Preserved the Union* (New York: Simon & Schuster, 2012), 165–166; Hoffer, *Webster and the Unfinished Constitution*, 133, 137–138. The Webster Desk is the original, preserved in the Old Senate Chamber, now a museum in the Capitol.

5 Remini, *Webster*, 673–674; Daniel Webster to Professor Moses Stuart, April 1850, in *The Writings and Speeches of Daniel Webster* (Boston: Little, Brown, 1903), 18:368.

Webster had the chance to clarify in the published version the next day. Which is the one that we should see as his view? How did doctrine "heal"? Not clear. How did wise counsel heal? That was very clear. The idea of the Senate as a deliberative body was not new; it was discussed at the constitutional convention. Webster pandered to the self-image of the senators. On this occasion it had a somewhat less celebratory sanguinary meaning—for the lower house was not only deadlocked, but deadlocked in raucous fashion.

> It is not to be denied that we live in the midst of strong agitations, and are surrounded by very considerable dangers to our institutions and government.[6]
>
> The imprisoned winds are let loose. The East, the North, and the stormy South combine to throw the whole ocean into commotion, to toss its billows to the skies, and disclose its profoundest depths. I do not affect to regard myself, Mr. President, as holding, or as fit to hold, the helm in this combat with the political elements; but I have a duty to perform, and I mean to perform it with fidelity, not without a sense of existing dangers, but not without hope. I have a part to act, not for my own security or safety, for I am looking out for no fragment upon which to float away from the wreck, if wreck there must be, but for the good of the whole, and the preservation of all; and there is that which will keep me to my duty during this struggle, whether the sun and the stars shall appear, or shall not appear for many days.

The metaphor of a captain on the deck of the ship of state, buffeted by winds from all quarters, rocked by "the stormy South," was pure Webster. The metaphor of the ship of state was familiar to his auditory. The first use of it was in Plato's *Republic*: "Imagine then a fleet or a ship in which there is a captain who is taller and stronger than any of the crew." Of course, Longfellow's ship had a captain on its deck, though the poem did not mention him. Webster had practiced the craft of the orator from his earliest days. Rhetoric, including public speaking, was one of the classic college subjects. Its instruction aimed to assist those students in future legal and ministerial careers. Webster already excelled at oratory

---

6 In the original, "of government," typical of the very modest changes.

because he was long used to entertain customers in his father's tavern with the recitation of Bible passages from memory. Little "Black Dan" (like his father, Daniel's complexion was dark, and that is how he introduced himself when he stood for entrance to Dartmouth) seemed a born orator. He honed his abilities in public speaking, whether innate or learned, at college. It was a heady time for oratory in the nation, changing from an exercise in "decorum, rational persuasion, and controlled appeals to the sentiments" to emotional excess. Law students especially absorbed the new canon of energy and expressiveness. Speaking in public, "Godlike Daniel" could shift rhythms, tones, and vocabulary so effortlessly that listeners did not perceive his many hours of preparation for each oration. The adult Webster's voice was described as rich and deep, always controlled, "majestic, almost superhuman." Compared to some of his congressional and courtroom peers, he spoke slowly, and that may have enabled him to go on for hours, sometimes for days.[7]

> I speak to-day for the preservation of the Union. "Hear me for my cause." I speak, to-day, out of a solicitous and anxious heart for the restoration to the country of that quiet and that harmony which make the blessings of this Union so rich and so dear to us all. These are the topics that I propose to myself to discuss; these are the motives, and the sole motives, that influence me in the wish to communicate my opinions to the Senate and the country; and if I can do anything, however little, for the promotion of these ends, I shall have accomplished all that I expect.[8]

As Webster looked about the room, what did he see? What was that quiet and harmonious life? He saw propertied white men. Daguerreotypes from the era allow us to see stiff but accurate representations of members of Congress. Portraits of other members also exist. They

---

7 Plato, *Republic*, VI.321, in *Dialogues of Plato, Translated into English*, ed. Benjamin Jowett (Oxford: Oxford University Press, 1875); Nan Johnson, "The Popularization of Nineteenth-Century Rhetoric: Elocution and the Private Learner," in *Oratorical Culture in Nineteenth-Century America: Transformation in the Theory and Practice of Rhetoric*, ed. Gregory Clark and S. Michael Halloran (Carbondale: University of Southern Illinois, 1993), 139–140; Christopher Grasso, *A Speaking Aristocracy: Transforming Public Discourse in Eighteenth-Century Connecticut* (Chapel Hill: University of North Carolina Press, 1999), 406, 407; "Black Dan," in S. J. Lyman, *Life of Daniel Webster* (New York: Appleton, 1855), 220. Text and notes from Hoffer, *Webster and the Unfinished Constitution*, 14.
8 In the original, "desire" instead of "expect."

stare out at us today with serious faces. (No one is smiling—too hard to maintain given the photographic process of the day.) They were the ruling class—lawyers, planters, speculators, former military officers, merchants—and the assumption was that the population (that mattered) was homogeneous. They were western European in ethnicity, almost all were Protestants. (The number of Catholics in the United States was small, but Irish migration after 1845 was driving the numbers up rapidly.) Nothing in Webster's speech suggests that diversity was valued; indeed, it was not noticed. Inclusion was dangerous. In fact, so many were left out of this calculus of blessing—women, Blacks, Native peoples—that one must assume Webster spoke only for and to a white, male, propertied class. After all, if he looked about the chamber, that is what he saw. This was not a harmonious Union but a fragmented, fragile confederation of interests, regions, and ruling cliques.[9]

> Mr. President, it may not be amiss to recur very briefly to the events which, equally sudden and extraordinary, have brought the political condition of the country to what it now is. In May, 1846, the United States declared war against Mexico. Our armies, then on the frontiers, entered the provinces of that republic, met and defeated all her troops, penetrated her mountain passes, and occupied her capital. The marine force of the United States took possession of her forts and her towns, on the Atlantic and on the Pacific. In less than two years a treaty was negotiated, by which Mexico ceded to the United States a vast territory, extending seven or eight hundred miles along the shores of the Pacific, and reaching back over the mountains, and across the desert, until it joins the frontier of the State of Texas.

Webster's was a patriotic history of the Mexican-American War that did not mention how President Polk and his Democratic allies had driven the war fever, how Whigs like Clay and Webster, both of whom lost sons in the war, had opposed it, and how the Wilmot Proviso had passed in the House but died in the Senate while ominously dividing the country along sectional lines.

---

9 This "Jacksonian democracy" was hardly a democracy at all. See, e.g., Alan Taylor, *American Republics: A Continental History of the United States, 1783–1850* (New York: Norton, 2021), 200–249.

It so happened, in the distracted and feeble condition of the Mexican government, that, before the declaration of war by the United States against Mexico had become known in California, the people of California, under the lead of American officers, overthrew the existing provincial government of California, the Mexican authorities, and ran up an independent flag. When the news arrived at San Francisco that war had been declared by the United States against Mexico, this independent flag was pulled down, and the stars and stripes of this Union hoisted in its stead. So, Sir, before the war was over, the forces of the United States, military and naval, had possession of San Francisco and Upper California, and a great rush of emigrants from various parts of the world took place into California in 1846 and 1847.

Here was a much more accurate depiction of the California "revolution" than Webster gave of the Mexican-American War, but again no mention of the diversity of the "people" of California. Some were holdovers from the Spanish years. Others were migrants from Mexico. A diminishing number were the original Native inhabitants. Some were Asians, and others were migrants from the United States, having arrived via the Overland Trail. California was what America would be.[10]

But now, behold another wonder. In January of 1848, the Mormons, or some of them, made a discovery of an extraordinarily rich mine of gold, or, rather, of a very great quantity of gold, hardly fit to be called a mine, for it was spread near the surface, on the lower part of the south, or American, branch of the Sacramento. They seem to have attempted to conceal their discovery for some time; but soon another discovery, perhaps of greater importance, was made of gold, in another part of the American branch of the Sacramento, and near Sutter's Fort, as it is called. The fame of these discoveries spread far and wide. They inflamed more and more the spirit of emigration towards California, which had already been excited; and persons crowded in hundreds, and flocked towards the Bay of San Francisco.

This, as I have said, took place in the winter and spring of 1848. The digging commenced in the spring of that year, and from that time to this

---

10 Or, actually, what most of eastern America already was: ethnic European ancestry farm families. John Mack Faragher, *Women and Men on the Overland Trail*, 2nd ed. (New Haven, CT: Yale University Press, 2001), 16–65.

the work of searching for gold has been prosecuted with a success not heretofore known in the history of this globe. We all know, Sir, how incredulous the American public was at the accounts, which reached us, at first, of these discoveries; but we all know, now, that these accounts received, and continue to receive, daily confirmation, and down to the present moment I suppose the assurances are as strong, after the experience of these several months, of mines of gold apparently inexhaustible in the regions near San Francisco, in California, as they were at any period of the earlier dates of the accounts.

It so happened, Sir, that, although, after the return of peace, it became a very important subject for legislative consideration and legislative decision, to provide a proper territorial government for California, yet differences of opinion in the counsels of the Government prevented the establishment of any such territorial government, at the last session of Congress. Under this state of things, the inhabitants of San Francisco and California, then amounting to a great number of people, in the summer of last year, thought it to be their duty to establish a local government. Under the proclamation of General [Bennet] Riley, the people chose delegates to a convention; that convention met at Monterey. They formed a constitution for the State of California, and it was adopted by the people of California in their primary assemblages. Desirous of immediate connection with the United States, its Senators were appointed and Representatives chosen, who have come hither, bringing with them the authentic Constitution of the State of California; and they now present themselves, asking, in behalf of their State, that it may be admitted into this Union as one of the United States.

Webster had done his homework. It had not been hard. Newspapers throughout the country had made the California gold rush a daily topic.[11]

This constitution, Sir, contains an express prohibition against slavery, or involuntary servitude, in the State of California. It is said, and I

---

11 H. W. Brands, *The Age of Gold: The California Gold Rush and the New American Dream* (New York: Random House, 2002), 127, 130.

suppose truly, that of the members who composed that Convention, some sixteen were natives of, and had been residents in, the slaveholding States, about twenty-two were from the non-slaveholding States, and the remaining ten members were either native Californians or old settlers in that country. This prohibition against slavery, it is said, was inserted with entire unanimity.

True enough, but at the same time, the Kentucky contingent at the California constitutional convention insisted, and the other delegates agreed, that the Constitution would bar the in-migration of "free negroes."[12]

And it is this circumstance, Sir, the prohibition of slavery by that Convention, which has contributed to raise, I do not say it has wholly raised, the dispute as to the propriety of the admission of California into the Union under this constitution. It is not to be denied, Mr. President, nobody thinks of denying that, whatever reasons were assigned at the commencement of the late war with Mexico, it was prosecuted for the purpose of the acquisition of territory, and under the alleged argument that the cession of territory was the only form in which proper compensation could be made to the United States by Mexico, for the various claims and demands which the people of this country had against that government. At any rate, it will be found that President Polk's message, at the commencement of the session of December, 1847, avowed that the war was to be prosecuted until some acquisition of territory should be made.

Ah, a poke at Polk. Webster had no use for the former president. Webster regarded Polk at best as a "man of mediocrity."[13]

And, as the acquisition was to be south of the line of the United States, in warm climates and countries, it was naturally, I suppose, expected by the South, that whatever acquisitions were made in that region would be added to the slaveholding portion of the United States. Very little of

12 Brands, *Age of Gold*, 279–280.
13 Remini, *Webster*, 609.

accurate information was possessed of the real physical character, either of California or New Mexico; and events have turned out as was not expected. Both California and New Mexico are likely to come in as free; and therefore some degree of disappointment and surprise has resulted. In other words, it is obvious that the question which has so long harassed the country, and at some times very seriously alarmed the minds of wise and good men, has come upon us for a fresh discussion; the question of slavery in these United States.

Climate and terrain were routinely linked to the expansion of slavery. Thus, the arid soil and desert climate of New Mexico and Arizona supposedly barred the expansion of slavery to those parts of the Mexican-American War acquisition. So said Clay. But slaves could work in mines, drive cattle, and clear land for settlement as well as plant and harvest cotton, as they did in East Texas.

What is more, discussions of slavery had never ended peacefully, not in Congress and not on the hustings. It was political dynamite. But California had lit the fuse, and Webster thought that words—his words, carefully chosen—could snuff the fuse out. There was a part of his career where he exulted in the adulation of his audiences. Perhaps it was the after-dinner alcohol that had fueled his self-importance. Clay, who could drink with any man, never had such illusions of godhood. Webster, however, did. This day Clay listened intently as Webster spoke. Calhoun was present as well.

> Now, Sir, I propose, perhaps at the expense of some detail and consequent detention of the Senate, to review historically this question, which, partly in consequence of its own importance, and partly, perhaps mostly, in consequence of the manner in which it has been discussed in one and the other portion of the country, has been a source of so much alienation and unkind feeling.

On this subject, Webster had notes. He had prepared them over the three days since Calhoun finished. These included, to judge from his speech, Jonathan Elliott's five volumes on the debates on the ratification of the Constitution and James Madison's notes on the debates at the convention. He may have shown his notes for the speech to Calhoun when he visited the ailing South Carolinian. Reading them deadened the speech, in part because he supposed that what he said was common knowledge. In fact, it was wrong on just about every count.[14]

> We all know, Sir, that slavery has existed in the world from time immemorial. There was slavery, in the earliest periods of history, in the Oriental nations. There was slavery among the Jews; the theocratic government of that people ordained no injunction against it. There was slavery among the Greeks; and the ingenious philosophy of the Greeks found, or sought to find, a justification for it exactly upon the grounds which have been assumed for such a justification in this country; that is, a natural and original difference among the races of mankind, and the inferiority of the black or colored race to the white. The Greeks justified their system of slavery upon that idea, precisely. They held the African, and in some parts the Asiatic, tribes to be inferior to the white race; but they did not show, I think, by any close process of logic, that, if this were true, the more intelligent and the stronger had therefore a right to subjugate the weaker.
>
> The more manly philosophy and jurisprudence of the Romans placed the justification of slavery on entirely different grounds.

At best, Webster was oversimplifying. Slavery was endemic in the ancient and early modern Mediterranean and Africa, but the conditions of the slaves and the powers of the masters varied from place to place and over time. Above all, there was no particular racial component to ancient slavery or African slavery. Europeans enslaved other Europeans and Africans enslaved other Africans. Slavery in these Old World places did not destroy personhood as it did in southern chattel slavery. For example, in Africa, slaves were debased in status but could be advisors to kings and even have slaves of their own.[15]

---

14 Jonathan Elliot, *The Debates in the Several State Conventions on the Adoption of the Federal Constitution* . . . (Philadelphia: Lippincott, 1835), 5v; James Madison, *Papers of James Madison* (Washington, DC: Langtree and O'Sullivan, 1840), vol. 3: reports of debates in the federal convention.

15 See, in general, David Brion Davis, *Inhuman Bondage: The Rise and Fall of Slavery in the New World* (New York: Oxford University Press, 2006); Joseph C. Miller, *The Problem of Slavery as History: A Global Approach* (New Haven, CT: Yale University Press, 2012); and Orlando Patterson, *Slavery and Social Death* (Cambridge, MA: Harvard University Press, 1982).

The Roman jurists, from the first and down to the fall of the empire, admitted that slavery was against the natural law, by which, as they maintained, all men, of whatsoever clime, color, or capacity were equal; but they justified slavery, first, upon the ground and authority of the law of nations, arguing, and arguing truly, that at that day the conventional law of nations admitted that captives in war, whose lives, according to the notions of the times, were at the absolute disposal of the captors, might, in exchange for exemption from death, be made slaves for life, and that such servitude might descend to their posterity. The jurists of Rome also maintained that by the civil law, there might be servitude or slavery, personal and hereditary; first, by the voluntary act of an individual, who might sell himself into slavery; secondly, by his being reduced into a state of slavery by his creditors in satisfaction of his debts; and, thirdly, by being placed in a state of servitude or slavery for crime.

While natural law held that all men were equal. the jus gentium (law of nations) and the jus civile (the Roman civil law) both sanctioned slavery. Slaves might come from other peoples, or slaves might be of Roman extraction. Webster had gotten this right. Whether his fellow senators cared was another matter. They were accustomed to Webster showing off.

At the introduction of Christianity, the Roman world was full of slaves, and I suppose there is to be found no injunction against that relation between man and man, in the teachings of the Gospel of Jesus Christ, or of any of his Apostles. The object of the instruction imparted to mankind by the founder of Christianity was to touch the heart, purify the soul, and improve the lives of individual men. That object went directly to the first fountain of all political and all social relations of the human race, as well as of all true religious feelings, the individual heart and mind of man.

The gospels in the New Testament accepted slavery. Paul in particular told masters to be humane. Slaves were bidden to be obedient. Manumission depended on the will of the master, as it was in ancient Rome.[16]

16 Alan Watson, *Slave Law in the Americas* (Athens: University of Georgia Press, 1989), 22–39.

Now, Sir, upon the general nature, and character, and influence of slavery, there exists a wide difference of opinion between the Northern portion of this country and the Southern. It is said on the one side that, if not the subject of any injunction or direct prohibition in the New Testament, slavery is a wrong; that it is founded merely in the right of the strongest; and that it is an oppression, like unjust wars, like all those conflicts by which a mighty nation subjects a weaker nation to its will; and that slavery, in its nature, whatever may be said of it in the modifications which have taken place, is not in fact according to the meek spirit of the Gospel. It is not "kindly affectioned"; it does not "seek another's, and not its own"; it does not "let the oppressed go free." These are sentiments that are cherished, and recently with greatly augmented force, among the people of the Northern States. They have taken hold of the religious sentiment of that part of the country, as they have more or less taken hold of the religious feelings of a considerable portion of mankind.

Webster was here representing his own as well as his northern neighbors' sentiments. It could have been an introduction to his earlier Senate speeches, for example, his second reply to Senator Robert Y. Hayne of South Carolina, on January 27, 1830. "I regard slavery as one of the greatest evils, both moral and political." No one would have been surprised if Webster reprised this refrain. But the very next passage sounded more like Calhoun than Webster.[17]

The South, upon the other side, having been accustomed to this relation between the two races all their lives, from their birth, having been taught, in general, to treat the subjects of this bondage with care and kindness, and I believe, in general, feeling for them great care and kindness, have not taken the view of the subject which I have mentioned. There are thousands of religious men, with consciences as tender as any of their brethren at the North, who do not see the unlawfulness of slavery; and there are more thousands, perhaps, that, whatsoever they may think of it in its origin, and as a matter depending upon natural right, yet take things as they are, and, finding slavery to be an established relation of the society

17 Webster, Speech in the Senate, January 27, 1830, in *Webster and Hayne's Celebrated Speeches* (Philadelphia: T. B. Peterson, 1830), 42, 43; Hoffer, *Webster and the Unfinished Constitution*, 113.

in which they live, can see no way in which, let their opinions on the abstract question be what they may, it is in the power of the present generation to relieve themselves from this relation. And, in this respect, candor obliges me to say, that I believe they are just as conscientious, many of them, and the religious people, all of them, as they are in the North who hold different opinions.

So, slavery was simply a difference of opinion? After all, Clay owned slaves and Calhoun owned slaves. Were they evil men? Were they not kind masters? (Clay was reputed to be so.) The more moderate (gradualist) abolitionists, earlier in the century, had taken this position: slavery was evil, but that did not mean that every master was evil. They could be persuaded to give up their slaves. As late of 1861, newly elected president Abraham Lincoln held this view. Note that in this scenario the slave had no opinion or did not voice an opinion, at least no opinion worth a white senator's notice. It was this approach that was the dominant view of slavery among American historians in the first forty years of the twentieth century. Slave narratives, slave testimony, firsthand accounts of slavery from slaves had no place in the work of leading historians like Ulrich Bonnell Phillips.[18]

Why, Sir, the honorable Senator from South Carolina, the other day, alluded to the separation of that great religious community, the Methodist Episcopal Church. That separation was brought about by differences of opinion upon this particular subject of slavery. I felt great concern, as that dispute went on, about the result; and I was in hopes that the difference of opinion might be adjusted, because I looked upon that religious denomination as one of the great props of religion and morals, throughout the whole country, from Maine to Georgia, and westward, to our utmost western boundary. The result was against my wishes and against my hopes. I have read all their proceedings and all their arguments; but I have never yet been able to come to the conclusion that there was any real ground for that separation; in other words, that any good could be produced by that separation. I must say I think there was some want of candor and charity.

---

18 U. B. Phillips, *American Negro Slavery* (New York: Appleton, 1918); Phillips, *Life and Labor in the Old South* (Boston: Little, Brown, 1929); on Phillips, see John David Smith, "The Life and Labor of Ulrich Bonnell Phillips," *Georgia Historical Quarterly* 70 (1986): 254–272.

The difference of opinion over the morality of slavery reached into religious practices and had split in two one of the country's largest churches—along sectional lines. The first Methodists in America were antislavery advocates. As Methodism grew institutionalized in the South, that message mutated to admonitions to be kind to slaves. "Primed by decades of proving themselves men of honor in recognizably southern ways, Baptists and methods rose readily to defend slavery in the 1830s, secession in the 1850s, and the hold cause of upholding both with force of arms in 1861." In 1840 the Baptists split over slavery, formalizing the schism in 1845 with the founding of the Southern Baptist Convention. In the same year, the so-called "southern schism" of Methodist Episcopal churches began in the North, with increased concern for the immorality of slavery and slaveholding among ministers. Presbyterian churches had already split over the issue. Southern congregations resented the moralizing of their northern brethren. Honor required that the southern churches depart the national body. By 1845, the schisms were complete. This did not mean that slaves had nowhere to worship. The Methodist Episcopal Church South, by the eve of the Civil War, had among its numbers almost half a million whites and nearly two hundred thousand Blacks—most of whom were slaves.[19]

Sir, when a question of this kind seizes on the religious sentiments of mankind, and comes to be discussed in religious assemblies of the clergy and laity, there is always to be expected, or always to be feared, a great degree of excitement. It is in the nature of man, manifested by his whole history, that religious disputes are apt to become warm, as men's strength of conviction is proportionate to their views of the magnitude of the questions. In all such disputes, there will sometimes men be found with whom every thing is absolute, absolutely wrong, or absolutely right.

There was that evil again—excitement. Both Clay and Calhoun had warned against it. Excitement was bad—it devoured reason. Was Webster arguing that religion led to unwanted passions? Or that the

---

19 Christine Heyrman, *Southern Cross: The Beginnings of the Bible Belt* (New York: Knopf, 1997), 249; *The Methodist Almanack for the Year of Our Lord 1861* (New York: Carlton and Porter, 1861), 26; C. C. Goen, *Broken Churches, Broken Nation* (Mercer, GA: Mercer University Press, 1985), 5, 71–75.

religious expressions of the abolitionists were a perversion of the pro-
prieties of worship?

They see the right clearly; they think others ought so to see it, and they
are disposed to establish a broad line of distinction between what is right,
and what is wrong. And they are not seldom willing to establish that line
upon their own convictions of truth and justice; and are ready to mark
and guard it, by placing along it a series of dogmas, as lines of boundary
on the earth's surface are marked by posts and stones. There are men who,
with clear perceptions, as they think, of their own duty, do not see how
too hot a pursuit of one duty may involve them in the violation of others,
or how too warm an embracement of one truth may lead to a disregard
of other truths equally important. As I heard it stated strongly, not many
days ago, these persons are disposed to mount upon some particular duty
as upon a war-horse, and to drive, furiously on and upon, and over, all
other duties that may stand in the way.

There are men who, in times of that sort, and in disputes of that sort,
are of opinion that human duties may be ascertained with the exactness
of mathematics. They deal with morals as with mathematics; and they
think what is right may be distinguished from what is wrong, with the
precision of an algebraic equation. They have, therefore, none too much
charity towards others who differ from them. They are apt, too, to think
that nothing is good but what is perfect, and that there are no compromises or modifications to be made in consideration of difference of opinion, or in deference to other men's judgment. If their perspicacious vision
enables them to detect a spot on the face of the sun, they think that a
good reason why the sun should be struck down from heaven. They prefer the chance of running into utter darkness, to living in heavenly light,
if that heavenly light be not absolutely without any imperfection.

There are impatient men; too impatient always to give heed to the
admonition of St. Paul, "that we are not to do evil that good may come";
too impatient to wait for the slow progress of moral causes in the
improvement of mankind. They do not remember that the doctrines and
the miracles of Jesus Christ have, in eighteen hundred years, converted
only a small portion of the human race; and among the nations that are
converted to Christianity, they forget how many vices and crimes, public
and private, still prevail, and that many of them, public crimes especially,

which are so clearly offenses against the Christian religion, pass without exciting particular indignation. Thus wars are waged, and unjust wars.

By this time, everyone knew who "these men" were—William Lloyd Garrison, Wendell Phillips, and the other "immediatist" abolitionists. Garrison warned, "The fire of God's indignation is kindling against us, and thick darkness covers the heavens, and the hour of retribution is at hand, but we are obstinate in our transgression, we refuse to repent." They demanded the end of slavery wherever it existed, not just the confinement of slavery to its present boundaries. In fact, they were a small minority of the abolitionist movement, were an even smaller segment of the Free Soil Party, and had little impact on the two major national parties. But that impact was growing, for the immediatist movement had captured public opinion in the North and raised great fear in the South.[20]

> I do not deny that there may be just wars. There certainly are; but it was the remark of an eminent person, not many years ago, on the other side of the Atlantic, that it was one of the greatest reproaches to human nature, that wars are sometimes just. The defence of nations sometimes causes a just war against the injustice of other nations.

Webster's first term as secretary of state (1841–1843) under presidents William Henry Harrison and John Tyler was a controversial one. He had succeeded in quieting the border conflict between the United States and Canada with the Webster-Ashburton Treaty of 1842, ending the Aroostook War on the Maine frontier and, on that basis, set the stage for ending the later quarrel over the Oregon Territory without bloodshed. He had avoided war when tempers might easily have led to war. The Mexican-American War, which he opposed, had cost him his beloved son. He did not see the heroism of war, although it might be necessary. When President Taylor died and Millard Fillmore reorganized the cabinet in June 1850, Webster was again named secretary of state. In the previous para-

---

20 William Lloyd Garrison, "Exposure of the American Colonization Society" (1832), in *Selections from the Writings and Speeches of William Lloyd Garrison* (Boston: R. F. Wallcott, 1852), 22. See, generally, Peter Charles Hoffer, *The Radical Advocacy of Wendell Phillips: Abolitionism, Democracy and Public Interest Law* (Kent, OH: Kent State University Press, 2024).

graph, he suggested that the most recent war, between the United States and Mexico, was one of defense, but it was still a reproach to human nature. The paragraph stood alone. He did not explore or explain what he meant, though contemporary observers would have understood it as another jab at Polk. He then turned back to the subject of his speech.

> Now, Sir, in this state of sentiment upon the general nature of slavery lies the cause of a great part of those unhappy divisions, exasperations, and reproaches, which find vent and support in different parts of the Union. Slavery does exist in the United States. It did exist in the States before the adoption of this Constitution, and at that time.
>
> And now let us consider, Sir, for a moment, what was the state of sentiment, North and South, in regard to slavery, at the time this Constitution was adopted. A remarkable change has taken place since; but what did the wise and great men of all parts of the country think of slavery, then? In what estimation did they hold it at the time when this Constitution was adopted? Now, it will be found, Sir, if we will carry ourselves by historical research back to that day, and ascertain men's opinions by authentic records still existing among us, that there was no great diversity of opinion between the North and South, upon the subject of slavery. And it will be found that both parts of the country held it equally an evil, a moral and political evil. It will not be found that, either at the North or at the South, there was much, though there was some, invective against slavery as inhuman and cruel.

Again, oversimplification and in many cases simply wrong. Many of the founding generation—John Adams, John Dickinson, Elbridge Gerry, John Jay, Gouverneur Morris, to name a few—held that slavery was wrong. But they acquiesced in the name of national unity in allowing slavery in parts of the Union where it already existed. After all, what was the alternative?[21]

> The great ground of objection to it was political; that it weakened the social fabric; that, taking the place of free labor, society became less strong

---

21 See, e.g., Sean Wilentz, *No Property in Man: Slavery and Anti-Slavery at the Nation's Founding* (Cambridge, MA: Harvard University Press, 2018).

and labor less productive; and, therefore, we find from all the eminent men of the time the clearest expression of their opinion that slavery is an evil. And they ascribed its existence here, not without truth, and not without some acerbity of temper and force of language, to the injurious policy of the mother country, who, to favor the navigator, had entailed these evils upon the Colonies. I need hardly refer, Sir, particularly to the publications of the day. They are matters of history on the record. The eminent men, the most eminent men, and nearly all the conspicuous politicians of the South, held the same sentiments; that slavery was an evil, a blight, a blast, a mildew, a scourge, and a curse. There are no terms of reprobation of slavery so vehement in the North at that day as in the South. The North was not so much excited against it as the South; and the reason is, I suppose, because there was much less of it at the North, and the people did not see, or think they saw, the evils so prominently as they were seen, or thought to be seen, at the South.

Here he is backpedaling a little because Webster knew that he had over-stated his case.

Then, Sir, when this Constitution was framed, this was the light in which the Convention viewed it. The Convention reflected the judgment and sentiments of the great men of the South. A member of the other House, whom I have not the honor to know, in a recent speech, has collected extracts from these public documents. They prove the truth of what I am saying, and the question then was, how to deal with it, and how to deal with it as an evil. Well, they came to this general result. They thought that slavery could not be continued in the country, if the importation of slaves were made to cease, and therefore they provided that after a certain period the importation might be prevented, by the act of the new government. Twenty years was proposed by some gentleman, a Northern gentleman, I think, and many of the Southern gentlemen opposed it as being too long. Mr. Madison, especially, was something warm against it. He said it would bring too much of this mischief into the country to allow the importation of slaves for such a period.

But Webster had to admit that the northern sentiment against the overseas slave trade, in 1787 carried on by the nations of Europe as well

as American ships, was widely shared. Virginia and other state delegation members agreed, although Georgia and South Carolina wanted the
ban imposed in 1808 rather than 1800. The northern gentleman, Gouverneur Morris of Pennsylvania, had wanted the word "slavery" included
in the ban, not to constitutionalize slavery but to acknowledge its evil.[22]

> Because we must take along with us, in the whole of this discussion, when
> we are considering the sentiments and opinions in which the constitu-
> tional provision originated, that the conviction of all men was, that if the
> importation of slaves ceased, the white race would multiply faster than
> the black race, and that slavery would therefore gradually wear out and
> expire. It may not be improper here to allude to that, I had almost said,
> celebrated opinion of Mr. Madison. You observe, Sir, that the term slave,
> or slavery, is not used in the Constitution. The Constitution does not re-
> quire that "fugitive slaves" shall be delivered up. It requires that "persons
> held to service in one State, and escaping into another, shall be delivered
> up." Mr. Madison opposed the introduction of the term; *slave*, or *slavery*,
> into the Constitution; for he said that he did not wish to see it recognized
> by the Constitution of the United States of America, that there could be
> property in men.

Like Clay and Calhoun, though a little more explicitly, Webster was
engaging in what is today called "originalism." By citing Madison by
name, no doubt with Madison's notes on the convention in hand, Webster was arguing that Madison's views were part of the Constitution, even
though, and even because, the word "slavery" was absent. The simplest
version of this is that the intentions of the framers themselves should
govern later interpretations. A later version was that the plain text of
the document, as understood at the time of its creation, should govern how subsequent generations understood the Constitution. Today,
law professors, political scientists, and historians hold varying positions
on whether these approaches to constitutional interpretation are even
workable. Originalism as a theory of constitutional interpretation was
easier for Webster and his generation than for its exponents in the twen-

---

22 Debate of August 21, 1787, in *The Records of the Federal Convention of 1787*, ed. Max Farrand
(New Haven, CT: Yale University Press, 1966), 2:364.

tieth and twenty-first centuries because they knew the framers, or at least used words in the same way as the framers' generation.[23]

> Now, Sir, all this took place at the Convention in 1787; but, connected with this, concurrent and contemporaneous, is another important transaction, not sufficiently attended to. The Convention for framing this Constitution assembled in Philadelphia in May, and sat until September, 1787. During all that time, the Congress of the United States was in session at New York. It was a matter of design, as we know, that the Convention should not assemble in the same city where Congress was holding its sessions. Almost all the public men of the country, therefore, of distinction and eminence, were in one or the other of these two assemblies; and I think it happened, in some instances, that the same gentlemen were members of both. If I mistake not, such was the case of Mr. Rufus King, then a member of Congress from Massachusetts, and at the same time a member of the Convention to frame the Constitution.

King, as it happened, was no friend to slavery, had a hand in excluding it from the Northwest Territory in 1787, and continued to oppose its extension in the Missouri controversy in 1819.[24]

> Now, it was in the summer of 1787, the very time when the Convention in Philadelphia was framing this Constitution, that the Congress in New York was framing the Ordinance of 1787. They passed that Ordinance on the 13th of July, 1787, at New York, the very month, perhaps the very day, on which these questions, about the importation of slaves and the character of slavery, were debated in the Convention at Philadelphia. And so far as we can now learn, there was a perfect concurrence of opinion between these respective bodies; and it resulted in this Ordinance of 1787, excluding slavery as to all the territory over which the Congress of the United States had jurisdiction, and that was, all the territory northwest of the Ohio.

---

23 Peter Charles Hoffer, *The Supreme Court Footnote: A Surprising History* (New York: New York University Press, 2024), 122–153.

24 Charles R. King, ed., *Life and Correspondence of Rufus King* (New York: Putnam, 1894), 1:129, 285; Rufus King, *Substance of Two Speeches in the Senate of the United States on the Missouri Bill* (New York: Kirk and Mercein, 1819), 17: "The term property, in its usual and common meaning, does not include slaves."

Given the opposition to the new federal Constitution in the Articles of Confederation Congress (the document was almost not sent to the states for ratification), Webster's version of events in New York City that fall seems a little misleading.[25]

> Three years before, Virginia and other States had made a cession of that great territory to the United States. And a most magnificent act it was. I never reflect upon it without a disposition to do honor and justice, and justice would be the highest honor, to Virginia, for the cession of her northwestern territory. I will say, Sir, it is one of her fairest claims to the respect and gratitude of the United States, and that, perhaps, it is only second to that other claim which attaches to her; that from her counsels, and from the intelligence and patriotism of her leading statesmen, proceeded the first idea put into practice of the formation of a general constitution of the United States.

Virginia was the most populous state at that time, the home of future presidents George Washington, Thomas Jefferson, James Madison, and James Monroe, and its leaders abjured slavery, while not all of them freeing their slaves. Washington provided for his slaves' freedom after the passing of his wife Martha. The Upper South's leaders expected slavery to die of its own accord, but that was before the cotton gin revolutionized short staple cotton commerce, and the Lower South need for slaves was supplied by the Upper South.[26]

> Now. Sir, the Ordinance of 1787 was applied thus to the whole territory over which the Congress of the United States had jurisdiction. It was adopted two years before the Constitution of the United States went into operation; because the Ordinance took effect immediately on its passage, while the Constitution of the United States, having been framed, was to be sent to the States to be adopted by their Conventions; and then a government was to be organized under it. This Ordinance, then, was

---

25 Pauline Maier, *Ratification: The People Debate the Constitution, 1787–1788* (New York: Simon & Schuster, 2010), 52–59.
26 Lacy K. Ford, *Deliver Us from Evil: The Slavery Question in the Upper South* (New York: Oxford University Press, 2009), 19–48.

in operation and force when the Constitution was adopted and the Government put in motion, in April, 1789.

Mr. President, three things are quite clear as historical truths. One is, that there was an expectation that, on the ceasing of the importation of slaves from Africa, slavery would begin to run out here. That was hoped and expected. Another is, that, as far as there was any power in Congress to prevent the spread of slavery in the United States, that power was executed in the most absolute manner, and to the fullest extent.[27]

The honorable member [Mr. Calhoun] said, the other day, that he considered this [Ordinance] as the first, in the series of measures, calculated to enfeeble the South, and deprive them of their just participation in the benefits and privileges of this government. He says, very properly, that it was enacted under the old Confederation and before this Constitution went into effect; but, my present purpose is only to say, Mr. President, that it was established with the entire and unanimous concurrence of the whole South. Why, there it stands!

The vote of every State in the Union was unanimous in favor of the Ordinance, with the exception of a single individual vote, and that individual vote was given by a Northern man. But, Sir, the Ordinance abolishing, or rather prohibiting, slavery northwest of the Ohio, has the hand and seal of every Southern member in Congress. So this ordinance was no aggression of the North on the South.

So, there was no evidence of aggression in the exclusion of slavery from the Northwest Territory.

The other and third clear historical truth is, that the Convention meant to leave slavery, in the States, as they found it, entirely under the authority and control of the States themselves.[28]

This was the state of things, Sir, and this the state of opinion, under which those very important matters were arranged, and those three important things done; that is, the establishment of the Constitution with

---

27 In the *Globe* appendix, the original added, "An honorable member whose health does not allow him to be here to-day." One of the members then spoke up, "He is here." And in fact Calhoun had attended that day. Webster continued, "I am very happy to hear that he is—may he long be in health and the enjoyment of it to serve his country."
28 A last sentence added in the published version.

a recognition of slavery as it existed in the States; the establishment of the ordinance prohibiting, to the full extent of all territory owned by the United States, the introduction of slavery into that territory, while leaving to the States all power over slavery in their own limits; and creating a power, in the new government, to put an end to the importation of slaves, after a limited period. And here, Sir, we may pause.[29]

Webster was defending the free states, in the process also defending his own position on the evils of slavery. He had extolled the virtues of free labor in his reply to Hayne, twenty years earlier. Now he was reprising it.

> We may reflect for a moment upon the entire coincidence and concurrence of sentiment, between the North and the South, upon all these questions, at the period of the adoption of the Constitution. But opinions, Sir, have changed, greatly changed, changed North, and changed South. Slavery is not regarded in the South now as it was then. . . . [Here Webster digressed to acknowledge the attention of Mr. Mason and paid a tribute to his distinguished grandfather.]

In fact, George Mason of Virginia owned many slaves and refused to sign the Constitution but was on record as despising slavery. In 1773 he wrote that slavery was "that slow Poison, which is daily contaminating the Minds & Morals of our People. Every Gentleman here [in Virginia] is born a petty Tyrant." Perhaps the tribute was a rebuke? In any case, that was then, and this was now. For the abolitionist movement was then but a single cloud on the horizon. Webster cast the change as one of opinion, not one of reform. For in the 1830s abolition was but one of a series of reform movements that had taken hold of the country, as in a ferment. Public education, the reform of prisons and asylums, the expansion of the franchise, temperance, a wide variety of utopian experiments in communal living and socialism, and the first stage of feminism had all made their appearance by 1850.[30]

---

29 Added to the published version.
30 George Mason, July 1773, extract from Virginia Charters, in *Papers of George Mason*, ed. Robert Allen Rutland (Chapel Hill: University of North Carolina Press, 1970), 173. On reform, see, e.g.,

Here we may pause. There was, if not an entire unanimity, a general concurrence of sentiment, running through the whole community, and especially entertained by the eminent men of all parts of the country. But soon
a change began, at the North and the South, and a severance of opinion
showed itself; the North growing much more warm and strong against slavery, and the South growing much more warm and strong in its support.
Sir, there is no generation of mankind whose opinions are not subject to
be influenced by what appear to them to be their present, emergent, and
exigent interests. I impute to the South no particularly selfish view in the
change which has come over her. I impute to her certainly no dishonest
view. All that has happened has been natural. It has followed those causes
which always influence the human mind and operate upon it.

Imputing nothing, but implying a great deal. Refusing to judge, but
the matter was not one of duplicity (or "dishonest") but a profound
change in southern opinion.

What, then, have been the causes which have created so new a feeling
in favor of slavery in the South, which have changed the whole nomenclature of the South on that subject, so that, from being thought and described in the terms I have mentioned and will not repeat, it has now
become an institution, a cherished institution in that quarter; no evil, no
scourge, but a great religious, social, and moral blessing, as I think I have
heard it latterly spoken of. I suppose this, Sir, is owing to the sudden uprising and rapid growth of the COTTON plantations of the South. So far
as any motive consistent with honor, justice, and general judgment could
act, it was the COTTON interest that gave a new desire to promote slavery, to spread it, and to use its labor. I again say that that was produced
by causes which we must always expect to produce like effects; the whole
interest of the South became connected, more or less, with it.

The worm in the bud was now revealed: it was "interest," in particular the rise of the cotton empire. (For Webster "interest," that is, self-
interest, was what partisanship was to Clay—his own as well as others'

Alice Felt Tyler, *Freedom's Ferment: Phases of American Social History to 1860* (Minneapolis:
University of Minnesota Press, 1944).

sin.) It was a cause whose effect was inevitable and irreversible. Again, that change was in the South, not the North, ignoring the dependence of northern textile interests on southern cotton production. Webster found that honor, justice, and general judgment had given way to the cotton interest. What had, in his previous account, been a difference of opinion, easily reversible, had now become an engine that could not be stopped. Economic self-interest drove opinion.

If we look back to the history of the commerce of this country at the early years of this government, what were our exports? Cotton was hardly, or but to a very limited extent, known. The tables will show that the exports of cotton for the years 1790 and 1791 were not more than forty or fifty thousand dollars a year. It has gone on increasing rapidly, until it may now, perhaps, in a season of great product and high prices, amount to a hundred millions of dollars. In the years I have mentioned, there was more of wax, more of indigo, more of rice, more of almost every article of export from the South, than of cotton. I think it is true when Mr. Jay negotiated the treaty of 1794 with England, that he did not know that cotton was exported at all from the United States; and I have heard it said, also, that the custom-house in London refused to admit cotton, upon an allegation that it could not be an American production, there being, as they supposed, no cotton raised in America. They could hardly think so now!

The rise of the cotton empire was coincident with the rise of the idea that slavery was a benevolent institution, good for the slave, good for the master, and good for the country. For cotton exports remade the map of slavery.[31]

Well, Sir, we know what followed. The age of cotton became the golden age of our Southern brethren. It gratified their desire for improvement and accumulation, at the same time that it excited it. The desire grew by what it fed upon, and there soon came to be an eagerness for other territory, a new area or new areas, for the cultivation of the cotton crop; and measures leading to this result were brought about rapidly, one after

---

31 Eric L. McKitrick, "The Defense of Slavery," in *Slavery Defended: The Views of the Old South*, ed. McKitrick (Englewood Cliffs, NJ: Prentice Hall, 1963), 1–5.

another, under the lead of Southern men at the head of the Government, they having a majority in both branches to accomplish their ends.

Cotton was not a crop friendly to the soil. It exhausted the nutrients in old fields. And so the cotton empire, like all empires, had to expand, conquer, or die. And with the acquisition of more fields would go the expansion of slave field labor.[32]

The honorable member from South Carolina observed that there has been a majority all along in favor of the North. If that be true, Sir, the North has acted either very liberally and kindly, or very weakly; for they never exercised that majority efficiently five times in the history of the Government, when a division, or trial of strength, arose. Never. Whether they were out-generaled, or whether it was owing to other causes, I shall not stop to consider; but no man acquainted with the history of the country can deny, that the general lead in the politics of the country, for three fourths of the period that has elapsed since the adoption of the Constitution, has been a Southern lead.

Back to politics—and the assertion that national politics favored the slave interest. One wonders whether Webster had become so enmeshed in his account that he forgot his original purpose—to save the Union. His narrative of the rise of the cotton empire was one step short of an assault. Still, no mention of northeastern textile manufacturing, supplying North and South with clothing, and abetting the cotton empire, and no mention of how finances of both regions were entangled with cotton prices (or how he represented the manufacturers in court).[33]

In 1802, in pursuit of the idea of opening a new cotton region, the United States obtained a cession from Georgia of the whole of her western territory, now embracing the rich and growing State of Alabama. In 1803, Louisiana was purchased from France, out of which the States of Loui-

---

32 Sven Beckert, *Empire of Cotton: A Global History* (New York: Knopf, 2014), 103.
33 Edward Baptist, *The Half Has Never Been Told: Slavery and the Making of American Capitalism* (New York: Basic Books, 2014), 312; Joshua D. Rothman, "The Contours of Cotton Capitalism: Speculation, Slavery, and Economic Panic," in *Slavery's Capitalism: A New History of American Economic Development*, ed. Sven Beckert and Seth Rockman (Philadelphia: University of Pennsylvania Press, 2016), 122–143.

siana, Arkansas, and Missouri, have been framed, as slaveholding States. In 1819 the cession of Florida was made, bringing in another region of slaveholding property and territory.

More territory for slavery at the behest of the slave interest in the federal government, and surely nothing for Calhoun to complain about, as Webster tore apart Calhoun's argument:

> Sir, the honorable member from South Carolina thought he saw in certain operations of the Government, such as the manner of collecting the revenue, and the tendency of measures calculated to promote emigration into the country, what accounts for the more rapid growth of the North than the South. He thinks they were not the operation of time, but to the system of government, and administration, established under this Constitution. That is matter of opinion.

The "manner of collecting the revenue" meant not the customs duties but the tariff, a rather nasty nod in the direction of Calhoun's part in the Nullification Crisis. But the growing power of the North was not some conspiracy among federal officials against the South as Calhoun then implied, but the natural effect of the immigration to the North of hundreds of thousands of Irish, Germans, and Scandinavians. They did not go to the South because the immigrants, like the free people already living in the North, did not want to compete with slaves. Did Calhoun want to reopen the overseas slave trade, to fill the South with more Africans?[34]

> To a certain extent it may be true; but it does seem to me that if any operation of the Government could be shown in any degree to have promoted the population, and growth, and wealth of the North, it is much more sure that there are sundry important and distinct operations of the Government, about which no man can doubt, tending to promote, and which absolutely have promoted, the increase of the slave interest and

---

34 That movement would come later in the 1850s. See, e.g., Ronald Takaki, "The Movement to Reopen the African Slave Trade in South Carolina," *South Carolina Historical Magazine* 66 (1965): 36–54; James Paisley Hendrix Jr., "The Efforts to Reopen the African Slave Trade in Louisiana" (thesis, Louisiana State University, 1968), https://repository.lsu.edu/gradschool_disstheses/8262.

the slave territory of the South. Allow me to say that it was not time that brought in Louisiana; it was the act of men. It was not time that brought in Florida; it was the act of men. And lastly, Sir, to complete these acts of men which have contributed so much to enlarge the area and the sphere of the institution of slavery, Texas, great and vast and illimitable Texas, was added to the Union as a slave State in 1845; and that, Sir, pretty much closed the whole chapter, and settled the whole account.

Concluding the section of his talk that the federal government had favored the interests of the South:

That closed the whole chapter, that settled the whole account, because the annexation of Texas, upon the conditions and under the guaranties upon which she was admitted, did not leave within the control of this Government an acre of land, capable of being cultivated by slave labor, between this Capitol and the Rio Grande or the Nueces, or whatever is the proper boundary of Texas, not an acre. From that moment, the whole country, from this place to the western boundary of Texas, was fixed, pledged, fastened, decided, to be slave territory forever, by the solemn guaranties of law. And I now say, Sir, as the proposition upon which I stand this day, and upon the truth and firmness of which I intend to act until it is overthrown, that there is not at this moment within the United States, or any territory of the United States, a single foot of land, the character of which, in regard to its being free-soil territory or slave territory, is not fixed by some law, and some irrepealable law, beyond the power of the action of the Government. Now, is it not so with respect to Texas? Why it is most manifestly so.

Law, not political interests, settled the question—a statement that reflected Webster's term as secretary of state. Treaties established boundaries, and according to the Constitution treaties were law. Texas's annexation was a treaty, between Texas and the United States. It was that simple.[35]

---

35 Or not. Actually, the status of treaties, in particular who could make them and who could break them, remains contested. See, e.g., Zechariah Chafee, "Amending the Constitution to Cripple Treaties," *Louisiana Law Review* 12 (1952): 345–382; Detlev Vagts, "The United States and Its Treaties: Observance and Breach," *American Journal of International Law* 95 (2001): 313–334.

The honorable member from South Carolina, at the time of the admission of Texas, held an important post in the Executive Department of the Government; he was Secretary of State. Another eminent person of great activity and adroitness in affairs, I mean the late Secretary of the Treasury [Mr. Walker], was a conspicuous member of this body, and took the lead in the business of annexation, in cooperation with the Secretary of State; and I must say that they did their business faithfully and thoroughly; there was no botch in it. They rounded it off, and made as close joiner-work as ever was exhibited. Resolutions of annexation were brought into Congress, fitly joined together, compact, firm, efficient, conclusive upon the great object which they had in view, and those resolutions passed.

In short, Calhoun should recognize that there was no wiggle room in the boundary of Texas.

Webster continued, "Allow me to read a part of these resolutions. It is the third clause of the second section of the resolution of the 1st of March, 1845, for the admission of Texas, which applies to this part of the case. That clause reads in these words:"

"New States, of convenient size, not exceeding four in number, in addition to said State of Texas, and having sufficient population, may hereafter, by the consent of said State, be formed out of the territory thereof, which shall be entitled to admission under the provisions of the Federal Constitution. And such States as may be formed out of that portion of said territory lying south of thirty-six degrees thirty minutes north latitude, commonly known as the Missouri Compromise line, shall be admitted into the Union with or without slavery, as the people of each State asking admission may desire; and in such State or States as shall be formed out of said territory north of said Missouri Compromise line, slavery or involuntary servitude (except for crime) shall be prohibited."

Now, what is here stipulated, enacted, and secured? It is, that all Texas south of 36° 30', which is nearly the whole of it, shall be admitted into the Union as a slave State. It was a slave State, and therefore came in as a slave State; and the guaranty is, that new States shall be made out of it, to the number of four, in addition to the State then in existence and admitted at that time by these resolutions, and that such States as are formed out of that portion of Texas lying south of 36° 30', may come in as slave States. I

know no form of legislation which can strengthen this. I know no mode
of recognition that can add a tittle [as in a jot and a tittle] of weight to it.

Making assurance doubly sure, again a characteristic of diplomatic
negotiations. One can see Webster settling the Maine boundary with
Lord Ashburton. Webster had turned the Senate floor into a room in
the State Department. But can Texas create new states out of its (yet
undetermined) western and northern borders? If so, was Webster willing to let that happen? As Texas was already a state and the Constitution
provided that no state could sever a part of itself, much less make that
part into a new state, without the permission of all the other states, this
was an impossibility. Texas could not do it. But Congress could with the
territories.

> I listened respectfully to the resolutions of my honorable friend from Ten-
> nessee [Mr. Bell]. He proposed to recognize that stipulation with Texas.
> But any additional recognition would weaken the force of it; because it
> stands here on the ground of a contract, a thing done for a consideration.
> It is a law founded on a contract with Texas, and designed to carry that
> contract into effect. A recognition, now, founded not on any consider-
> ation or any contract, would not be so strong as it now stands on the face
> of the resolution.

The analogy was to a civil contract—the presumption was that Texas,
seeking to enter the Union, had made the offer, and Congress had accepted it. Before he was secretary of state, Webster had had a thriving
legal practice, a large part of which involved contracts. Some of these
cases entailed public corporate contracts, that is, monopolies. But also a
reference to the Constitution itself, as a contract that was binding. Webster's powers of argument, by implication and aside, by analogy and stipulation, were in full display here. But had Congress actually contracted
with Texas to form new states out of territory not yet extracted from
Mexico? After all, the war with Mexico had not yet even begun when the
treaty of annexation was approved.

> Now, I know no way, I candidly confess, in which this government, acting
> in good faith, as I trust it always will, can relieve itself from that stipula-

tion and pledge, by any honest course of legislation whatever. And therefore I say again, that, so far as Texas is concerned, in the whole of that
State south of 36° 30', which, I suppose, embraces all the territory capable
of slave cultivation, there is no land, not an acre, the character of which is
not established by law; a law which cannot be repealed without the violation of a contract.[36]

And he throws in a good faith argument, a concept from the equity
side of the docket. One had to act in good faith to the other party (also
known as the "clean hands doctrine") for the court to hear one's suit. It
certainly looks like Webster is conceding to the South a lot more than
Clay had, and one wonders if Webster still had hopes that with southern
support he could become the nation's chief executive.

I hope, Sir, it is now apparent that my proposition, so far as it respects
Texas, has been maintained, and that the provision in this article is clear
and absolute; and it has been well suggested by my friend from Rhode
Island, that that part of Texas which lies north of 36° 30' of north latitude
and which may be formed into free States. This is dependent, in like manner, upon the consent of Texas, herself a slave State.

Webster's approach was now clear. It was a legal brief, argued before
the court of the Senate. It likened the Senate to the English House of
Lords, the highest court in that land. In a legal brief, one dealt with arguments one by one, stuck to the facts of the case, and when finished with
one point, went on to the next. Of course the Senate was not a court, but
habits from a lifetime of arguing in courts shaped Webster's style.

Now, Sir, how came this? How came it to pass that within these walls,
where it is said by the honorable member from South Carolina that the
free States have always had a majority, this resolution of annexation, such
as I have described it, obtained a majority in both houses of Congress? Sir,
it obtained that majority by the great number of Northern votes added
to the entire Southern vote, or at least nearly the whole of the Southern
votes. The aggregate was made up of Northern and Southern votes. In the

---

36 Added to the published version "and plain disregard of the public faith."

House of Representatives it stood, I think, about eighty Southern votes
for the admission of Texas, and about fifty Northern votes for the admission of Texas. In the Senate the vote stood for the admission of Texas
twenty-seven, and twenty-five against it; and of those twenty-seven votes,
constituting the majority, no less than thirteen came from the free States,
and four of them were from New England. The whole of these thirteen
Senators, constituting within a fraction, you see, one half of all the votes
in this body for the admission of this immeasurable extent of slave territory, were sent here by free States.

One won one's case in a lawsuit by mastering the details of the litigation. Webster was showing his mastery of those details.

Sir, there is not so remarkable a chapter in our history of political events,
political parties, and political men, as is afforded by this admission of a
new slave-holding territory, so vast that a bird cannot fly over it in a week.
[Laughter.] New England, as I have said, with some of her own votes,
supported this measure. Three fourths of the votes of the liberty-loving
Connecticut were given for it in the other house, and one half here. There
was one vote for it from Maine, but I am happy to say not the vote of the
honorable member who addressed the Senate the day before yesterday
(Mr. Hamlin), and who was then a Representative from Maine in the
House of Representatives: but there was a vote or two from Maine, aye,
and there was one vote for it from Massachusetts, given by a gentleman
then representing, and now living in, the district in which the prevalence
of Free Soil [the idea, not the political party] sentiment for a couple of
years or so has defeated the choice of any member to represent it in Congress. Sir, that body of Northern and Eastern men who gave those votes
at that time are now seen taking upon themselves, in the nomenclature of
politics, the appellation of the Northern Democracy. They undertook to
wield the destinies of this empire and their policy was, and they persisted
in it, to bring into this country and under this government all the territory they could. They did it, in the case of Texas, under pledges, absolute
pledges, to the slave interests, and they afterwards lent their aid in bringing in these new conquests, to take their chances for slavery or freedom.[37]

---

37 In the *Globe* appendix, "if I may call a republic an empire."

Webster was a Whig and could not resist the chance to label the northern Democrats as traitors to the section. Webster had in days past argued against cheap land prices for western settlement, one of the major policies of the Democratic Party. Here he attached their "Manifest Destiny" plan of expansion to the Pacific to the expansion of slavery, wherein the Republic became an empire. Republics were good, empires were bad.

My honorable friend from Georgia, in March, 1847, moved the Senate to declare that the war ought not to be prosecuted for the dismemberment of Mexico. The whole of the Northern Democracy voted against it. He did not get a vote from them. It suited the patriotic and elevated sentiments of the Northern Democracy to bring in a world from among the mountains and valleys of California and New Mexico, or any other part of Mexico, and then quarrel about it; to bring it in, and then endeavor to put upon it the saving grace of the Wilmot Proviso.[38]

Webster's oratory often involved snide attacks, innuendos, and insults, which he veiled in satirical language and mocking gestures. He raised his voice, or lowered it, when he engaged in these, all added to dramatic effect. The oration thus became a theatrical performance. Here "patriotic and elevated sentiments" was exactly the reverse. His listeners (except those he pilloried) loved the show.

There were two eminent and highly respectable gentlemen from the North and East, then leading gentlemen in the Senate—I refer, and I do so with entire respect, for I entertain for both of those gentlemen, in general, high regard to Mr. [John] Dix of New York and Mr. [John Milton] Niles of Connecticut—who both voted for the admission of Texas. They would not have that vote any other way than as it stood; and they would have it as it did stand. I speak of the vote upon the annexation of Texas.

Dix was a Democrat, voted for the annexation of Texas, and lost his seat in 1849 to Whig William Henry Seward. John Milton Niles was an-

---

38 A reference to John M. Berrien, a Georgia Whig, who believed that slavery, though not mentioned in it, was a founding principle of the Constitution. Nevertheless, he opposed the war with Mexico. Royce C. McCrary, "Georgia Politics and the Mexican War," *Georgia Historical Quarterly* 60 (1976): 211–227.

other Democrat, from Connecticut. He declined to run for reelection in 1849.

> Those two gentlemen would have the resolution of annexation just as it is, without amendment; and they voted for it just as it is, and their eyes were all open to its true character. The honorable member from South Carolina [Calhoun] who addressed us the other day was then Secretary of State. His correspondence with Mr. [William] Murphy, the Charge d'Affaires of the United States in Texas, had been published. That correspondence was all before those gentlemen, and the Secretary had the boldness and candor to avow in that correspondence, that the great object sought by the annexation of Texas was to strengthen the slave interest of the South. Why, Sir, he said so in so many words.

Calhoun, back in his seat to hear Webster, was not too weak or too distracted by pain to demand a chance to defend himself and his conduct as secretary of state from 1844 to 1845.

> CALHOUN: Will the honorable Senator permit me to interrupt him for a moment?
> [WEBSTER]: Certainly.
> CALHOUN: I am very reluctant to interrupt the honorable gentleman; but, upon a point of so much importance, I deem it right to put myself "rectus in curia" [set the record straight]. I did not put it upon the ground assumed by the Senator. I put it upon this ground: that Great Britain had announced to this country, in so many words, that her object was to abolish slavery in Texas, and, through Texas, to accomplish the abolition of slavery in the United States and the world. The ground I put it on was, that it would make an exposed frontier, and, if Great Britain succeeded in her object, it would be impossible that that frontier could be secured against the aggressions of the Abolitionists; and that this government was bound, under the guaranties of the Constitution, to protect us against such a state of things.

Seriously? Had Britain such an aim, it would have surprised Webster, for he and the British ambassador had just concluded a border treaty that had no such clause. So he replied to Calhoun,

That comes, I suppose, Sir, to exactly the same thing. It was, that Texas must be obtained for the security of the slave interest of the South.
CALHOUN: Another view is very distinctly given.

Webster had seen the correspondence in the State Department, where he served, and he was not going to allow Calhoun to claim authority based on the latter's term as secretary of state following Webster. This was high drama, two former secretaries of state revealing to the public correspondence that should have been kept secret.

> WEBSTER: That was the object set forth in the correspondence of a worthy gentleman not now living, who preceded the honorable member from South Carolina in the Department of State. There repose on the files of the Department, as I have occasion to know, strong letters from Mr. Upshur [Abel P. Upshur, secretary of state from 1843 to 1844] to the United States minister in England, and I believe there are some to the same minister from the honorable Senator himself, asserting to this effect the sentiments of this government; namely, that Great Britain was expected not to interfere to take Texas out of the hands of its then existing government and make it a free country.

The last thrust home: Webster saying that he saw the evidence, the Calhoun letters. How? Calhoun served after Webster and Upshur. Diplomatic correspondence was a state secret. But these letters, as Webster said, were made public during the Texas annexation debate in Congress.

> But my argument, my suggestion, is this; that those gentlemen who composed the Northern Democracy when Texas was brought into the Union saw clearly that it was brought in as a slave country, and brought in for the purpose of being maintained as slave territory, to the Greek Kalends.[39]
> I rather think the honorable gentleman who was then Secretary of State might, in some of his correspondence with Mr. Murphy, have suggested that it was not expedient to say too much about this object,

---

39 Greek Kalends: forever, or a time that would never arrive; a Roman slur on the Greeks never paying their debts. Webster is showing off again.

lest it should create some alarm. At any rate, Mr. Murphy wrote to him that England was anxious to get rid of the constitution of Texas, because it was a constitution establishing slavery; and that what the United States had to do was to aid the people of Texas in upholding their constitution; but that nothing should be said which should offend the fanatical men of the North. But, Sir, the honorable member did avow this object himself, openly, boldly, and manfully; he did not disguise his conduct or his motives.

The honorable gentleman being Calhoun. Instead of saying plainly that Calhoun's letters proved his point, Webster praised Calhoun's conduct (though not his opinions) as open, bold, and manly. How could Calhoun object to that?

[CALHOUN: Never, never.]
WEBSTER: What he means he is very apt to say.
[CALHOUN: Always, always.]
WEBSTER: And I honor him for it.
    This admission of Texas was in 1845. Then, in 1847 "*flagrante bello*" [during the war] between the United States and Mexico, the proposition I have mentioned was brought forward by my friend from Georgia, and the Northern Democracy voted steadily against it. Their remedy was to apply to the acquisitions, after they should come in, the Wilmot Proviso. What follows? These two gentlemen, worthy and honorable and influential men, and if they had not been they could not have carried the measure, these two gentlemen, members of this body, brought in Texas, and by their votes they also prevented the passage of the resolution of the honorable member from Georgia, and then they went home and took the lead in the Free Soil party. And there they stand, Sir!

Calhoun quieted, Webster returned to his attack on the northern Democrats who voted for annexation.

They leave us here, bound in honor and conscience by the resolutions of annexation; they leave us here, to take the odium of fulfilling the obligations in favor of slavery which they voted us into, or else the greater odium of violating those obligations, while they are at home making capital and rousing speeches for free soil and no slavery. And therefore I say, Sir, that there is not a chapter in our history, respecting public measures and public men, more full of what would create surprise, more full of what does create, in my mind, extreme mortification, than that of the conduct of the Northern Democracy on this subject.

The northern Democrats were two-faced, according to Webster, at home arguing for free soil and in Congress voting for the extension of slavery. Webster was mortified by such duplicity, none of it cloaked in manful boldness. Who were the targets? Plainly Lewis Cass and Stephen Douglas. Why did they act in this fashion? Presumably to win support in the North and the South for their presidential bids.

Mr. President, sometimes, when a man is found in a new relation to things around him and to other men, he says the world has changed, and that he has not changed. I believe, Sir, that our self-respect leads us often to make this declaration in regard to ourselves when it is not exactly true. An individual is more apt to change, perhaps, than all the world around him. But, under the present circumstances, and under the responsibility which I know I incur by what I am now stating here, I feel at liberty to recur to the various expressions and statements, made at various times, of my own opinions and resolutions respecting the admission of Texas, and all that has followed.

Webster, however, had changed his opinion on the same issue and had to exculpate himself. Like some black hole, his speech pulled into itself bits of personal politics, history, law, and moralizing. He had prepared notes but did not read from a text. Instead, he extemporized. People in the room knew to whom and what he referred, but listening to him today, it is much harder to know exactly where he was going. Fortunately, sometimes he tells us.

Sir, as early as 1836, or in the early part of 1837, there was conversation and correspondence between myself and some private friends on this project of annexing Texas to the United States; and an honorable gentleman with whom I have had a long acquaintance, a friend of mine, now perhaps in this chamber, I mean General [James] Hamilton, of South Carolina, was privy to that correspondence.

There is another story here, only part of which Webster shared. The letters were private, perhaps when Webster was still thinking about running for the presidency, and reassuring potential southern supporters that he would not block the annexation of Texas. Saying that the letters were "private" meant that they were not intended as campaign fodder. Saying that Hamilton, who was a "friend" and an "honorable gentleman," did not excuse him from revealing to the public correspondence to which he was "privy." Hamilton was something of a conniver and operator himself, and had allied himself with Webster on a number of occasions.[40]

I had voted for the recognition of Texan independence, because I believed it to be an existing fact, surprising and astonishing as it was, and I wished well to the new republic; but I manifested from the first utter opposition to bringing her, with her slave territory, into the Union. I happened, in 1837, to make a public address to political friends in New York, and I then stated my sentiments upon the subject. It was the first time that I had occasion to advert to it; and I will ask a friend near me to have the kindness to read an extract from the speech made by me on that occasion. It was delivered in Niblo's Garden, in 1837.

Mr. Greene read this extract from the speech to which Senator Webster referred:[41]

"Gentlemen, we all see that, by whomsoever possessed, Texas is likely to be a slave-holding country; and I frankly avow my entire unwillingness to do any thing which shall extend the slavery of the African race on this continent, or add other slave-holding States to the Union.

---

40 James Hamilton Jr. of South Carolina was a former governor of the state during the Nullification Crisis and the mayor of Charleston during the Denmark Vesey conspiracy. He had loaned money to Texas and was its agent during the annexation proceedings. Robert Tinkler, *James Hamilton of South Carolina* (Baton Rouge: Louisiana State University Press, 2004), 181, 239.
41 Albert C. Greene was a Whig senator from Rhode Island and an ally of Webster's. Webster had asked Greene to read, just as Clay had asked Underwood to read and Calhoun had asked Mason to read. Having another read a portion or all of a speech was a gesture of trust and friendship. It also gave Webster a chance to rest his voice.

"When I say that I regard slavery in itself as a great moral, social, and political evil, I only use language which has been adopted by distinguished men, themselves citizens of slave-holding States.

"I shall do nothing, therefore, to favor or encourage its further extension. We have slavery already amongst us. The Constitution found it in the Union; it recognized it, and gave it solemn guaranties.

"To the full extent of those guaranties we are all bound, in honor, in justice, and by the Constitution. All the stipulations contained in the Constitution in favor of the slave-holding States which are already in the Union ought to be fulfilled, and, so far as depends on me, shall be fulfilled, in the fullness of their spirit, and beyond the reach of Congress. It is a concern of the States themselves; they have never submitted it to Congress, and Congress has no rightful power over it.

"I shall concur, therefore, in no act, no measure, no menace, no indication of purpose, which shall interfere or threaten to interfere with the exclusive authority of the several States over the subject of slavery as it exists within their respective limits. All this appears to me to be matter of plain and imperative duty.

"But when we come to speak of admitting new States, the subject assumes an entirely different aspect. Our rights and our duties are then both different. . . .

"I see, therefore, no political necessity for the annexation of Texas to the Union; no advantage to be derived from it; and objections to it of a strong, and, in my judgment, decisive character."

[WEBSTER]: I have nothing, Sir, to add to, or to take from, those sentiments. That speech, the Senate will perceive, was made in 1837. The purpose of immediately annexing Texas at that time was abandoned or postponed; and it was not revived with any vigor for some years. In the meantime it happened that I had become a member of the executive administration, and was for a short period in the Department of State. The annexation of Texas was a subject of conversation, not confidential, with the President and heads of departments, as well as with other public men. No serious attempt was then made, however, to bring it about. I left the Department of State in May, 1843, and shortly after I learned, though by means which were no way connected with official information, that a design had been taken up of bringing Texas, with her slave territory and population, into this Union.

Webster was not confessing or conceding anything. Instead, he was acting as a lawyer defending a client (Webster himself) in the court of public opinion. He produced evidence of where he was and what he did. Thus he made clear that he was not revealing any state secret—his means being "in no way connected with official information." When the annexation question was revisited, he still opposed it.

> I was in Washington at the time, and persons are now here who will re-member that we had an arranged meeting for conversation upon it. I went home to Massachusetts and proclaimed the existence of that pur-pose, but I could get no audience and but little attention. Some did not believe it, and some were too much engaged in their own pursuits to give it any heed. They had gone to their farms or to their merchandise, and it was impossible to arouse any feeling in New England, or in Massa-chusetts, that should combine the two great political parties against this annexation; and, indeed, there was no hope of bringing the Northern Democracy into that view, for their leaning was all the other way. But, Sir, even with Whigs, and leading Whigs, I am ashamed to say, there was a great indifference towards the admission of Texas, with slave territory, into this Union.
>
> The project went on. I was then out of Congress. The annexation reso-lutions passed on the 1st of March, 1845; the legislature of Texas complied with the conditions and accepted the guaranties; for the language of the resolution is, that Texas is to come in "upon the conditions and under the guaranties herein prescribed." I was returned to the Senate in March, 1845, and was here in December following, when the acceptance by Texas of the conditions proposed by Congress was communicated to us by the President, and an act for the consummation of the union was laid before the two houses. The connection was then not completed. A final law, doing the deed of annexation ultimately, had not been passed; and when it was put upon its final passage here, I expressed my opposition to it, and recorded my vote in the negative; and there that vote stands, with the observations that I made upon that occasion.

Bold and manful, if a little more detail than required, the defense ended, the client was exonerated. This portion of the speech had shifted from support of Clay to a defense of Webster's own conduct. He obviously intended this from the start, having given to Senator Greene the pieces of his earlier speeches and asked Greene to be prepared to read them—again, just as a lawyer would.

> It has happened that, between 1837 and this time, on various occasions, I have expressed my entire opposition to the admission of slave States, or the acquisition of new slave territories, to be added to the United States. I know, Sir, no change in my own sentiments, or my own purposes, in that respect. I will now ask my friend from Rhode Island to read another extract from a speech of mine made at a Whig Convention in Springfield, Massachusetts, in the month of September, 1847.

Webster, like Clay but unlike Calhoun, had been flexible over the years, but now, in the closing days of his career, Webster wanted to show his steadfastness to principle: "no change in my own sentiment, or my own purposes." Webster's speeches were invariably printed, and thus the evidence of his changing views on this occasion was incontrovertible. In a superb attempt at distraction, he had given Greene the portion of the print version to read to show his earlier antislavery views, hopefully to avert attention from his present stance.

> [MR. GREENE]: "We hear much just now of a 'panacea' for the dangers and evils of slavery and slave annexation, which they call the 'Wilmot Proviso.' That certainly is a just sentiment, but it is not a sentiment to found any new party upon. It is not a sentiment on which Massachusetts Whigs differ. There is not a man in this hall who holds to it more firmly than I do, nor one who adheres to it more than another.
> I feel some little interest in this matter, Sir. Did not I commit myself in 1837 to the whole doctrine, fully, entirely? And I must be permitted to say that I cannot quite consent that more recent discoverers should claim the merit and take out a patent.
> I deny the priority of their invention. Allow me to say, Sir, it is not their thunder.
> We are to use the first and last and every occasion which offers to oppose the extension of slave power.

But I speak of it here, as in Congress, as a political question, a question for statesmen to act upon. We must so regard it. I certainly do not mean to say that it is less important in a moral point of view, that it is not more important in many other points of view; but as a legislator, or in any official capacity, I must look at it, consider it, and decide it as a matter of political action."

[WEBSTER]: On other occasions, in debates here, I have expressed my determination to vote for no acquisition, or cession, or annexation, north or south, east or west. My opinion has been, that we have territory enough, and that we should follow the Spartan maxim, "Improve, adorn what you have," seek no further. I think it was in some observations that I made on the three-million loan bill that I avowed this sentiment. In short, Sir, it has been avowed quite as often, in as many places, and before as many assemblies, as any humble opinions of mine ought to be avowed.

Ever the New Englander, concerned about the dilution of strength in Congress of the New England delegation, Webster had consistently resisted the acquisition of new lands. He was a supporter of internal improvements, however.

But now that, under certain conditions, Texas is in the Union, with all her territory, as a slave State, with a solemn pledge, also, that, if she shall be divided into many States, those States may come in as slave States south of 36° 30', how are we to deal with this subject? I know no way of honest legislation, when the proper time comes for the enactment, but to carry into effect all that we have stipulated to do.

Necessity had required Webster to acquiesce. Necessity was a defense against a suit for breach of contract. Here the breach was Webster going back on his word.

I do not entirely agree with my honorable friend from Tennessee [Mr. Bell], that, as soon as the time comes when she is entitled to another representative, we should create a new State. On former occasions, in creating new States out of Territories, we have generally gone upon the idea that, when the population of the territory amounts to about sixty thousand, we would consent to its admission as a State. But it is quite a different thing when a State is divided, and two or more States made out of it. It does not follow in such a case that the same rule of apportionment should be applied. That, however, is a matter for the consideration of Congress, when the proper time arrives.

John Bell of Tennessee was a lawyer and at first a supporter of Andrew Jackson. He later broke with the president and became a Whig politician. He owned slaves, but consistently opposed the expansion of slavery. He would have allowed California to enter, and Texas to be split into three states, two of which, to keep the balance in the Senate, would be slave states. It was this plan to which Webster referred.[42]

I may not then be here; I may have no vote to give on the occasion; but I wish it to be distinctly understood, that, according to my view of the matter, this government is solemnly pledged, by law and contract, to create new States out of Texas, with her consent, when such States are formed out of Texan territory lying south of 36° 30', to let them come in as slave States. That is the meaning of the resolution which our friends, the Northern Democracy, have left us to fulfill; and I, for one, mean to fulfill it, because I will not violate the faith of the Government.

Another reference to Webster's advanced age: "I may not then be here." But he was not "distinct" at all, and Webster immediately clarified his position.

What I mean to say is, that the time for the admission of new States formed out of Texas, the number of such States, their boundaries, the requisite amount of population, and all other things connected with the admission, are in the free discretion of Congress except this; to wit, that, when new States formed out of Texas are to be admitted, they have a right, by legal stipulation and contract, to come in as slave States.[43]

---

42 Joseph H. Parks, "John Bell and the Compromise of 1850," *Journal of Southern History* 9 (1943): 328–356. Again, was Webster agreeing to the plan or merely referring to it? Not clear.

43 None of the final phrase appeared in the original, in the *Globe*. Webster was again giving more to the South than he had, although other alterations in the printed version actually took away from this gift. Webster was trying to please two masters—northern free soil opinion and southern leadership.

Congress, when a state applies, has the power to define its boundaries, requisite amount of population, and other things. Henry Clay gave Congress no such discretion. Was Webster opening the door to Congress considering itself free to shift the borders of California—perhaps keeping everything south of 36° 30' as a territory, and a potential slave territory? But he did not favor the admission of slave states, so how was this consistent? Better to move on to portions of the newly acquired territory that were not parts of Texas. Lawyers are debaters, and the other side in litigation must be out debated when both sides present oral argument in court. Shifting the focus of the argument is a common debate tactic, but not so effective in a court of law. Which was Congress?

> Now, as to California and New Mexico, I hold slavery to be excluded from these territories by a law even superior to that which admits and sanctions it in Texas. I mean the law of nature, of physical geography, the law of the formation of the earth. That law settles for ever, with a strength beyond all terms of human enactment, that slavery cannot exist in California or New Mexico. Understand me, Sir; I mean slavery as we regard it; slaves in gross, of the colored race, transferable by sale and delivery, like other property.

Historians have not noticed that it was first Webster, rather than New York senator William Henry Seward, who rested his argument against slavery on a superior law to any made in Congress. This higher law was the law of nature, a law that "settled forever" the exclusion of slavery from California and New Mexico (including Arizona, Colorado, and Utah). Slavery could not exist in the Southwest, rather than slaves could be brought into the region, because the law of nature forbade it. Was Webster speaking of climate? He did not say so. He also omitted here the issue with Mexican law that Clay had raised.[44]

> I shall not discuss the point, but leave it to the learned gentlemen who have undertaken to discuss it; but I suppose there is no slave of that de-

---

44 Senator William Henry Seward of New York's "Higher Law" speech was delivered in Congress on March 11, 1850. Seward, long an antislavery leader, favored the admission of Texas. His view that the Constitution was not the last word when it came to human rights raised a furor in the Senate, led by James Mason of Virginia. Peter Charles Hoffer, *Seward's Law: Country Lawyering, Relational Rights, and Slavery* (Ithaca, NY: Cornell University Press, 2023), 57–76.

scription in California now. I understand that *"peonism,"* a sort of penal servitude, exists there, or rather a sort of voluntary sale of a man and his offspring for debt, as it is arranged and exists in some parts of California and some provinces of Mexico. But what I mean to say is, that African slavery, as we see it among us, is as utterly impossible to find itself, or to be found in California and New Mexico, as any other natural impossibility.

But Webster drew back from a natural-law-based absolute to a geographical postulate—slavery "as we know it" could not "find itself" in California and New Mexico. Although, in fact, it had existed in both places in the past. Without saying so, Webster was making a distinction between slave gang labor and domestic slaves, whose presence in Spanish Empire haciendas was common.[45]

California and New Mexico are Asiatic in their formation and scenery. They are composed of vast ridges of mountains, of great height, with broken ridges and deep valleys. The sides of these mountains are entirely barren; their tops capped by perennial snow. There may be in California, now made free by its constitution, and no doubt there are, some tracts of valuable land. But it is not so in New Mexico. Pray, what is the evidence which every gentleman must have obtained on this subject, from information sought by himself or communicated by others?[46]

I have inquired and read all I could find, in order to acquire information on this important question. What is there in New Mexico that could, by any possibility, induce any body to go there with slaves? There are some narrow strips of tillable land on the borders of the rivers; but the rivers themselves dry up before midsummer is gone. All that the people can do in that region, is to raise some little articles, some little wheat for their tortillas, and that by irrigation. And who expects to see a hundred black men cultivating tobacco, corn, cotton, rice, or any thing else, on lands in New Mexico, made fertile only by irrigation?

---

45 James F. Brooks, *Captives and Cousins: Slavery, Kinship, and Community in the Southwest Borderlands* (Chapel Hill: University of North Carolina Press, 2002), 234–235, 327–328; Stacey L. Smith, *Freedom's Frontier: California and the Struggle over Unfree Labor, Emancipation, and Reconstruction* (Chapel Hill: University of North Carolina Press, 2013), 17.
46 Actually, the vegetation is more Mediterranean than Asiatic, but Webster meant foreign to a New Englander.

Nature determined the outcome of the debate, according to Webster. That California had slavery under Spanish rule was left out of the equation. That portions of New Mexico had slavery under Spanish rule, and still had slavery under the Comanche, was similarly absent from all he could read and learn from his inquiries.

> I look upon it, therefore, as a fixed fact, to use an expression current at this day, that both California and New Mexico are destined to be free, so far as they are settled at all, which I believe, in regard to New Mexico, will be very little for a great length of time; free by the arrangement of things by the Power above us. I have therefore to say, in this respect also, that this country is fixed for freedom, to as many persons as shall ever live in it, by as irrepealable and more irrepealable a law, than the law that attaches to the right of holding slaves in Texas; and I will say further, that if a resolution, or a law, were now before us to provide a territorial Government for New Mexico, I would not vote to put any prohibition into it whatever. The use of such a prohibition would be idle, as it respects any effect it would have upon the territory; and I would not take pains to reaffirm an ordinance of Nature, nor to reenact the will of God. I would put in no Wilmot Proviso for the mere purpose of a taunt or a reproach. I would put into it no evidence of the votes of superior power; for no purpose but to wound the pride, even whether a just pride, a rational pride, or an irrational pride, to wound the pride of the gentlemen who belong to Southern States. I have no such object, no such purpose.

Webster, having divined the will of God and the fact of nature, explained that he would therefore allow the territorial government of New Mexico to permit slavery. That is, he would not vote with the Free Soilers, although he had condemned their own twisted logic. What justified his own illogic? He would not "insult" the settlers of New Mexico by substituting his will for theirs. One has to conclude that Webster in 1850 was no longer the Webster of 1830—of the two speeches in reply to Senator Hayne. That Webster could sustain the logic of an argument through many hours; this Webster was struggling.[47]

---

47 Webster's replies to Senator Robert Y. Hayne of South Carolina in 1830 over the management of western lands anticipated many of the arguments of Free Soil. Christopher Childers, *The*

They would think it a taunt, an indignity; they would think it to be an act taking away from them what they regard as a proper equality of privilege; and whether they expect to realize any benefit from it or not, they would think it at least a plain theoretic wrong; that something more or less derogatory to their character and their rights had taken place. I propose to inflict no such wound upon any body, unless something essentially important to the country, and efficient to the preservation of liberty and freedom, is to be effected.

Therefore, I repeat, Sir, and I repeat it because I wish it to be understood, that I do not propose to address the Senate often on this subject. I desire to pour out all my heart in as plain a manner as possible; and I say, again, therefore, that if a proposition were now here for a Government for New Mexico, and it was moved to insert a provision for the prohibition of slavery, I would not vote for it.

To conclude—the question of the subdivision of Texas was settled. But Webster had hardly begun. He was repeating himself on an issue that was not central to Clay's resolutions but was central to Calhoun's objections—California had to come in as a free state.

Now, Mr. President, I have established, so far as I proposed to go into any line of observation to establish, the proposition with which I set out, and upon which I propose the stand or fall; and that is, that the whole territory of the States in the United States, or in the newly acquired territory of the United States, has a fixed and settled character, now fixed and settled by law, which cannot be repealed; in the case of Texas without a violation of public faith, and by no human power in regard to California or New Mexico; that, therefore, under one or other of these laws, every foot of land in the States or in the Territories has already received a fixed and decided character.

Sir, if we were now making a Government for New Mexico, and any body should propose a Wilmot Proviso, I should treat it exactly as Mr. Polk treated that provision for excluding slavery from Oregon. Mr. Polk was known to be in opinion decidedly averse to the Wilmot Proviso; but

Webster-Hayne Debate: Defining Nationhood in the Early American Republic (Baltimore: Johns Hopkins University Press, 2018), 104.

he felt the necessity of establishing a Government for the Territory of
Oregon; and, though the proviso was in it, he knew it would be entirely
nugatory; and, since it must be entirely nugatory, since it took away no
right, no describable, no estimable, no weighable or tangible right of the
South, he said he would sign the bill for the sake of enacting a law to form
a government in that Territory, and let that entirely useless, and, in that
connection, entirely senseless, proviso remain.

Then back to his antislavery roots. Students of his career, like many of
his contemporaries, did not credit the sincerity of these views, given his
support for the fugitive slave bill. But his dislike of slavery was genuine.

Sir, we hear much of the annexation of Canada; and if there be any man,
any of the Northern Democracy, or any one of the Free Soil party, who
supposes it necessary to insert a Wilmot Proviso in a territorial government of New Mexico, that man would of course be of opinion that it is
necessary to protect the everlasting snows of Canada from the foot of
slavery by the same overspreading wing of an act of Congress. Sir, wherever there is a substantive good to be done, wherever there is a foot of
land to be staid back from becoming slave territory, I am ready to assert
the principle of the exclusion of slavery. I am pledged to it from the year
1837; I have been pledged to it again and again; and I will perform those
pledges; but I will not do a thing unnecessarily that wounds the feelings
of others, or that does to my own understanding.

Having established that he was not in favor of extending slavery, he
turned to the matter of a new fugitive slave law. His recitation of mutual
sectional recrimination bore a remarkable similarity to Clay's.

Mr. President, in the excited times in which we live, there is found to exist
a state of crimination and recrimination between the North and South.
There are lists of grievances produced by each; and those grievances, real
or supposed, alienate the minds of one portion of the country from the
other, exasperate the feelings, and subdue the sense of fraternal affection, patriotic love, and mutual regard. I shall bestow a little attention, Sir,
upon these various grievances existing on the one side and on the other.
I begin with complaints of the South.

By complaints of the South Webster meant those in Calhoun's speech. It was Calhoun and his southern cohort who threatened disunion. Webster had long cast himself as the defender of Union. It was thus up to him to mollify the South while not antagonizing the North.

> I will not answer, further than I have, the general statements of the honorable Senator from South Carolina, that the North has grown upon the South in consequence of the manner of administering this government, in the collecting of its revenues, and so forth. These are disputed topics, and I have no inclination to enter into them. But I will state these complaints, especially one complaint of the South, which has in my opinion just foundation; and that is, that there has been found at the North, among individuals and among legislators, a disinclination to perform fully, their constitutional duties in regard to the return of persons bound to service who have escaped into the free States. In that respect, it is my judgment that the South is right, and the North is wrong.

On the most slender of grounds Webster agreed with Calhoun. Webster had already made himself an object of attack in Massachusetts among immediate abolition advocates. But after this speech, they would pour a torrent of abuse on his head. He must have anticipated that event, but he pressed on anyway.

> Every member of every Northern legislature is bound by oath, like every other officer in the country, to support the Constitution of the United States; and this article of the Constitution, which says to these States, that they shall deliver up fugitives from service, is as binding in honor and conscience as any other article. No man fulfills his duty in any legislature who sets himself to find excuses, evasions, escapes from this constitutional obligation. I have always thought that the Constitution addressed itself to the legislatures of the States or to the States themselves. It says that those persons escaping to other States "shall be delivered up," and I confess I have always been of the opinion that it was an injunction upon the States themselves. When it is said that a person escaping into another State, and becoming therefore within the jurisdiction of that State, shall be delivered up, it seems to me the import of the clause is, that the State itself, in obedience to the Constitution, shall cause him to be delivered

up. That is my judgment. I have always entertained that opinion, and I
entertain it now.

He was disagreeing with justice Joseph Story's opinion in *Prigg v.
Pennsylvania* (1842). In *Prigg*, a slave catcher who carried a Black family from Pennsylvania to Maryland violated the Pennsylvania anti-
kidnapping law. In striking down the state law because it violated the
1793 Fugitive Slave Act, Story, no friend to slavery, opined that states
were not bound to enforce the federal law of 1793.[48]

But when the subject, some years ago, was before the Supreme Court of the
United States, the majority of the judges held, that the power to cause fugitives
from service to be delivered up was a power to be exercised under the authority of this Government. I do not know, on the whole, that it may not have been
a fortunate decision. My habit is to respect the result of judicial deliberations,
and the solemnity of judicial decisions. But, as it now stands, the business of
seeing that these fugitives are delivered up resides in the power of Congress
and the national judicature, and my friend at the head of the Judiciary Committee [James Mason], has a bill on the subject now before the Senate [which
in fact became the Fugitive Slave Law of 1850] with some amendments to it,
which I propose to support, with all its provisions, to the fullest extent. And I
desire to call the attention of all sober-minded men, of all conscientious men,
in the North, of all men who are not carried away by any fanatical idea or by
any false idea whatever, to their constitutional obligations.[49]

---

48 *Prigg v. Pennsylvania*, 41 U.S. 539 (1842).
49 The bill was an amendment to the Fugitive Slave Bill Clay proposed. It became the bill the
Senate passed. Mason was as ardent a proslavery advocate as Calhoun. Robert W. Young, *Senator
James Murray Mason: Defender of the Old South* (Knoxville: University of Tennessee Press, 1989),
35–55. Webster's speech here was a source of confusion. Was he supporting the bill or trying to
amend it? The different versions of his speech at this point are unclear. *Boston Atlas*, an antislavery
publication, editorialized on May 8, 1850, that the speech as published didn't say what Webster really
said, because the word *"which"* was placed wrong. He did not say, "My friend at the head of the
Judiciary Committee has a bill on the subject, now before the Senate, with some amendments to it,
which I propose to support, with all its provisions to the fullest extent." According to the paper,
Webster said, "My friend at the head of the Judiciary Committee has a bill on the subject, now
before the Senate, *which*, with some amendments to it, I propose to support, with all its provisions
to the fullest extent." And according to the paper, at the time Webster had three amendatory
provisions on his desk; and he had shown them to other members of the Senate interested in the
question. But he did not indicate their substance in either his speech (per the *Globe*) or the
published version of the speech.

So, the men and women in government who aided and abetted fugitive slaves were fanatics? The word has many connotations. Closest to Webster's meaning was "radicals."

> I put it to all the sober and sound minds at the North as a question of morals, and a question of conscience. What right have they, in their legislative capacity, or any other capacity, to endeavor to get round this Constitution, to embarrass the free exercise of the rights secured by the Constitution to the persons whose slaves escape from them? None at all; none at all. Neither in the forum of conscience, nor before the face of the Constitution, are they justified, in my opinion.

Well, perhaps not fanatics, then, but indifferent to the rights of the slave owners. Unless he is talking about members of free state legislatures acting in their legislative capacity. But some of these men were both antislavery activists out of doors and members of state legislatures.

> Of course it is a matter for their consideration. They probably, in the turmoil of the times, have not stopped to consider of this. They have followed what seemed to be the current of thought and of motives, as the occasion arose, and they neglected to investigate fully the real question, and to consider their constitutional obligations; as, I am sure, if they did consider, they would fulfill them with alacrity.

The abolitionists were unthinking, or unable to investigate fully the real question? Or was Webster's target antislavery, a much broader segment of northern opinion? Webster knew that for twenty years at least, abolitionists had been investigating every aspect of slavery itself. They went to Britain, which had ended slavery in its empire, to share ideas. They interrogated former slaves and helped runaways to tell their stories. They were anything if not neglectful. But for Webster this was a contest of ideas—of adherence to the fugitive slave clause of the Constitution versus adherence to moral obligations outside of the law. If, as Webster himself had said on many prior occasions, slavery violated moral law, were the abolitionists not justified in aiding the runaway?

Therefore, I repeat, Sir, that here is a ground of complaint against the North well founded, which ought to be removed, which it is now in the power of the different departments of this Government to remove; which calls for the enactment of proper laws authorizing the judicature of this Government, in the several States, to do all that is necessary for the recapture of fugitive slaves, and for the restoration of them to those who claim them. Wherever I go, and whenever I speak on the subject, and when I speak here I desire to speak to the whole North, I say that the South has been injured in this respect, and has a right to complain; and the North has been too careless of what I think the Constitution peremptorily and emphatically enjoins upon her as a duty.

The South had been injured—but how? Arguing that the slave South would have lost property and labor does not include the possibility, as the South discovered after the Civil War, that free labor is also highly productive. By mere words from the writings and lips of a handful of men and women? Had the abolitionists tried to steal southerners' property from southern lands? Had there been any act of aggression that violated southern states' laws? After all, slavery existed only where law permitted it, and law did not permit it in the free states. This doctrine of ultra vires, where southern domestic slave law reached out of the South into the free states, faced the problem of the Full Faith and Credit Clause of the Constitution: should northern freedom laws reach into the South? Some southern states allowed that they did—slaves taken to a free state and allowed to reside there were considered free when they returned to the slave state of their origins. But after 1850, this southern willingness to allow freedom to the returnees vanished.[50]

Complaint has been made against certain resolutions that emanate from Legislatures at the North, and are sent here to us, not only on the subject of slavery in this District, but sometimes recommending Congress to consider the means of abolishing slavery in the States. I should be sorry to be called upon to present any resolutions here which could not be referrable to any committee or any power in Congress; and, therefore, I

---

50 The 282 "freedom suits" from Missouri included *Rachel v. William Walker* (1836) and the doctrine of "once free, always free." See Ann Twitty, *Before Dred Scott: Slavery and Legal Culture in American Confluence* (New York: Cambridge University Press, 2016).

should be unwilling to receive from the Legislature of Massachusetts any instructions to present resolutions expressive of any opinion whatever on the subject of slavery, as it exists at the present moment in the States, for two reasons: because, first, I do not consider that the Legislature of Massachusetts has any thing to do with it; and next, I do not consider that I, as her representative here, have any thing to do with it.

Webster separated himself from John Quincy Adams, who had passed away two years earlier after leading the crusade to allow the reading of antislavery petitions in Congress. Adams was a hero to the abolitionists. Had Webster forgotten that he had read the very same petitions in the Senate in 1836? The reference to state legislative action criticized the "personal liberty laws" of Vermont and New York (1842), and personal liberty court decisions in Massachusetts and other northern states.[51]

Sir, it has become, in my opinion, quite too common; and if the Legislatures of the States do not like that opinion, they have a great deal more power to put it down than I have to uphold it; it has become, in my opinion, quite too common a practice for the State Legislatures to present resolutions here on all subjects, and to instruct us on all subjects. There is no public man that requires instruction more than I do, or who requires information more than I do, or desires it more heartily; but I do not like to have it come in too imperative a shape.

Webster did not want state legislatures to tell him what to do, even though it was state legislatures who chose senators? They should not present resolutions to the federal body whose members they selected? Well, at least not so often and so insistently, although southern state legislatures were doing it too.

I took notice, with pleasure, of some remarks upon this subject made the other day in the Senate of Massachusetts, by a young man of talent and character, of whom the best hopes may be entertained. I mean Mr. [George Stillman] Hillard. He told the Senate of Massachusetts that he

---

51 Peter Charles Hoffer, *John Quincy Adams and the Gag Rule, 1835–1850* (Baltimore: Johns Hopkins University Press, 2017), 74; Thomas D. Morris, *Free Men All: The Personal Liberty Laws of the North, 1780–1861* (Chicago: University of Chicago Press, 1974).

would vote for no instructions, whatever, to be forwarded to members of Congress, nor for any resolutions to be offered, expressive of the sense of Massachusetts, as to what her members of Congress ought to do. He said, that he saw no propriety in one set of public servants giving instructions and reading lectures to another set of public servants. To their own master all of them must stand or fall, and that master is their constituents.

Curiouser and curiouser, for the state legislative resolutions sent to the Senate were the product of popular agitation in the states. They were very much the voice of "their constituents." To quote George Stillman Hillard in his support was even more remarkable, for Hillard was a Free Soil Democrat, a law partner of radical abolitionist Charles Sumner, and a respected patron of literary figures like Nathaniel Hawthorne and Henry Wadsworth Longfellow. Hillard did support the compromise, in the end.

I wish these sentiments could become more common, a great deal more common. I have never entered into the question, and never shall, about the binding force of instructions. I will, however, simply say this: if there be any matter pending in this body, while I am a member of it, in which Massachusetts has an interest of her own not adverse to the general interests of the country, I shall pursue her instructions with gladness of heart and with all the efficiency which I can bring to the occasion. But if the question be one which affects her interest, and at the same time equally affects the interest of all the other States, I shall no more regard her particular wishes or instructions than I should regard the wishes of a man who might appoint me an arbitrator, or referee, to decide some question of important private right.[52]

Having voiced his opposition to legislative instructions that he disliked, Webster reversed course and said that he would gladly support such instructions if they aided the general interest. In other words, he would support those instructions that he supported.

---

52 The published version added to "important private right" the words "between him and his neighbor, and then instruct me to decide in his favor." The difference is really one of emphasis—the legislature acting as its own referee. But this is what legislation often did—act in the public good to give to some and take from others, for example, in granting the right-of-way to railroads through private property.

If ever there was a Government upon earth it is this Government; if ever there was a body upon earth it is this body, which should consider itself as composed by agreement of all, each member appointed by some, but organized by the general consent of all, sitting here, under the solemn obligations of oath and conscience, to do that which they think to be best for the good of the whole.

The general good was the good of the whole—that is, the Union—not the good of a particular section or of single states. This was another poke at Calhoun's theory of concurrent majorities. The general interest, like the general good, was of course the great goal of government. Webster might have been citing French Enlightenment philosopher Jean-Jacques Rousseau. The problem was that the two sections did not agree on the general good of slavery for the country, which was what was at stake. Webster is trying to avoid using the word "slavery," although slavery is the brooding omnipresence whose shadow falls over everything here.[53]

Then, Sir, there are the abolition societies, of which I am unwilling to speak, but in regard to which I have very clear notions and opinions. I do not think them useful. I think their operations for the last twenty years have produced nothing good or valuable. At the same time, I know thousands of their members to be honest and good men; perfectly well-meaning men. They have excited feelings; they think they must do something for the cause of liberty; and in their sphere of action, they do not see what else they can do, than to contribute to an abolition press, or an abolition society, or to pay an abolition lecturer.

The abolition lecturer extraordinaire was the lawyer Wendell Phillips, scion of the Boston Brahmin class, who wrote and spoke against slavery. He was part of the circle around William Lloyd Garrison's American Anti-Slavery Society in Boston, but Phillips was more than a Garrison clone. Phillips was also an advocate of rights for women, workingmen, and immigrants. Even more galling to Webster, Phillips advocated Mas-

---

53 Stephen Hahn, *Forging America: A Continental History of the United States* (New York: Oxford University Press, 2024), 1:481. (The "battle lines" were drawn over slavery's expansion.)

sachusetts leaving the Union because the Constitution was a pact with
the evil slavocracy. Phillips would lead the attack on Webster when the
latter supported the new Fugitive Slave Law.[54]

> I do not mean to impute gross motives even to the leaders of these societ-
> ies, but I am not blind to the consequences of their proceedings. I cannot
> but see what mischiefs their interference with the South has produced.
> And is it not plain to every man? Let any gentleman who doubts of that,
> recur to the debates in the Virginia House of Delegates in 1832, and he
> will see with what freedom a proposition made by Mr. Jefferson Ran-
> dolph for the gradual abolition of slavery was discussed in that body.

The reference is to the Nat Turner rebellion of 1831, in which a Virginia slave preacher led a violent raid across plantations south of the
James River, and which resulted in over 60 whites and over 120 Blacks
dying. Trials afterward convicted more slaves, and when Turner was finally captured, his trial was something of a spectacle. Afterward, Virginia tightened its slave laws. There was no evidence that northern
abolitionism had anything to do with the uprising.[55]

> Every one spoke of slavery as he thought; very ignominious and disparag-
> ing names and epithets were applied to it. The debates in the [Virginia]
> House of Delegates on that occasion, I believe, were all published. They
> were read by every colored man who could read, and to those who could
> not read, those debates were read by others. At that time Virginia was
> not unwilling or afraid to discuss this question, and to let that part of her
> population know as much of the discussion as they could learn. That was
> in 1832. As has been said by the honorable member from South Carolina,
> these abolition societies commenced their course of action in 1835. It is
> said, I do not know how true it may be, that they sent incendiary publica-

---

54 Hoffer, *Radical Advocacy of Wendell Phillips*, 53.
55 Some Virginians believed that abolitionist William Lloyd Garrison's *The Liberator*, a newspaper
that began publication in January 1831, had inspired the revolt. "Letter to the Editor," *The Liberator*,
September 10, 1831. There was no truth to that conspiratorial notion. Kenneth S. Greenberg, *Nat
Turner: A Slave Rebellion in History and Memory* (New York: Oxford University Press, 2003), 151,
152 (Garrison believed in peaceful abolition and rejected calls for the violent overthrow of slavery);
Patrick H. Breen, *The Land Shall Be Deluged in Blood: A New History of the Nat Turner Revolt* (New
York: Oxford University Press, 2015), 252n35.

tions into the slave States; at any rate, they attempted to arouse, and did arouse, a very strong feeling; in other words, they created great agitation in the North against Southern slavery. Well, what was the result?

The timeline here was confused—how did the 1835 petition campaign to end slavery in the District of Columbia abet the Nat Turner rebellion in 1831? Webster's error. The petitions were sent to members of Congress and did not fall into the hands of slaves, except for one remarkable petition presented to the House by John Quincy Adams that purposed to come from slaves and was greeted with horror by southern representatives.[56]

> The bonds of the slaves were bound more firmly than before, their rivets were more strongly fastened. Public opinion, which in Virginia had begun to be exhibited against slavery, and was opening out for the discussion of the question, drew back and shut itself up in its castle. I wish to know whether any body in Virginia can, now, talk as Mr. Randolph, Governor McDowell, and others talked openly, and sent their remarks to the press, in 1832? We all know the fact, and we all know the cause; and every thing that these agitating people have done has been, not to enlarge, but to restrain, not to set free, but to bind faster, the slave population of the South.

So—the abolitionists should cease their agitation because lawmakers in the South used the agitation to pass more stringent slavery laws? This is an example of the "heckler's veto" in which a speaker is silenced because a heckler disrupts the speech. Anti-abolitionist mobs in the North had used this tactic with success in the 1830s, but by 1850 it was far less common. But Webster recognized the power of the heckler, as his subsequent remarks on the abolitionist press revealed.

> That is my judgment. Sir, as I have said, I know many abolitionists in my own neighborhood, very honest, good people, misled, as I think, by strange enthusiasm; but they wish to do something, and they are called on to contribute, and they do contribute; and it is my firm opinion this

---

56 Hoffer, *Gag-Rule*, 36.

day, that within the last twenty years as much money has been collected and paid to the abolition societies, abolition presses, and abolition lecturers, as would purchase the freedom of every slave, man,
woman and child, in the State of Maryland, and send them all to Liberia. I have no doubt of it. But I have yet to learn that the benevolence
of these abolition societies has at any time taken that particular turn.
[Laughter.]

As for the Maryland figures, according to the 1840 census, Maryland
had 89,405 slaves. At $250 apiece—about half the value that southern
men assigned to their human property—we are talking $22,373,350.
Allow $30 each to carry them to Liberia, with no provision to keep them
alive when they get there, and the sum rises to $25,058,600. Think of
it—$25 million over the twenty years that Webster mentions is over $1.25
million a year, or $3,500 a day coming into the abolition movement. Ab-
surd. The implication was that abolitionists used the funds they raised
for illicit purposes, an accusation that Webster muted by saying that he
knew abolitionists and they were simply misguided. They were no longer fanatics, one supposes.[57]

Again, Sir, the violence of the press is complained of. The press violent! Why, Sir, the press is violent everywhere. There are outrageous
reproaches in the North against the South, and there are reproaches
no better in the South against the North. Sir, the extremists of both
parts of this country are violent; they mistake loud and violent talk for
eloquence and for reason. They think that he who talks loudest reasons
best. And this we must expect, when the press is free, as it is here, and
I trust always will be; for, with all its licentiousness and all its evil, the
entire and absolute freedom of the press is essential to the preservation
of government on the basis of a free constitution. Wherever it exists
there will be foolish paragraphs and violent paragraphs in the press,
as there are, I am sorry to say, foolish speeches and violent speeches in
both houses of Congress.

---

57 Maryland State Archives, "Legacy of Slavery in Maryland" (n.d.), 1840 census, https://msa.
maryland.gov/msa/mdslavery/html/research/census1840.html. The calculation of the value of
slaves is my own.

Time for some humor. The literature of the antebellum period regularly coupled oratory with comedy, particularly on the stage.[58]

> In truth, Sir, I must say that, in my opinion, the vernacular tongue of the country has become greatly vitiated, depraved, and corrupted by the style of our Congressional debates. [Laughter.] And if it were possible for those debates to vitiate the principles of the people as much as they have depraved their tastes, I should cry out, "God save the Republic!"

Humorous aside finished, Webster returned to the centerpiece of his speech. Nothing so far, even his defense of his about-face on the admission of Texas, should have so roiled the waters of his native state as his stance on the fugitive slave question.

> Well, in all this I see no solid grievance, no grievance presented by the South, within the redress of the government, but the single one to which I have referred; and that is, the want of a proper regard to the injunction of the Constitution for the delivery of fugitive slaves.
>
> There are also complaints of the North against the South. I need not go over them particularly. The first and gravest is, that the North adopted the Constitution, recognizing the existence of slavery in the States, and recognizing the right, to a certain extent, of the representation of slaves in Congress, under a state of sentiment and expectation which does not now exist; and that, by events, by circumstances, by the eagerness of the South to acquire territory and extend her slave population, the North finds itself, in regard to the relative influence of the South and the North, of the free States and the slave States, where it never did expect to find itself when they agreed to the compact of the Constitution. They complain, therefore, that, instead of slavery being regarded as an evil, as it was then, an evil which all hoped would be extinguished gradually, it is now regarded by the South as an institution to be cherished, and preserved, and extended; an institution which the South has already extended to the utmost of her power by the acquisition of new territory.

---

58 See, e.g., Emily Banta, "Sovereign Pleasures: Comic Play in Antebellum America" (PhD diss., Rutgers University, 2021).

One step forward, one step back: Calhoun had no legitimate grievance against free soil, as at the time of the ratification of the Constitution slavery was regarded as an evil in both North and South. This was
another example of Webster's version of originalism. By reminding his
audience that southern framers viewed slavery with distaste, he poked
Calhoun one more time.

> Well, then passing from that, every body in the North reads; and every
> body reads whatsoever the newspapers contain; and the newspapers,
> some of them, especially those presses to which I have alluded, are careful
> to spread about among the people every reproachful sentiment uttered
> by any Southern man bearing at all against the North; every thing that
> is calculated to exasperate, to alienate; and there are many such things,
> as every body will admit, from the South, or some portion of it, which
> are disseminated among the reading people, and they do exasperate, and
> alienate, and produce a most mischievous effect upon the public mind at
> the North.

The South had almost put itself out of court by exaggerating every
criticism of it in northern newspapers. At the same time, such commentary in northern papers fomented anti-southern (as opposed to antislavery) opinions. Here Webster was blaming the newspapers for the
growing sectional animosity. It was true that the invention of the rotary
newspaper press and the resulting "penny press" newspapers had enabled the spread of political venom. Webster and other politicians allied
themselves with newspaper publishers, and some publishers were themselves politicians. Newspapers routinely aligned themselves with this or
that political party or faction.[59]

> Sir, I would not notice things of this sort appearing in obscure quarters;
> but one thing has occurred in this debate which struck me very forcibly.
> An honorable member from Louisiana addressed us the other day on this
> subject. I suppose there is not a more amiable and worthy gentleman in
> this chamber, nor a gentleman who would be more slow to give offense

---

59 David L. Jameson, "Newspapers and the Press" (Nineteenth Century Newspapers, 2008), www.
gale.com.

to anybody, and he did not mean in his remarks to give offense. But what did he say? Why, Sir, he took pains to run a contrast between the slaves of the South and the laboring people of the North, giving the preference, in all points of condition, and comfort, and happiness, to the slaves of the South. The honorable member, doubtless, did not suppose that he gave any offense, or did any injustice. He was merely expressing his opinion. But does he know how remarks of that sort will be received by the laboring people of the North?

Senator Pierre Soulé may have been the culprit. A naturalized American citizen, lawyer, and Democrat, Soulé was chosen by President Pierce in 1853 to serve as US ambassador to Spain, where he evidently took his pistol, for he was involved in a duel there. He was not the only one brandishing firearms in the Senate. Foote of Mississippi threatened Thomas Hart Benton with a pistol, but Benton refused the offer to duel. The argument itself was a mainstay of southerners' defense of slavery as a positive good, as compared to the political revolutions, crime, and impoverishment in "free society."[60]

Why, who are the laboring people of the North? They are the North. They are the people who cultivate their own farms with their own hands; freeholders, educated men, independent men. Let me say, Sir, that five-sixths of the whole property of the North is in the hands of the laborers of the North; they cultivate their farms, they educate their children, they provide the means of independence. If they are not freeholders, they earn wages; these wages accumulate, are turned into capital, into new freeholds, and small capitalists are created. That is the case, and such the course of things among the industrious and frugal. And what can these people think when so respectable and worthy a gentleman as the member from Louisiana undertakes to prove that the absolute ignorance and the abject slavery of the South are

---

60 J. Preston Moore, "Pierre Soule: Southern Expansionist and Promoter," *Journal of Southern History* 21 (1955): 203–223; James P. Coleman, "Two Irascible Antebellum Senators: George Poindexter and Henry S. Foote," *Journal of Mississippi History* 46 (February 1984): 17–27. The enslaved had it better according to the positive defense of slavery: George Fitzhugh, *A Sociology for the South; or, The Failure of Free Society* (Richmond, VA: A. Morris, 1854), iii; revived in Robert William Fogel and Stanley L. Engerman, *Time on the Cross: The Economics of American Negro Slavery* (Boston: Little, Brown, 1974), 1:109–117.

more in conformity with the high purposes and destiny of immortal, rational, human beings, than the educated, the independent, free labor of the North?[61]

Webster's defense of free labor and the northern worker against all calumny was another part of the speech often skipped by his critics. It recalled his "second reply to Hayne" in 1831. By free labor, Webster meant the family farmer as well as the urban workman and the village artisan. Their virtues of industry and frugality might—though he did not make the comparison explicit—be favorably compared to the indolence that slavery induced in the slave and his master.[62]

There is a more tangible and irritating cause of grievance at the North. Free blacks are constantly employed in the vessels of the North, generally as cooks or stewards. When the vessel arrives at a Southern port, these free colored men are taken on shore, by the police or municipal authority, imprisoned, and kept in prison, till the vessel is again ready to sail. This is not only irritating, but exceedingly unjustifiable and oppressive. Mr. Hoar's mission, some time ago, to South Carolina, was a well-intended effort to remove this cause of complaint. The North thinks such imprisonments illegal and unconstitutional; and as the cases occur constantly, and frequently, they regard it as a great grievance.[63]

The episode was widely covered in the northern press. It had been featured in Clay's speech. To repeat: The South Carolina Negro Seaman's Act of 1822 followed the Denmark Vesey conspiracy. Under the act, free Black sailors arriving on ships in Charleston Harbor were arrested and jailed until the ships sailed. Ship captains had to pay for the expense. These sailors were free men, and the act was intended to prevent their congregation with free Black South Carolinians. When the act was challenged in federal circuit court, US Supreme Court justice William Johnson ruled that it violated the Constitution, but Charleston officials continued to enforce the act. When Secretary of State John

---

61 Again, Pierre Soulé.
62 See, e.g., Eric Foner, *The Story of American Freedom* (New York: Norton, 1999), 68.
63 The concluding sentence appeared in the published version but not the *Globe* version. Perhaps it was an attempt to appear more balanced. This balancing act was very hard to perform, evidently.

Quincy Adams, followed by the US Supreme Court, followed by Adams as president-elect told South Carolina not to enforce the act, the governor and the state legislature officially refused to comply. The entire episode was a prelude to the Nullification Crisis of 1828. In 1844, Samuel Hoar was sent by Massachusetts to act as an intermediary to free sailors from the state and was threatened with jail himself.[64]

> Now, Sir, so far as any of these grievances have their foundation in matters of law, they can be redressed, and ought to be redressed; and so far as they have their foundation in matters of opinion, in sentiment, in mutual crimination and recrimination, all that we can do is to endeavor to allay the agitation, and cultivate a better feeling and more fraternal sentiments between the South and the North.

Webster's version of Clay's appeal to moderation.

> Mr. President, I should much prefer to have heard from every member on this floor declarations of opinion that this Union could never be dissolved, than the declaration of opinion by anybody that, in any case, under the pressure of any circumstances, such a dissolution was possible. I hear with pain, and anguish, and distress, the word "secession," especially when it falls from the lips of those who are patriotic, and known to the country, and known all over the world, for their political services. Secession! Peaceable secession! Sir, your eyes and mine are never destined to see that miracle. The dismemberment of this vast country without convulsion! The breaking up of the fountains of the great deep without ruffling the surface! Who is so foolish, I beg everybody's pardon, as to expect to see any such thing? Sir, he who sees these States, now revolving in harmony around a common center, and expects to see them quit their places and fly off without convulsion, may look the next hour to see the heavenly bodies rush from their spheres, and jostle against each other in the realms of space, without causing the crush of the universe.

---

64 Philip M. Hamer, "Great Britain, the United States, and the Negro Seaman Acts, 1822–1848," *Journal of Southern History* 1 (1935): 1–28; Michael A. Schoeppner, *Moral Contagion: Black Atlantic Sailors, Citizenship, and Diplomacy in Antebellum America* (New York: Cambridge University Press, 2019), 50–52, 54, 150–156.

Webster returned, in the final hour of his address, to the place where Clay ended his—with the frightening prospect of secession. Again, like Clay, he saw the nation and the Union as one and inseparable and fore-saw a parade of horrors resulting from secession.

There can be no such thing as a peaceable secession. Peaceable secession is an utter impossibility. Is the great Constitution under which we live, covering this whole country; is it to be thawed and melted away by seces-sion, as the snows on the mountains melt under the influence of a vernal sun, disappear almost unobserved, and run off? No, Sir! No, Sir! I will not state what might produce the disruption of the Union; but, Sir, I see as plainly as I see the sun in heaven, what that disruption itself must pro-duce; I see that it must produce war, and such a war as I will not describe *in its twofold character.*

Like the Roman lawyer and politician Cicero in his famous oration against Mark Anthony, Webster said he would not describe such a war, then proceeded to do so. Classic. It would be a shame to break into Webster's peroration, so moving and eloquent as it was. But one should note how it illustrated his mastery of classical oratory. For example, he repeated the word "secession" over and over, each time adding to its opprobrium. This is the trope of repetition. Samuel Taylor Coleridge's "Rime of the Ancient Mariner" (1834) offers a famous example: "Alone, alone, all, all alone, Alone on a wide wide sea! And never a saint took pity on My soul in agony."

Peaceable secession! Peaceable secession! The concurrent agreement of all members of this great republic to separate! A voluntary separation, with alimony on one side and on the other. Why, what would be the re-sult? Where is the line to be drawn? What States are to secede? What is to remain American? What am I to be? An American no longer? Am I to become a sectional man, a local man, a separatist? with no country in common with the gentlemen who sit around me here, or who fill the other House of Congress? Heaven forbid! Where is the flag of the re-public to remain? Where is the eagle still to tower? Or is he to cower, and shrink, and fall to the ground? Why, Sir, our ancestors, our fathers and our grandfathers, those of them that are yet living amongst us with prolonged lives, would rebuke and reproach us; and our children and our grandchildren would cry out shame upon us, if we, of this generation, should dishonor these ensigns of the power of the Government and the harmony of that Union, which is every day felt among us with so much joy and gratitude.

What is to become of the army? What is to become of the navy? What is to become of the public lands? How is each of the thirty States to defend itself? I know, although the idea has not been stated distinctly, there is to be, or it is supposed possible that there should be, a Southern Confederacy. I do not mean, when I allude to this statement, that any one seriously contemplates such a state of things. I do not mean to say that it is true, but I have heard it suggested elsewhere, that that idea has originated a design to separate. I am sorry, Sir, that it has ever been thought of, talked of, or dreamed of, in the wildest flights of human imagination. But the idea, so far as it exists, must be of a separation, assigning the slave States to one side, and the free States to the other.

Sir, there is not, I may express myself too strongly, perhaps, but some things, some moral things, are almost as impossible as other natural or physical things; and I hold the idea of a separation of these States, those that are free to form one government, and those that are slaveholding to form another, as a moral impossibility. We could not separate the States by any such line, if we were to draw it. We could not sit down here today and draw a line of separation that would satisfy any five men in the country. There are natural causes that would keep and tie us together, and there are social and domestic relations which we could not break if we would, and which we should not if we could.

Sir, nobody can look over the face of this country at the present moment, nobody can see where its population is the most dense and growing, without being ready to admit, and compelled to admit, that ere long America will be in the valley of the Mississippi.

Well, now, Sir, I beg to inquire what the wildest enthusiast has to say on the possibility of cutting that river in two, and leaving free States at its source, and its branches, and slave States down near its mouth, each forming a separate government? Pray, Sir, pray, sir, let me say to the people of this country that these things are worthy of their pondering and of their consideration. Here, Sir, are five millions of freemen in the free States north of the river Ohio: Can any body suppose that this population can be severed, by a line that divides them from the territory of a foreign and an alien government, down somewhere, the Lord knows where, upon the lower banks of the Mississippi?

Webster's political geography here was the reverse of Calhoun's. Both men saw the Mississippi as the engine of progress. Both celebrated population growth in the states bordering the river. The invention of the steamboat had transformed commercial traffic on the River. But Webster saw that traffic carrying the grains and livestock of free farmers, where Calhoun saw the river carrying giant bales of cotton. Severing the river traffic at the border of slavery made no sense to both men, but they drew different conclusions from that insight.

What would become of Missouri? Will she join the arrondissement of the slave States? Shall the man from the Yellow Stone and the Platte be connected, in the new Republic, with the man who lives on the southern extremity of the Cape of Florida? Sir, I am ashamed to pursue this line of remark. I dislike it, I have an utter disgust for it. I would rather hear of natural blasts and mildews, war, pestilence, and famine, than to hear gentlemen talk of secession. To break up! To break up this great Government, to dismember this glorious country, to astonish Europe with an act of folly such as Europe for two centuries has never beheld in any Government or any People! No, Sir; no, Sir! There will be no secession! Gentlemen are not serious when they talk of secession.

Sir, I hear there is to be a convention held at Nashville. I am bound to believe that if worthy gentlemen meet at Nashville in convention their object will be to adopt counsels conciliatory; to advise the South to forbearance and moderation, and to advise the North to forbearance and moderation; and to inculcate principles of brotherly love and affection, and attachment to the Constitution of the country as it now is. I believe, if the convention meet at all, it will be for this purpose; for certainly, if they meet for any purpose hostile to the Union, they have been singularly inappropriate in their selection of a place. I remember, Sir, that, when the treaty was concluded between France and England, at the peace of Amiens, a stern old Englishman and an orator, who regarded the conditions of the peace as ignominious to England, said in the House of Commons, that if King William could know the terms of that treaty, he would turn in his coffin! Let me commend this saying of Mr. Windham, in all its emphasis and in all its force, to any persons, who shall meet at Nashville for the purpose of concerting measures for the overthrow of this Union, over the bones of Andrew Jackson!

Jackson was the founder, or at least the most important figure, of the Democratic Party. Webster's reference was thus a backhanded criticism of the Senate's Democratic majority. See how you have betrayed the legacy of Jackson, Webster implied. After all, in the Nullification Crisis of 1828–1833, Jackson had threatened to send gunboats to Charleston Harbor if South Carolina blocked the collection of the customs duties there.[65]

Sir, I wish now to make two remarks, and hasten to a conclusion. I wish to say, in regard to Texas, that if it should be, hereafter, at any time, the pleasure of the Government of Texas to cede to the United States a portion, larger or smaller, of her territory which lies adjacent to New Mexico, and north of [sic] 34 deg. Latitude, to be formed into free States, for a fair equivalent in money or in the payment of her debt, I think it an object well worth the consideration of Congress, and I shall be happy to concur in it myself, if I should be in the public counsels of the country at that time.

I have one other remark to make. In my observations upon slavery as it has existed in the country, and as it now exists, I have expressed no opinion of the mode of its extinguishment or melioration. I will say, however, though I have nothing to propose, because I do not deem myself so competent as other gentlemen to take any lead, that if any gentleman from the South shall propose a scheme of colonization, to be carried on by this government upon a large scale, for the transportation of free colored people to any colony or any place in the world, I should be quite disposed to incur almost any degree of expense to accomplish that object. Nay, Sir, following an example set more than twenty years ago by a great man, then a Senator from New York, I would return to Virginia, and through her for the benefit of the whole South, the money received from the lands and territories ceded by her to this Government, for any such

65 Arthur Schlesinger Jr.'s Age of Jackson (Boston: Little, Brown, 1945), 306–307, 95–96; William W. Freehling, Prelude to Civil War: The Nullification Controversy in South Carolina, 1816–1836 (New York: Harper & Row, 1966), 186–188.

purpose as to relieve, in whole or in part, or in any way to diminish or deal beneficially with, the free colored population of the Southern States.

The great man from New York was Rufus King. Here he wore a somewhat different face from that Clay portrayed. A lawyer, veteran politician, diplomat, and constitutional framer, King was the last of the Federalists and an outspoken opponent of slavery. He was an active member of the American Colonization Society. The proposal was compensation to slaveholders, one of the linchpins of the colonization project. But the American Colonization Society project had been a nonstarter from its inception in 1816, as I have already indicated in the comments on Clay's proposal for compensation.[66]

> I have said that I honor Virginia for her cession of this territory. There have been received into the treasury of the United States eighty millions of dollars, the proceeds of the sales of the public lands ceded by her. If the residue should be sold at the same rate, the whole aggregate will exceed two hundred millions of dollars. If Virginia and the South see fit to adopt any proposition to relieve themselves from the free people of color among them, or such as may be made free, they have my free consent that the Government shall pay them any sum of money out of its proceeds, which may be adequate to the purpose.

This was a reference to the debate in the Virginia House of Delegates, in 1832, after the Nat Turner uprising the previous year. Some members in that legislature from the western part of the state wanted to use public funds to pay for and relocate the state's slaves to the colony of Liberia, on the west coast of Africa. The project fit the American Colonization Society plan. Many of the founders of the ACS, including Richard Bland Lee and Bushrod Washington, were Virginians. In 1840, Henry Clay was the group's president. In 1850, Virginia even set aside funds to colonize free Blacks. But slaveholders in the eastern part of the state had found a market for their slaves in the newly developed cotton lands of Mississippi and Alabama.[67]

---

66 Robert Ernst, *Rufus King, American Federalist* (Chapel Hill: University of North Carolina Press, 2012), 392.
67 Eric Burin, *Slavery and the Peculiar Institution: A History of the American Colonization Society* (Gainesville: University Press of Florida, 2008).

And now, Mr. President, I draw these observations to a close. I have spoken freely, and I meant to do so. I have sought to make no display; I have sought to enliven the occasion by no animated discussion, nor have I attempted any train of elaborate argument. I have wished only to speak my sentiments, fully and at large, being desirous, once and for all, to let the Senate know, and to let the country know, the opinions and sentiments which I entertain on all these subjects. These opinions are not likely to be suddenly changed. If there be any future service that I can render to the country, consistently with these sentiments and opinions, I shall cheerfully render it. If there be not, I shall still be glad to have had the opportunity to disburden my conscience from the bottom of my heart, and to make known every political sentiment that therein exists.

Like Clay, Webster offered his services to the nation, eschewing personal ambition. Setting aside the ego-centric nature of some of his address, he really was a patriot.

And now, Mr. President, instead of speaking of the possibility or utility of secession, instead of dwelling in these caverns of darkness, instead of groping with those ideas so full of all that is horrid and horrible, let us come out into the light of day; let us enjoy the fresh air of Liberty and Union; let us cherish those hopes which belong to us; let us devote ourselves to those great objects that are fit for our consideration and our action; let us raise our conceptions to the magnitude and the importance of the duties that devolve upon us; let our comprehension be as broad as the country for which we act, our aspirations as high as its certain destiny; let us not be pigmies in a case that calls for men. Never did there devolve on any generation of men higher trusts than now devolve upon us, for the preservation of this Constitution, and the harmony and peace of all who are destined to live under it.

This was a call to return to the patriotism of the fathers, something like the Jeremiads of the Puritan ministry at the end of the 1600s. Then, the preachers feared, the piety that had sailed across the Atlantic with the first Puritans had withered into lust for profit and lands. The congregations must be called back to their old piety. So Webster, who grew up in the twilight of that Puritan errand, recalled its fervor in this secular sermon.

Let us make our generation one of the strongest and brightest links in that golden chain, which is destined, I fondly believe, to grapple the people of all the States to this Constitution for ages to come. We have a great, popular, constitutional government, guarded by law, and by judicature, and defended by the whole affections of the people. No monarchical throne presses these States together; no iron chain of military power encircles them; they live and stand under a government popular in its form, representative in its character, founded upon principles of equality, and so constructed, we hope, as to last for ever.

Were it not for slavery and were he not on the Senate floor, Webster's peroration might have been the closing words of any Fourth of July address. He was familiar with these, having delivered them. The references to "liberty," popular government, and the principles of equality suggested that slavery was no part of the "ages to come." Thus both he and Calhoun had seen the future, albeit from different angles of repose.

In all its history it has been beneficent; it has trodden down no man's liberty; it has crushed no State. Its daily respiration is liberty and patriotism; its yet youthful veins are full of enterprise, courage, and honorable love of glory and renown. Large before, the country has now, by recent events, become vastly larger. This republic now extends, with a vast breadth, across the whole continent. The two great seas of the world wash the one and the other shore. We realize, on a mighty scale, the beautiful description of the ornamental border of the buckler of Achilles:—

"Now, the broad shield complete, the artist crown'd
With his last band, and poured the ocean round;
In living silver seem'd the waves to roll,
And beat the buckler's verge, and bound the whole."

So Achilles's belt was the Union? Did Webster not know what happened to Achilles—armor notwithstanding? In any case, Webster's speech was a reply to Calhoun more than to Clay, and that was obvious from its reception. In his concessions to Calhoun, Webster seemed to many antislavery advocates as a Judas to the cause of emancipation. Perhaps, as one modern commentator believes, Webster's approach was not political at all but personal. Calhoun was an old rival for the crown of senatorial debate, and Webster thought that he could win it once and for all. But perhaps Calhoun had won the debate after all, for Calhoun had never spelled out in detail what the white southern grievances were, and Webster did just that—attacking antislavery far more thoroughly than did Calhoun. He had, in effect, fallen into a trap that Calhoun (whether intentionally or inadvertently) had set. Or perhaps Webster was simply out of touch with growing antislavery popular opinion in the North. In any case, he did not have the last word. Calhoun sat through Webster's speech, making a few comments. Surely he was pleased by the concessions Webster had made to southern complaints. Webster weathered a storm of protest in a vessel filled with the plaudits of his friends. Clay's resolutions were almost—almost—forgotten.[68]

At first, out of doors, Webster's speech was greeted with applause. Webster orchestrated a publicity blitz, arranging for copies to be sent all over the country. Then the criticism began. Abolitionist newspapers began to pick at the speech like the harpies at Prometheus's chained body. When Webster was condemned by many politicians in Massachusetts, his friends there rallied to his support and he made every effort to explain himself in an exhaustive speaking trip after the debate had closed in the Senate. Members of the Massachusetts legislature rejected a resolution condemning his actions, and several hundred New York businessmen sent him a letter of thanks and a gold watch. To another correspondent, Webster gushed, "I cannot well say how much pleasure it gave me to see a name, so much venerated and beloved by me as yours is, on the letter recently received by me from friends in Boston and its vicinity, approving the general object and character of my speech in the Senate." Webster had, he offered, his "support for the constitution and the fundamental principles of the government under which" they lived. Webster revised the speech to remove particularly contentious remarks and arranged for the printing of two hundred thousand pamphlet copies in Washington; half of these were mailed out under his Senate frank. Additional quantities were printed throughout the country as Webster traveled widely, wrote editorials, met with legislators, and addressed huge crowds at public meetings.[69]

---

68 Sean Wilentz, *The Rise of American Democracy: Jefferson to Lincoln* (New York: Norton, 2005), 641.
69 Remini, *Webster*, 675–677.

Conclusion

When Words Mattered

IN 1919, with the earth's wounds still raw from the Great War, Irish poet W. B. Yeats lamented, "Things fall apart; the centre cannot hold; / Mere anarchy is loosed upon the world, / The blood-dimmed tide is loosed, and everywhere / The ceremony of innocence is drowned; / The best lack all conviction, while the worst / Are full of passionate intensity." In the winter of 1850, this was the prospect—a bloodletting exchange of words, followed by a civil war—that stoked the fears of Clay, Calhoun, and Webster. A compromise, embedded in a series of laws, saved the Union. Legal words saved the Union.[1]

But why should we pay attention to Clay's, Calhoun's, and Webster's words when, in conventional historical scholarship, the debate over the admission of California was merely prelude to the Civil War, an "impending crisis" on the "road to Civil war"? Most historians agree that as slavery "continued to gnaw at the nation's vitals," southern radicals had hesitated to preach disunion until "the crisis of 1850 strengthened their hand." Coupled to their accounts of the debate over the Wilmot Proviso, historians of the 1850s trace an unstoppable declension into secession and domestic insurrection. If the Compromise of 1850 gave the nation a brief breathing spell, an "armistice," the language of the three speeches suggests that everyone was holding their breath. But hindsight, the gift of Apollo to the historians, too easily mistakes drama for narrative. Events are too complex for that.[2]

---

1 William Butler Yeats, "The Second Coming" (1919), *The Dial*, November 1920, 466.
2 Fergus Bordewich, *America's Great Debate: Henry Clay, Stephen A. Douglas, and the Compromise that Preserved the Union* (New York: Simon & Schuster, 2012), 369; Avery O. Craven, *The Coming of the Civil War* (Chicago: University of Chicago Press, 1957), 273; David Potter, *The Impending Crisis: America Before the Civil War, 1848–1861* (New York: Harper & Row, 1976), 30, 90; Joanne B. Freeman, *The Field of Blood: Violence in Congress and the Road to Civil War* (New York: Farrar, Straus and Giroux, 2018), 208–266.

The fate of Clay's resolutions did not remain in his own hands. In his speech, he offered support to anyone and anything that would arrive in the same place—survival of the Union. Henry Foote of Mississippi tried to bundle them into an "omnibus," and at first Clay objected. Foote then proposed a committee of thirteen to work out a compromise, and Clay agreed to serve. Again, Clay pleaded for moderation, leading the committee of thirteen, whose creation he had originally opposed. Stirring the pot, in New Mexico statehood advocates were demanding their voice be heard in Congress. With all in doubt, the "omnibus" was defeated. But all was not lost. Calhoun passed away at the end of March. In July, President Taylor suddenly died. Webster was once again secretary of state, this time in President Millard Fillmore's cabinet. Illinois Democrat Stephen Douglas, who like Webster and Clay hungered for the presidency, now stepped forward to propose a solution—vote the parts of Clay's proposal separately, northern senators voting for admission of California, southern senators for the Fugitive Slave Law, with some northern Democrats, like Douglas, acting as swing votes. After four months of debates on the floor and deals in the back rooms of party leaders, the bills passed. A torrent of words had flowed, and a compromise was had.[3]

* * *

I have said that bringing these three speeches together reveals attributes of political thinking that viewing the three in isolation or merely summarizing them would veil. These men truly believed that words—in particular their words—could save the nation. Had not oratory helped them get elected? Would not the words of great men, leaders, wise men, trusted men bind what partisanship, ambition, and recrimination were tearing asunder, to borrow Calhoun's metaphor. It was a faith in the power of oratory and a belief that leadership mattered that was central to the thinking of the antebellum period. The speeches, read together, reveal the central tenets of that thinking. Moderation, compromise, trading favors were successful

3 John C. Waugh, *On the Brink of Civil War: The Compromise of 1850 and How It Changed the Course of American History* (Wilmington, DE: Scholarly Resources, 2003), 127–128; Potter, *Impending Crisis*, 102, 108–113; Michael F. Holt, *The Political Crisis of the 1850s* (New York: Wiley, 1978), 85.

tactics, radicalism and demagoguery were not. Radical political parties could not win the presidency or control of Congress. But putting the speeches together demonstrates once and for all the centrality of slavery in the political consciousness of the nation's leaders. No matter the starting point of the speech, slavery found its way to the center. Other issues orbited slavery, like planets in the solar system about the sun. Slavery shaped the other themes in the speeches. But slavery undercut moderation, compromise, and traded favors.

Slavery was not the only subject of antebellum senatorial oratory. Another was the attention that all of the speakers gave to history, in particular legal and political history. History mattered to all three men. They knew that they would be part of American history and were consciously shaping their reputation. Moreover, they shared the need to found their arguments on historical narrative. They went back to the colonial period, to the confederation, to the fashioning of land policy and the Northwest Ordinance, to the framing of the federal Constitution, to the first decades of the new nation, to the Missouri Compromise, and to the Mexican-American War. They deployed historical episodes as evidence and supplied the motives of the founders. Clay, who was the most informal of all the speakers, nevertheless tried to recall dates and the language of earlier legislation; Webster ranged over history like a professor in the classroom. Calhoun's entire speech was a history of southern views. History mattered.

In addition, law mattered. All of these men were lawyers, and all but Calhoun had extensive courtroom experience. While much of the nuts and bolts of writing and submitting legal papers to the clerks of the courts was left to their junior associates, argument in court was theirs. One can see how that experience shaped their speeches. They did not just express opinions, particularly the opinions of their constituents. Instead, they made arguments that looked a good deal like appellate court briefs. That is, every point was buttressed with evidence, repeated, and refashioned. The speeches thus had a formulaic quality, authority coming not just from the status of the men but from their analysis of the law. The absence of personal attacks may also have stemmed from courtroom experience. Lawyers knew that attacks on other counsel in the courtroom not only were frowned upon (after all, one's opponent today could be one's co-counsel tomorrow) but also could result in contempt citations from the bench. Thus, all three of the speakers avoided direct personal attacks on other members of the Senate. This self-imposed limitation was not true of every senator, however.

In their jurisprudence, the three men were all originalists. That is, all of them attributed authority to the framers' words, assuming that they, who were not there at the framing of the Constitution and had no special insight into the framers' thinking, nevertheless could know with certainty what the framers meant. How could the three do this? Presumably the answer lay in a shared political culture, a culture of revolutionary republicanism in which terms had not changed in the two generations from 1787 to 1850. In effect, they claimed the language and ideas of the framers as their inheritance.[4]

Third, because at the time the speeches were taken as a whole, from their varied perspective, all three of the senators demonstrated how important the Union was and what it symbolized. If words could not close the gap of sectional differences much as Clay and Webster wished or settle the issues on terms that satisfied Calhoun, the speeches offered a temporary bridge. They sought to keep working, to find a solution. The thinking of the antebellum period, unlike that after the Civil War, was optimistic. Solutions to problems could be found in a world of practicality and enterprise.[5]

Fourth, what the dismantling and recombining of the speeches in the present format shows to us is something that we, even gifted with hindsight, may have missed. The speakers, all national politicians, assumed that in a shared culture politicians could find ways to bridge sectional differences. Rational men, acting in rational fashion, could find common ground. The enemy was passionate self-interest. But we can see how a government system supposed to check and balance such interest—James Madison's defense of the Constitution in *Federalist* No. 10—did as it was designed. A body of senior politicians sitting in a gathering designed to allow deliberation—the Senate—did exactly what Madison predicted.

---

4 They assumed that they could determine the intent of the framers from their writings because they shared the same political culture. Whether this was true is another matter. See Peter Charles Hoffer, *The Supreme Court Footnote: A Surprising History* (New York: New York University Press, 2024), 122–124.

5 David E. Shi, "Antebellum Optimism," in *Facing Facts: Realism in American Thought and Culture, 1850–1920* (New York: Oxford University Press), 15–25. It was a white man's optimism, to be sure, but these were white men.

And here again is why it mattered that Clay and Webster had large legal practices. Even the most successful lawyer knew that some cases could not be won—but they could be settled. Resolving disputes short of bringing suit was the most common way lawyers represented clients' interests. By contrast, although trained as a lawyer, Calhoun did not practice, and his intransigence was abetted by his lack of practice at resolving disputes. Still, for all three the solution to the crisis lay in law—a stiffer federal Fugitive Slave Law.[6]

Finally, the old age of speakers gave their words greater meaning. Antebellum America venerated old age—it was a sign of God's blessing. When Clay, Calhoun, and Webster were growing up, the New England elder and the southern planter patriarch were the living repositories of custom and paternal authority. This gave them confidence that their words would have an impact. Not that Clay, Calhoun, and Webster dwelt on their own ages, although they did recognize the debilities of old age. Clay recognized the advanced season of his life and did not wish to live to see the dissolution of the Union. He feared his death was imminent, although it was not quite so near. In his remarks, Calhoun lamented, "Crying Union, Union, the glorious Union! Can no more prevent disunion than the cry of 'Health, health, glorious health' on the part of the physician can save a patient lying dangerously ill." Webster too added that he "might not be here" the next day. In fact, Clay, Calhoun, and Webster were very old men who were ailing. Calhoun died on March 31, 1850, aged sixty-eight years. Webster died on October 24, 1852, aged seventy. Clay died on June 29, 1852, aged seventy-five. White male life expectancy, if one lived past the age of twenty, was a mere forty years of age. They had already lived many years beyond that. They saw the crisis in those terms—the death of the Union seemed near, secession seemed a very real possibility, and they quivered at the prospect. There was something heroic in their efforts, standing for hours (save Calhoun), speaking loud enough for the chamber to echo their words. Physically daunting, emotionally draining, intellectually demanding, with the Senate and the nation hanging on their every word, their speeches were epic performances.[7]

---

6 Deborah Rhode, *Lawyers as Leaders* (New York: Oxford University Pres, 2013), 65–66.

7 David Hackett Fischer, *Growing Old in America* (New York: Oxford University Press, 1978), 3–25; David S. Heidler and Jeanne T. Heidler, *Henry Clay: The Essential American* (New York:

Given their authors' stage of life, the speeches represented the passing of the baton from one generation to the next. Clay, Calhoun, and Webster knew the founders of the Republic and had worked alongside them. By April 1850, the next generation of leaders, like William Henry Seward of New York and Jefferson Davis of Mississippi, were already seated in the Senate. To them would pass the final question of the survival of the Union.[8]

* * *

Five separate acts derived from Clay's eight resolutions passed between September 9 and September 20, 1850. The acts defining the borders of Texas and the admission of California were finalized. The debts were settled. Ending the slave auction in the District, the long-standing aim of abolitionists, was a victory offset by the continuing legality of slavery there. But instead of quieting the waters, the Fugitive Slave Act of 1850 further roiled the nation's politics. Mobs of antislavery agitators freed runaways from slave catchers in the North. Northern free states passed laws insisting on due process rights for suspected runaways, in order to protect their own Black citizens from false arrests. Northern state courts sometimes refused to cooperate with federal courts. Southern leaders began to seriously contemplate secession; although the Nashville convention in 1850 did not lead to secession, its momentum gained force through the 1850s, as did abolitionism.[9]

The issue of slavery's expansion to the West continued to cause disputes, as the Utah Territory law, allowing immigrants to choose slavery or freedom for their future, hinted. When the Kansas Territory was established, the question arose again. In 1854, Stephen Douglas, whose compromise had ended the California crisis, reintroduced Michi-

Random House, 2010), 480.

8 Some scholars, particularly after World War I, claimed that the third generation blundered into war. For that argument, see James G. Randall, "The Blundering Generation," *Mississippi Valley Historical Review* 27 (1940): 12.

9 Abolitionism relied on moral suasion rather than mob action, but as the 1850s progressed, some abolitionists took antislavery to the streets. James Brewer Stewart, *Holy Warriors: The Abolitionists and American Slavery*, 2nd ed. (New York: Hill & Wang, 1997), 157–158; Peter Charles Hoffer, *The Radical Advocacy of Wendell Phillips: Abolitionism, Democracy, and Public Interest Law* (Kent, OH: Kent State University Press, 2024), 51–72; typical of the personal liberty acts was Massachusetts's 1855 law guaranteeing habeas corpus protection for incarcerated Blacks. Massachusetts, *Acts and Resolves of the General Court of Massachusetts* (Boston: State Printer, 1855), 924.

gan senator Lewis Cass's old plan to allow the settlers of the territory to decide—the same as the Utah provision. Popular sovereignty in the Kansas-Nebraska Act of 1854 repealed the Missouri Compromise line of no slavery north of 36° 30' and hurled Kansas and the nation into a violent controversy. A "bleeding Kansas" divided by pro- and antislavery forces would not become a state until the first year of the Civil War.[10]

Words had saved the Union from internecine warfare in 1850, but incautious words could also be a provocation to violent acts. The weakness of words—the inflammatory potential of senatorial oratory—reached a crescendo in 1856, when Massachusetts senator Charles Sumner's two-day speech titled "The Crime Against Kansas" resulted in his public assault on the floor of the Senate chamber. His voice was only briefly silenced by the beating, although he did not return to his post for three years. His attacker, South Carolina congressman Preston Brooks, was celebrated in the South and denounced in the North. Brooks was expelled from Congress and immediately reelected, but died shortly thereafter from a sickness. The nation did not heal either.[11]

Slavery in the 1850s was like the giant squid in Jules Verne's science fiction novel *Twenty Thousand Leagues Under the Seas* (1871). The squid's tentacles nearly destroyed Captain Nemo's submarine, the *Nautilus*. "It was a squid of colossal dimensions, fully eight meters long. It was traveling backward with tremendous speed in the same direction as the Nau-

---

10 Roy F. Nichols, "The Kansas–Nebraska Act: A Century of Historiography," *Mississippi Valley Historical Review* 43 (1956): 187–212; Nicole Etcheson, *Bleeding Kansas: Contested Liberty in the Civil War Era* (Lawrence: University Press of Kansas, 2004), 1–8 (struggle was really about white liberty); Thomas Goodrich, *War to the Knife: Bleeding Kansas, 1854–1861* (London: Stackpole, 1998), 7–25 (struggle was about slavery).

11 Williamjames Hull Hoffer, *The Caning of Charles Sumner* (Baltimore: Johns Hopkins University Press, 2012). Consider the vitriol of his indictment of the slave power: "But the criminal also must be dragged into day, that you may see and measure the power by which all this wrong is sustained. From no common source could it proceed. In its perpetration was needed a spirit of vaulting ambition which would hesitate at nothing; a hardihood of purpose which was insensible to the judgment of mankind; a madness for Slavery, which should disregard the constitution, the laws, and all the great examples of our history; also a consciousness of power such as comes from the habit of power; a combination of energies found only in a hundred arms directed by a hundred eyes; a control of Public Opinion, through venal pens and a prostituted press; an ability to subsidize crowds in every vocation of life—the politician with his local importance, the lawyer with his subtle tongue, and even the authority of the judge on the bench; and a familiar use of men in places high and low, so that none, from the President to the lowest border postmaster, should decline to be its tool;—all these things and more were needed; and they were found in the Slave Power of our Republic." *The Crime Against Kansas; Speech of Charles Sumner, May 19, 1856* (Boston: Jewett, 1956), 7.

tilus. It gazed with enormous, staring eyes that were tinted sea green. Its eight arms (or more accurately, feet) were rooted in its head, which has earned these animals the name cephalopod; its arms stretched a distance twice the length of its body and were writhing like the serpentine hair of the Furies. You could plainly see its 250 suckers, arranged over the inner sides of its tentacles and shaped like semispheric capsules." So slavery reached out its tentacles, and its suckers attached to every public issue and threatened to drag the nation, like the *Nautilus*, to its doom.

And therein lies a final irony of the 1850 crisis. Words—embodied in law—had saved the nation, but that law was the Fugitive Slave Act of 1850. Without its passage, the Deep South probably would have seceded. President Taylor would have used force to reknit the Union, but Taylor had passed away. Millard Fillmore was made of softer stuff. The congressional lawyers had once more found a compromise, but compromise with the devil of slavery could not last, and the law was provocation in the North.[12]

---

12 For the fear was that slavery would soon become national. Sumner, again: "But this enormity, vast beyond comparison, swells to dimensions of wickedness which the imagination toils in vain to grasp, when it is understood that for this purpose are hazarded the horrors of intestine feud, not only in this distant Territory, but everywhere throughout the country. Already the muster has begun. The strife is no longer local, but national. Even now, while I speak, portents hang on all the arches of the horizon, threatening to darken the broad land, which already yawns with the mutterings of civil war." *Crime Against Kansas*, 6. And the war came.

ACKNOWLEDGMENTS

I AM grateful once again to Mark W. Summers and N. E. Hull for their comments on the manuscript, and to the two readers for the press for their kind words and critical insights. At NYU Press, Clara Platter was the very model of a modern acquisitions editor (a nod to W. S. Gilbert). Joseph Dahm was a superb copy editor. Remaining errors are of course mine.

APPENDIX

The Compromise Acts (Partial List)

An Act for the admission of the State of California into the Union

WHEREAS the people of California have presented a constitution and asked admission into the Union, which constitution was submitted to Congress by the President of the United States, by message dated February thirteenth, eighteen hundred and fifty, and which, on due examination, is found to be republican in its form of government:

Be it enacted by the Senate and House of Representatives of the United States of America in Congress assembled, That the State of California shall be one, and is hereby declared to be one, of the United States of America, and admitted into the Union on an equal footing with the original States in all respects whatever.

SEC. 2. And be it further enacted, That, until the representatives in Congress shall be apportioned according to an actual enumeration of the inhabitants of the United States, the State of California shall be entitled to two representatives in Congress.

SEC. 3. And be it further enacted, That the said State of California is admitted into the Union upon the express condition that the people of said State, through their legislature or otherwise, shall never interfere with the primary disposal of the public lands within its limits, and shall pass no law and do no act whereby the title of the United States to, and right to dispose of, the same shall be impaired or questioned; and that they shall never lay any tax or assessment of any description whatsoever upon the public domain of the United States, and in no case shall non-resident proprietors, who are citizens of the United States, be taxed higher than residents; and that all the navigable waters within the said State shall be common highways, and forever free, as well to the inhabitants of said State as to the citizens of the United States, without any tax, impost, or duty therefor: Provided, That nothing herein contained shall be construed as recognizing or rejecting the propositions tendered by the people of California as articles of compact in the ordinance adopted by the convention which formed the constitution of that State.

APPROVED, September 9, 1850.

Texas Boundary Settlement

An act proposing to the State of Texas the establishment of her northern and western boundaries, the relinquishment by the said State of all territory claimed by her exterior to said boundaries and of all her claims upon the United States, and to establish a Territorial government for New Mexico. . . .

First, the State of Texas will agree that her boundary on the north shall commence at the point at which the meridian of 100 degrees west from Greenwich is intersected by the parallel of 36 degrees 30' north latitude, and shall run from said point due west to the meridian of 103 degrees west from Greenwich; thence her boundary shall run due south to the thirty-second degree of north latitude; thence on the said parallel of 32 degrees of north latitude to the Rio Bravo del Norte, and thence with the channel of said river to the Gulf of Mexico.

Second. The State of Texas cedes to the United States all her claim to territory exterior to the limits and boundaries which she agrees to establish by the first article of this agreement.

Third. The State of Texas relinquishes all claim upon the United States for liability of the debts of Texas and for compensation or indemnity for the surrender to the United States of her ships, forts, arsenals, customhouses, custom-house revenue, arms and munitions of war, and public buildings with their sites, which became the property of the United States at the time of the annexation.

Fourth. The United States, in consideration of said establishment of boundaries, cession of claim to territory, and relinquishment of claims, will pay to the State of Texas the sum of $10,000,000 in a stock bearing 5 per cent interest, and redeemable at the end of fourteen years, the interest payable half-yearly at the Treasury of the United States.

APPROVED September 6, 1850

An Act to establish a Territorial Government for Utah

Be it enacted by the Senate and House of Representatives of the United States of America in Congress assembled, That all that part of the territory of the United States included within the following limits, to wit: bounded on the west by the State of California, on the north by the Territory of Oregon, and on the east by the summit of the Rocky Mountains, and on the south by the thirty-seventh parallel of north latitude, be, and the same is hereby, created into a temporary government, by the name of the Territory of Utah; and, when admitted as a State, the said Territory, or any portion of the same, shall be received into the Union, with or without slavery, as their constitution may prescribe at the time of their admission: Provided, That nothing in this act contained shall be construed to inhibit the government of the United States from dividing said Territory into two or more Territories, in such manner and at such times as Congress shall deem convenient and proper, or from attaching any portion of said Territory to any other State or Territory of the United States. . . .

APPROVED, September 9, 1850.

An Act to amend, and supplementary to, the Act entitled "An Act respecting Fugitives from Justice, and Persons escaping from the Service of their Masters," approved February twelfth, one thousand seven hundred and ninety-three

. . . SEC. 2. And be it further enacted, That the Superior Court of each organized Territory of the United States shall have the same power to appoint commissioners to take acknowledgements of bail and affidavits and to take depositions of witnesses in civil causes, which is now possessed by the Circuit Court of the United States; and all commissioners who shall hereafter be appointed for such purposes by the Superior Court of any organized Territory of the United States, shall possess all the powers, and exercise all the duties, conferred by law upon the commissioners appointed by the Circuit Courts of the United States for similar purposes, and shall moreover exercise and discharge all the powers and duties conferred by this act.

SEC. 3. And be it further enacted, That the Circuit Courts of the United States, and the Superior Courts of each organized Territory of the United States, shall from time to time enlarge the number of commissioners, with a view to afford reasonable facilities to reclaim fugitives from labor, and to the prompt discharge of the duties imposed by this act.

SEC. 4. And be it further enacted, That the commissioners above named shall have concurrent jurisdiction with the judges of the Circuit and District Courts of the United States, in their respective circuits and districts within the several States, and the judges of the Superior Courts of the Territories, severally and collectively, in term-time and vacation; and shall grant certificates to such claimants, upon satisfactory proof being made, with authority to take and remove such fugitives from service or labor, under the restrictions herein contained, to the State or Territory from which such persons may have escaped or fled.

... SEC. 6. And be it further enacted, That when a person held to service or labor in any State or Territory of the United States, has heretofore or shall hereafter escape into another State or Territory of the United States, the person or persons to whom such service or labor may be due, or his, her, or their agent or attorney, duly authorized, by power of attorney, in writing, acknowledged and certified under the seal of some legal officer or court of the State or Territory in which the same may be executed, may pursue and reclaim such fugitive person, either by procuring a warrant from some one of the courts, judges, or commissioners aforesaid, of the proper circuit, district, or county, for the apprehension of such fugitive from service or labor, or by seizing and arresting such fugitive, where the same can be done without process, and by taking, or causing such person to be taken, forthwith before such court, judge, or commissioner, whose duty it shall be to hear and determine the case of such claimant in a summary manner; and upon satisfactory proof being made, by deposition or affidavit, in writing, to be taken and certified by such court, judge, or commissioner, or by other satisfactory testimony, duly taken and certified by some court, magistrate, justice of the peace, or other legal officer authorized to administer an oath and take depositions under the laws of the State or Territory from which such person owing service or labor may have escaped, with a certificate of such magistracy or other authority, as aforesaid, with the seal of the proper court or officer thereto attached, which seal shall be sufficient to establish the competency of the proof. . . .

SEC. 7. And be it further enacted, That any person who shall knowingly and willingly obstruct, hinder, or prevent such claimant, his agent or attorney, or any person or persons lawfully assisting him, her, or them, from arresting such a fugitive from service or labor, either with or without process as aforesaid, or shall rescue, or attempt to rescue such fugitive from service or labor, from the custody of such claimant, his or her agent or attorney, or other person or persons lawfully assisting as aforesaid, when so arrested, pursuant to the authority herein given and declared; or shall aid, abet, or assist such person so owing service or labor as aforesaid, directly or indirectly, to escape from such claimant, his agent or attorney, or other person or persons legally authorized as aforesaid; or shall harbor or conceal such fugitive, so as to prevent the discovery and arrest of such person, after notice or knowledge of the fact that such person was a fugitive from service or labor as aforesaid, shall, for either of said offences, be subject to a fine not exceeding one thousand dollars, and imprisonment not exceeding six months, by indictment and conviction before the District Court of the United States for the district in which such offence may have been committed.

APPROVED September 9, 1850

An Act to suppress the Slave Trade in the District of Columbia

Be it enacted by the Senate and House of Representatives of the United States of America in Congress assembled, That from and after the first day of January, eighteen hundred and fifty-one, it shall not be lawful to bring into the District of Columbia any slave whatever, for the purpose of being sold, or for the purpose of being placed in depot, to be subsequently transferred to any other State or place to be sold as merchandize. And if any slave shall be brought into the said District by its owner, or by the authority or consent of its owner, contrary to the provisions of this act, such slave shall thereupon become liberated and free.

SEC. 2. And be it further enacted, That it shall and may be lawful for each of the corporations of the cities of Washington and Georgetown, from time to time, and as often as may be necessary, to abate, break up, and abolish any depot or place of confinement of slaves brought into the said District as merchandize, contrary to the provisions of this act, by such appropriate means as may appear to either of the said corporations expedient and proper. And the same power is hereby vested in the Levy [tax] Court of Washington county, if any attempt shall be made, within its jurisdictional limits, to establish a depot or place of confinement for slaves brought into the said District as merchandize for sale contrary to this act.

APPROVED, September 20, 1850.

INDEX

Page numbers in italics indicate Figures.

ABOUT THE AUTHOR

P ETER CHARLES HOFFER is Distinguished Research Professor of History at the University of Georgia. He has authored and coauthored more than twenty books, including *Clio Among the Muses: Essays on History and the Humanities*, *The Historians' Paradox: The Study of History in Our Time*, and *The Clamor of Lawyers: The American Revolution and the Crisis in the Legal Profession*.